GUNS IN LAW

A VOLUME IN
The Amherst Series in Law,
Jurisprudence, and Social Thought

EDITED BY
Austin Sarat
Martha Merrill Umphrey
Lawrence Douglas

GUNS IN LAW

Edited by
Austin Sarat
Lawrence Douglas
Martha Merrill Umphrey

University of Massachusetts Press
Amherst and Boston

ISBN 978-1-62534-429-8 (paper); 428-1 (hardcover)

Designed by Jack Harrison
Set in Scala
Printed and bound by Maple Press, Inc.

Cover design by Frank Gutbrod
Cover art by Alya Gaciyeva, *untitled* (colorized by Frank Gutbrod), Shutterstock.com.

Library of Congress Cataloging-in-Publication Data

Names: Sarat, Austin, editor. | Douglas, Lawrence, editor. | Umphrey, Martha
    Merrill, editor.
Title: Guns in law / Edited by Austin Sarat, Lawrence Douglas, Martha Merrill
    Umphrey.
Description: Amherst : University of Massachusetts Press, 2019. | Series: The
    amherst series in law, jurisprudence, and social thought | Includes
    bibliographical references and index. |
Identifiers: LCCN 2018051830 (print) | LCCN 2018052027 (ebook) | ISBN
    9781613766781 (ebook) | ISBN 9781613766798 (ebook) | ISBN 9781625344281
    (hardcover) | ISBN 9781625344298 (pbk.)
Subjects: LCSH: Firearms—Law and legislation—United States. | Gun
    control—United States. | United States. Constitution. 2nd Amendment.
Classification: LCC KF3941 (ebook) | LCC KF3941 .G88 2019 (print) | DDC
    344.7305/33—dc23
LC record available at https://lccn.loc.gov/2018051830

British Library Cataloguing-in-Publication Data
A catalog record for this book is available from the British Library.

To my son Ben with gratitude for his warm and kind heart
(A.S.)

Contents

Acknowledgments

This book is based on a seminar series conducted at Amherst College during 2016–17. Thanks to Megan Estes for her extraordinary work in making this series happen. We are grateful to our colleagues David Delaney and Adam Sitze for their intellectual companionship and to our students in Amherst College's Department of Law, Jurisprudence, and Social Thought for their interest in the issues addressed in this book. We would like to express our appreciation for generous financial support provided by Amherst College's Corliss Lamont Fund.

GUNS IN LAW

The Contested Legal Meanings of Guns

Austin Sarat, Lawrence Douglas, and Martha Merrill Umphrey
with John Malague and Lorenzo Villegas

If, as Max Weber said, the state is defined by its "monopoly of the legitimate use of physical force,"[1] then the widespread diffusion of guns in a society would seem to challenge that monopoly and the state itself. In responding to this challenge, what attitude should states take toward private ownership of firearms? Should they prohibit or permit such ownership? Should they allow private ownership but tightly regulate it? And what about the conditions under which guns can be used?

Given the importance of these questions, it is not surprising that political theorists since Plato and Aristotle have considered the meaning and significance of allowing citizens to bear arms (whether guns or not) and the challenges doing so poses to, and for, political and legal authority. Plato noted that an armed citizenry is one of the conditions that allows for the emergence of a democracy,[2] and Aristotle considered the possession of arms a fundamental source of political power and believed that each citizen should work, participate in political affairs, and bear arms.[3] Tyrants, Aristotle wrote, "mistrust the people and deprive them of their arms."[4]

The writings of the Roman politician and lawyer Cicero link the right to bear arms and self-defense as well as defense of the state.[5] "There exists a law," Cicero said,

> not written down anywhere, but inborn in our hearts, a law which comes to us not by training or custom or reading, a law which has come to us not from theory but from practice, not by instruction but by natural intuition. I refer to the law which lays down that, if our lives are endangered by plots or violence or armed robbers or enemies, any and every method of protecting ourselves is morally right.[6]

Later, Machiavelli, Hobbes, Locke, and Rousseau discussed the importance of militias, the use of arms in self-preservation, and the role that weapons play in protecting democratic governments.[7]

Today the problems private possession of weapons pose for law and the state are more acute than they have ever been. This is especially true in the United States with its constitutional protection of the "right to bear arms" and where there now are more guns than there are citizens.[8] Ownership of firearms is not evenly held among the American people, and it marks a significant cultural and political cleavage.[9]

The challenge that guns pose is reflected in the reasons Americans give for needing firearms. Unlike in earlier generations when gun ownership was significantly lower and the primary reason for ownership was "recreation," today most gun owners say that they "own guns for protection."[10] Surveys show that gun owners tend to have less faith in government than those who do not own guns.[11] Thus widespread gun ownership is a symbolic vote of no confidence in prevailing structures of public authority and symptomatic of a growing culture of "private justice."[12]

Guns give their owners a feeling of safety in an era in which economic and political power seem to be uncertain at best. As Elizabeth Anker notes,

> Gun ownership . . . often carries the implicit promise of counteracting increasing economic and social insecurity. Owning, and especially carrying, a gun buffers against declining sovereignty. If sovereignty, classically defined, is the final authority to make decisions within a given sphere, then gun owners feel as if they can restore their personal capacity for self-determination and success against a backdrop of waning sovereignty.[13]

Carrying a gun, Anker suggests, "reinstantiates a type of individual sovereignty when other forms of sovereign power seem out of reach."[14] It is an expression of what she calls "mobile sovereignty"[15] and a source of "omnipotent power" that masks or removes insecurities and feelings of inadequacy or helplessness.[16] A gun "makes a little man feel big, a stupid man feel clever, a frightened man brave, and an insecure man feel sure."[17] In Anker's view, "Gun ownership . . . has become a way for people, especially white men who make up the vast majority of owners, to feel as if they are personally sovereign over many of the precarious yet confusing economic and political experiences that shape their daily lives."[18]

Political and legal authorities respond to these assertions of personal sovereignty in different ways. In some places, they try to contain them by imposing stringent regulations. In others, they accommodate those assertions with a growing array of permissions and protections for firearm possession. In June 2017, in a telling example of such accommodation, more than two dozen Pennsylvania state legislators introduced a bill to make gun owners a so-called "protected class" under the state's Human Rights Act.[19] Even though Pennsylvania is an open carry state, without licensing, registration, or waiting periods, the bill's sponsors wanted to extend a range of protections to gun owners and prevent employers or anyone else from forbidding the possession of guns on their property.

The idea of gun owners as a protected class is an unusual and, in some ways, odd idea since the other classes already protected under the act focus on attributes of persons and their social identities (race, ethnicity, age, or disability) rather than what they possess. As one news report put it, "Essentially, employers would have to treat gun ownership as they do disabilities and make sure that they treat employees who own and carry guns equal to those who need assistive devices such as wheelchairs."[20]

For gun rights activists, the Pennsylvania legislation is simply a logical extension of the constitutionally protected "right to bear arms." In their view, that right extends to all people in any context. "The people" referred to by the Second Amendment suggests that the right is universal. Others think that the Pennsylvania legislation reflects a misunderstanding of that amendment, which, they argue, was designed solely to ensure that the federal government did not interfere with the prerogative of states to have their own militias.[21]

Guns and Gun Laws in American History

The kind of debate occasioned by the Pennsylvania proposal and efforts to understand the meaning of the Second Amendment are often framed explicitly in historical terms. What did the "right to bear arms" mean at the time of its ratification? What can we learn by examining legal sources that would have been available to those who proposed and ratified the amendment?[22]

Such historical inquiries often start with the English Bill of Rights, the first statement of individual rights and liberties to expressly reference the right of citizens to arms.[23] Initially that right allowed Protestants, many of whom had been disarmed by England's Catholic King James, to own weapons. Subsequently, American colonists used the English Bill of Rights to support their claims to possess guns and organize the militias that would later be instrumental in the American Revolution.

Gun rights advocates argue that because the English Bill of Rights protected an individual's right to bear arms, its American counterpart should be understood to do the same.[24] Opponents counter that the English Bill of Rights protected a collective, not personal, right. Moreover, they point out that gun owners were subject to many legal restrictions.[25]

State constitutions that predated the Second Amendment suggest that the right to bear arms was closely linked to a concern about the dangers that having a national standing army would pose to the states. To take one example from the Virginia Bill of Rights:

> That a well-regulated militia, composed of the body of the people, trained to arms, is the proper, natural, and safe defense of a free state; that standing armies, in times of peace, should be avoided, as dangerous to liberty; and that in all cases the military should be under strict subordination to, and governed by, the civil power.[26]

Moreover, many other state constitutions contained provisions protecting the militia. Four of them explicitly protected the right to keep and bear arms "for the common defense" or "for the defense of the state."[27] Only Vermont and Pennsylvania protected their citizens' right to bear arms both "for the defense of *themselves* and the state."[28]

When the federal constitution was submitted to the states, ratifying conventions in New Hampshire, Virginia, New York, and North Carolina wanted an amendment that would protect state-controlled militias and an armed citizenry. The different versions of the Second Amendment discussed during those conventions included phrases like "no person religiously scrupulous of bearing arms, shall be compelled to render military service in person" and explicitly linked the right to bear arms to "the common defense." In addition, between 1774 and 1821, during debates first in the Continental Congress and subsequently in the U.S. Congress, the language about bearing arms was used exclusively to refer to military matters.[29]

Early federal and state legislation suggests both that bearing arms in a militia was considered to be a civic duty and that gun regulation was customary.[30] Cities such as Boston prohibited citizens from keeping a loaded gun in their homes, whereas New York and Philadelphia banned the firing of guns within city limits. Certain groups—Catholics and African Americans—were not allowed to own guns.[31]

Gun control legislation continued to be enacted after the ratification of the Constitution and Bill of Rights. Cities and states passed such legislation in response to the rising number of murders, assassinations, and shootings across the country. Kentucky, Louisiana, Indiana, Georgia, Virginia, Alabama, and Ohio all passed laws designed to curb or outlaw carrying concealed weapons.[32] These early laws restricted the time, place, and manner that weapons could be carried. By the 1830s, some states passed laws banning entire classes of weapons and restricting their sale. Yet the history of the law's treatment of guns was by no means linear. Other states introduced robust provisions protecting the right to own guns for self-defense, and some people began to argue that the Second Amendment guaranteed a right to private gun ownership.[33]

During the nineteenth century the contest between these views was also played out in the judicial arena, where courts were asked to overturn various gun regulatons. In one of the most important of those cases, *Bliss v. Commonwealth*, a Kentucky court struck down that state's law banning concealed weapons. The court held that gun ownership was an individual right which could not be subject to even reasonable regulation.[34] This ruling produced a strong backlash, and Kentucky eventually amended its constitution to overrule *Bliss* and ban concealed weapons.[35]

The start of the twentieth century witnessed another wave of gun regulation. One example of such regulation occurred when New York City passed the Sullivan Act, which required a license for people wanting to possess firearms small enough to be concealed.[36] West Virginia, New Jersey, Michigan, Indiana, Oregon, California, New Hampshire, North Dakota, and Connecticut all passed similar legislation within the next decade.[37] In addition, the National Firearms Act of 1934 taxed the manufacture, sale, and transfer of weapons (such as shotguns and machine guns) associated with gangsters and bootleggers.[38] The Federal Firearms Act of 1938 established a licensing system for gun dealers.[39]

In a 1939 case, *U.S. v. Miller*, the Supreme Court held that the Second Amendment protected the right to bear arms only in conjunction with service in a militia and upheld federal gun regulation.[40] The *Miller* court developed a two-pronged test to evaluate Second Amendment claims: those claiming a right to bear arms had to show that their weapon (1) bore some relation to militia activity and (2) that it was required as part of militia service.[41] Following *Miller*, many lower courts used this test to uphold national and state gun laws.[42]

A New Understanding of the Second Amendment

Miller's approach domesticated guns and brought them fully within a Weberian conception of the state. As a result, guns were well regulated throughout the twentieth century. Moreover, significant gains were made in curbing gun violence with the passage of the federal Gun Control Act of 1968 and the Brady Handgun Violence Prevention Act of 1993. Lower courts also relied on—and even expanded—*Miller*'s collective rights interpretation of the Second Amendment.

However, gun rights advocates and conservative lobbying organizations did not give up on the individual rights approach. They soon achieved important legislative and judicial victories. Among them was the 1986 Firearms Owners' Protection Act, which limited the federal government's ability to regulate gun sales and to require inspections of gun dealers. In addition, in 1997, the Supreme Court struck down a provision of the Brady Act requiring law enforcement officers to perform background checks on prospective handgun buyers.[43]

Pro-gun forces achieved their greatest victory a decade later in *Heller v. District of Columbia*, when the U.S. Supreme Court decided, for the first time in American history,[44] that the Second Amendment protects the right of an individual to possess a firearm for personal defense. Writing for the majority, Justice Scalia argued that the Amendment's prefatory language—"A well-regulated Militia, being necessary to the security of a free State"—merely announced the purpose of the underlying right to bear arms without limiting it.[45] Scalia's originalist opinion purported to derive this interpretation from history, tradition, and colonial practice.

In 2010, the Supreme Court revisited the meaning of the Second Amendment and considered whether it applied to the states. In *McDonald v. Chicago*, a 5–4 majority held that the right to bear arms was a "fundamental" right applicable to the states. It ruled that Chicago's handgun ban violated the Second Amendment.[46]

Heller and *McDonald* opened the court system to a flood of litigation concerning the scope of permissible regulation. Since 2008, over 1,000 Second Amendment cases have been brought to the lower courts.[47] Gun-rights advocates have won significant victories and further expanded the realm of mobile sovereignty associated with possession of a gun. For example, in 2011, the Seventh Circuit Court of Appeals struck down a Chicago law banning firing ranges within the city limits. Two years later, the same court ruled that Illinois was required to revise its gun laws to allow concealed carry of firearms.[48]

At the same time, lower courts have upheld gun regulations in 94 percent of the cases they have heard.[49] Laws banning assault weapons, requiring background checks and firearm registration, and forbidding certain persons from owning firearms have survived court challenges.

Among the most controversial issues to come before the courts since *Heller* is the question of whether or not the Second Amendment protects the right to carry a weapon outside the home. In 2014, the U.S. District Court for the District of Columbia ruled that a complete ban on carrying firearms in public was "unconstitutional under any level of scrutiny."[50] In response, the Metropolitan Chief of Police decided to issue permits only if an applicant demonstrated "just cause" and registered the weapon with the police department.

But gun advocates continued to press for less restrictive regulation, and, in *Wrenn v. District of Columbia,* a federal judge ordered D.C. to further relax its gun laws. He held that the Second Amendment protects a "right to carry an operable handgun outside the home for self-defense."[51] Finding that there was not a reasonable relationship between D.C.'s regulation and a reduction in the risk of violent crime, the court ruled that the "just cause" requirement was unconstitutional.[52] However, the D.C. Court of Appeals vacated the order, thus leaving D.C.'s permit regime intact.[53]

Gun advocates challenged the same law again in *Grace v. District of Columbia,* and, on May 17, 2016, D.C.'s Federal District Court granted a preliminary injunction against the "just cause" requirement.[54] However, the D.C. Court of Appeals quickly issued a stay that allowed the district to keep its permit regime in effect until all appeals were exhausted.[55] Either *Wrenn* or *Grace* could provide the Supreme Court the opportunity to rule on whether or not the Second Amendment protects a right to carry a weapon outside the home.[56]

In the wake of *Heller* and *McDonald,* the right to own a gun now is equal to any other right in the Constitution and Bill of Rights. One consequence is that by 2013, thirty-seven states were issuing concealed carry permits to private citizens—a dramatic increase from the 1986, when the number was eight states.[57] Still, the ease of obtaining a permit varies considerably. For example, New York, New Jersey, Maryland, and California require applicants to demonstrate "good" or "special" cause in order to obtain a concealed carry permit.[58] Twenty-four states require applicants to undergo live-fire training at a firing range.[59] A few states allow anyone who can legally possess a firearm to carry it concealed—in public—without a permit or a license.[60] At the same time, the number of states that flatly outlawed the carrying of a gun fell from sixteen to zero.[61] In addition, in thirty states individuals have no duty to retreat from a threat anywhere they are lawfully present.[62]

As these developments suggest, *Heller* and *McDonald* paved the way for the kind of legal accommodation of guns that the Pennsylvania human rights legislation sought to provide. In so doing, they opened the way to the flowering of, and gave legal sanction to, "mobile sovereignty." Such an assertion of individual rights may open the way for a twenty-first century equivalent of the "Abolitionist Theory" of the right to bear arms, which gained traction in the mid-nineteenth century. Under that theory, the Second Amendment protects not only the right of personal self-defense, but also the right to revolt by an armed militia.[63]

Gun Violence

We are reminded of the challenge that guns pose to the state and law by the stark reality that 33,559 people were killed with firearms in 2014.[64] Sixty-two percent of those deaths were suicides.[65] States with the highest number of guns have 3.8 times more firearm suicide deaths than those with the lowest number of guns.

Moreover, in 2014, there were 10,945 gun murders across in the United States,[66] and guns were involved in 60 percent of all homicides.[67] Guns have been involved in 77 percent of all mass killings in the United States since 2006.[68] Gun ownership is associated with an increased likelihood of involvement in a violent confrontation and an increased probability that that confrontation will be fatal.[69]

Comparing the United States and other developed countries highlights the distinctive character of America's gun violence and the challenge guns pose to American law.[70]

The depth of this challenge is suggested by the fact that the population of the United States owns significantly more firearms than other developed nations.[71] There are 88.8 guns for every 100 people in the United States, compared to 33.1 guns per 100 people in Norway, 30.8 in Canada, 15 in Australia, and 6.2 in the United Kingdom. The United States experiences significantly higher firearm homicide rates as well. Annually, there are 3.54 firearm homicides per 100,000 people in the United States. In Norway that rate is 0.1, in Canada it is 0.38, in Australia it is 0.16, and in the United Kingdom that rate is 0.06.[72] Moreover, while the United States has 5 percent of the world's population, it has 31 percent of the world's public mass shootings.[73]

American law's response to the challenges posed by guns and gun violence has changed over time as our conception of the meanings and uses of guns and gun ownership have changed. Like other rights, gun rights are embedded in a continuing struggle over the boundaries of permissible regulation and the permissible uses of guns. Much of that struggle is reflected in arguments about the Second Amendment, arguments not put to rest by *Heller*.

The work collected in this book takes up those arguments and explores new avenues for engaging with them. It turns to history, offers new conceptions of the Second Amendment's meaning, and explores the arenas in which contests over gun rights play out. Our contributors also examine the complex world of law's efforts to regulate guns and their uses and show that the popularity of guns in America is related to growing concerns that the state is, and will be, unable to protect its citizens.[74]

The first chapter, by Saul Cornell, takes up arguments about the meaning of the Second Amendment, especially the uses of originalism in its interpretation. It offers a critique of what the author calls originalist "law office history." Cornell describes the "vast confluence" of right-wing scholarship and gun lobby efforts that were devoted to overturning the idea that the Second Amendment protects only a collective right. Much of the rhetoric surrounding the Second Amendment merely recycles "tired," originalist arguments. In Cornell's view, it is now hard to distinguish Second Amendment scholarship from politically motivated amicus briefs. To break this scholarly deadlock, he suggests that we abandon the ahistorical view of originalism that drives this pro-gun scholarship.

Finding a truly originalist meaning of the Second Amendment requires "discovering what it meant to Americans in 1791, and how it related to a specific set of fears and aspirations rooted in eighteenth century ideas and social realities." A faithful, historical study of the Second Amendment would show that no certain meaning exists. If this historical ambiguity was taken seriously in Second Amendment jurisprudence, a critical part of Justice Scalia's justification for *Heller* would crumble.

Cornell shows the complexity of the original meaning of the right to bear arms by focusing on the right to travel armed in public. He turns to the Statute of Northampton (SON) as a case study. Enacted in England in 1328, the SON provided that

> no man great nor small, of what condition soever he be, except the king's servants in his presence, and his ministers in executing of the king's precepts, or of their office, and such as be in their company assisting them, and also [upon a cry made for arms to keep the peace, and the same in such places where such acts happen,] be so hardy to come before the King's justices, or other of the King's ministers doing their office, with force and arms, nor bring no force in affray of the peace, nor to go nor ride armed by night or by day, in fairs, markets, nor in the presence of the justices or other ministers, nor in no part elsewhere, upon pain to forfeit their armour to the King, and their bodies to prison at the King's pleasure.[75]

Much like the Second Amendment, the SON has been subject to wildly different interpretations. One interpretation views it as a prohibition on armed public travel with a select few exceptions. Another interpretation holds that it allowed open carry unless it was done with malicious intent.

At the time of the SON's enactment, merely carrying arms would have been considered an affront to the king, doubting either his willingness or ability to protect his subjects. Only in certain circumstances, especially when far from populated areas where a person could not reasonably expect to be protected by the king, was it acceptable to be armed. This, Cornell argues, provides strong support for the first interpretation of the SON. The second interpretation he argues is an example of ahistorical, originalist defenses of weapons rights (of the kind used by Scalia in *Heller*) that improperly impose norms from another time period on a provision's framers.

The next chapter explores some neglected meanings of gun ownership and gun regulations in American culture as a way of understanding the Second Amendment. Darrell A. H. Miller contends that today gun owners equate guns and personal safety. Guns make them *feel* safer, but they also may identify them with a group of outsiders, or signal disapproval of the government or social order. All these meanings highlight the challenges that guns pose to the state and to law.

Heller identifies self-defense as the core of the Second Amendment, but this, Miller suggests, provides an incomplete explanation of the right to bear arms. While *Heller* allows regulations to prohibit convicted felons from owning guns, it did not say that felons waive their right to protect themselves. Similarly, the decision does not invalidate the regulation of weapons such as short-barreled shotguns, which would be especially useful for self-defense.

Miller turns to *Heller* and *McDonald* to try to identify the most important justifications for gun rights. He examines three: (1) protection from tyranny, (2) safety (a bit broader than self-defense), and (3) "some social benefit like a culture that protects human dignity or autonomy."

The first (protection from tyranny) does not offer an adequate justification for an individual right to possess guns. For one thing, no one whose government respects gun rights need be concerned with tyranny. And even if tyranny was a legitimate concern, no serious jurist has contended that the Second Amendment permits possession of weapons that would actually be effective against a standing army.

The next justification (safety) is based on what Miller calls a "marketplace of violence," the idea that the gun owners with good intentions will overwhelm gun owners with bad intentions. A marketplace, however, sometimes requires government intervention to prevent market failures. Indeed, *Heller* recognizes this and approves of regulations concerning felons, the mentally ill, and "presumptively lawful" locations such as schools, churches, and polling places.

The last justification suggests that guns create, what Miller labels, a "second best allocation of decision-making authority." Yet, as he notes, the social contract requires citizens to surrender their right to judge and punish others.

Miller concludes that the Second Amendment should be understood only to bar the government from disarming the population. Beyond this, Miller notes, disarming some "discrete and insular minority" would certainly violate equality norms. In the end, to fully understand the meaning and value of the Second Amendment we must recognize its expressive value and the fact that guns create an aura of power or respect and offer a marker of identity for those who own and carry them.

Chapter 3, by Katherine Shaw, continues to explore the meaning and interpretive practices surrounding the Second Amendment. It examines the role state and local government officials can have in the "ongoing, iterative story of development, contestation, and mobilization around guns and the Constitution." Shaw draws on the theory of popular constitutionalism, the idea that citizens should have a role in constitutional interpretation, and analyzes the way this theory impacts the Second Amendment.

She claims that popular constitutionalism played a surprisingly significant role in both *District of Columbia v. Heller* and *McDonald v. City of Chicago*. Although *Heller* purported to be a purely originalist opinion, Shaw argues that it was actually a product of what Reva Siegel has called the "constitutional politics of the twentieth century." As the public came to see the Second Amendment in terms of individual rights, the Court too drifted in that direction.

Shaw notes that state and local officials actively supported that view in both *Heller* and *McDonald*. Thirty state attorneys general filed an amicus brief in *Heller* arguing for an individual right. Only five state AGs wrote in support of the District of Columbia. What happened in *McDonald* was even more significant. Thirty-eight state AGs supported incorporation of the Second Amendment.

After *McDonald* and *Heller*, local and state law enforcement officials worked to preserve and even expand the rights announced in those cases, in spite of the difficulties such a reading might pose to law enforcement. For example, following the Aurora movie theater shooting in 2012, Colorado's state legislature passed a gun safety law requiring mandatory background checks and banned high-capacity magazines. Some county sheriffs announced that they would not enforce that new law, which they did not believe comported with the Second Amendment. Other sheriffs sued Colorado's governor, demanding that federal courts invalidate the law.

Shaw ends with a brief discussion of concealed carry "reciprocity," an idea she says has a decent chance of being enacted into law. One version of such a bill would require all states to recognize concealed carry permits issued in other states. This would allow states that interpret the Second Amendment in one way, in essence, to impose their interpretation on other states.

Chapter 4 turns away from the doctrinal and interpretive contests surrounding the Second Amendment to examine the impact of regulation on the level of gun violence in America. Carl T. Bogus begins by acknowledging that America is plagued by gun violence. However, this is not, he claims, a symptom of some exceptionally violent culture. It is instead a product of the proliferation of handguns. So why won't America take any serious steps to reduce the number of handguns in circulation? The answer Bogus suggests is that most people are stuck on the idea that gun violence can be stopped if we sort out the "good guys" from the "bad guys." Both sides of the gun control debate fall prey, he suggests, to this way of thinking.

The National Rifle Association disseminated a study that purported to show a correlation between the number of concealed carry permits issued and reductions in crime to advance its own version of the good guy/bad guy theory. Guns, the NRA claimed, pose no real danger when they are in the hands of "law abiding" citizens.[76]

Bogus also explores the way good guy/bad guy thinking plays out in response to mass shootings. These shootings have become the "new normal" since the Charles Whitman shooting at the University of Texas in 1966. According to the Guns Violence Archive, mass shootings now occur at an average rate of one per day. Can we identify and filter out the people who are going to commit these shootings? Bogus says no. Psychological profiling will be remarkably ineffective, as there is little overlap between those with serious psychological disorders and those who actually commit mass shootings. The same is true of criminal background checks, since many of these offenders are breaking the law for the first time. Given the myriad complexities involved with the process of buying a gun, it is impossible to reliably make the distinction on which the good guy/bad guy model depends.

Bogus looks at the implications of that model for gun regulation. He argues that regulation can work and has worked elsewhere. However, for regulation to work, much needs to be done to get beyond the framing of the issue in terms of good guys and bad guys. As a result, those seeking effective gun regulation need to take the "long view." Effective gun control will not happen any time soon.

The next chapter looks at gun regulation from the perspective of those called upon to enforce it. Jennifer Carlson examines the socio-legal realities that shape police enforcement of gun laws in order to highlight the "limits of law as often conceptualized by policymakers."

She interviewed police chiefs in California and hypothesized that police, seeing widespread gun ownership as a complicating factor in their profession, would favor stricter gun control policies. As it turns out, police identity and jurisdiction play an important role in officers' views on guns and gun control. Police officers are not cogs mindlessly enforcing policy developed elsewhere, and they are not simply professionals looking to make their jobs easier. They are actors in a complex and dynamic policy field.

California's concealed carry law grants discretion to law enforcement officials to decide whether there is "good cause" for issuing the licenses. Some police chiefs think about their control over issuing licenses in terms of resources. They express concerns over the time-consuming nature of the licensing process, or the funding it requires, and choose to delegate the issuing responsibility to the county sheriff. Other chiefs are concerned with political ramifications of issuing licenses. Still others simply want to assert local jurisdiction.

Despite these differences, Carlson found a striking consensus in the way chiefs see themselves and the policymakers responsible for promulgating gun regulation. They believe that their hands-on experience and common sense gives them an advantage over lawmakers in crafting effective policy. Reflecting the duality that Bogus discussed, they feel that lawmakers frequently ignore the clear (to them) division between good guys with guns and bad guys with guns.

While not all chiefs opposed gun control measures, all of them expressed disdain for a political process that does not sufficiently punish and target the "bad guys." Their self-proclaimed ability to distinguish "good guys" and "bad guys" gives the police moral authority and symbolic capital and allows them to "demarcate jurisdictional boundaries against policymakers." Such demarcation of boundaries expresses the self-conceptions of those charged with enforcing legislative policy and, in turn, helps explain how gun control policy plays out as it does.

The last chapter in this book focuses on women and guns and complicates common notions of how ordinary citizens understand gun rights.

Scholarship generally has focused on individuals and their beliefs and neglected the web of relationships in which those beliefs are embedded. Laura Beth Nielsen argues that in order to gain an adequate grasp of gun rights we must appreciate the extent to which those rights interact with cherished relationships.

Nielsen identifies three major types of what she calls "good moms with guns" (a term she uses to describe mothers who want to be the best possible parents and see gun ownership as related to those maternal efforts). The first type is "committed." These women grew up with guns and always intended to have them in their homes. Many have a sentimental attachment to guns rooted in their own early experiences. They value the right to have a gun in case they need it but also carefully plan safety measures to protect children from guns in the home.

The next type of good mom with guns Nielsen calls "compromising." Although initially opposed to having guns in their homes, these mothers made concessions to their husbands who wanted to have them, but also attempted to leverage those concessions in order to demand safe storage. Some continue to believe that guns are both undesirable and unnecessary even as they compromise those beliefs.

The third type of good moms with guns is "converted." Although they did not initially plan to have guns in their homes, these moms married men who did. Unlike the compromising moms, however, they now fully embrace gun ownership. They have come to believe that owning a gun is vital to keeping their children safe. The converted mothers all have serious concerns (accurate or not) about their safety and the safety of their children and the belief (accurate or not) that owning a gun will alleviate that risk.

All the mothers whom Nielsen interviewed believe that they have a right to own a gun. Interestingly, however, they also support background checks and assault weapons bans. They view themselves and their guns in the context of emotionally significant familial relationships. This relational context, Nielsen contends, needs to be part of the way we think about the debate, about guns, and the challenges they pose to the state and to law.

Taken together, the contributions to this book suggest that those challenges are rooted in different views of history, the practices of legal and social institutions, and the self-conceptions and relationships associated with owning, or being asked to regulate, guns. From Supreme Court justices to mothers, guns are sources of profound attachment and also great contention. The work collected here suggests that how law responds to that attachment and contention will be as important in the future as it has been throughout American history.

Notes

1. See Max Weber, "Politics as a Vocation" (1919), 1, http://anthropos-lab.net/wp/wp -content/uploads/2011/12/Weber-Politics-as-a-Vocation.pdf.

2. Plato, *Republic,* trans. E. Cornford (New York: Oxford University Press, 1945), 280–81.

3. Stephen P. Halbrook, *That Every Man Be Armed: The Evolution of a Constitutional Right,* rev. ed. (Albuquerque: University of New Mexico Press, 2013), 7.

4. Aristotle, *The Politics,* trans. Benjamin Jowett (1999), Book 5, chap. 10, http://socserv2 .mcmaster.ca/~econ/ugcm/3ll3/aristotle/Politics.pdf. Julius Caesar's account of the Gallic wars demonstrates how disarming the populace allowed a tyrant to take power. Halbrook, *That Every Man,* 14

5. Marcus Tullius Cicero, *Selected Political Speeches,* trans. Michael Grant (New York: Penguin, 1969).

6. Marcus Tullius Cicero, *Murder Trials,* trans. Michael Grant (New York: Penguin, 1975), 279.

7. See Vickie B. Sullivan, *Machiavelli, Hobbes, and the Formation of a Liberal Republicanism in England* (New York: Cambridge University Press, 2006).

8. See Christopher Ingraham, "There Are Now More Guns Than People in the United States," *Washington Post,* October 5, 2015, https://www.washingtonpost.com/news /wonk/wp/2015/10/05/guns-in-the-united-states-one-for-every-man-woman-and-child -and-then-some/?utm_term=.7dd8d3d22ddf. John Donohue notes that "the U.S. is by far the world leader in the number of guns in civilian hands." See "How US Gun Control Compares to the rest of the World," *The Conversation,* June 19, 2017, https:// theconversation.com/how-us-gun-control-compares-to-the-rest-of-the-world-79490. Also, the number of guns manufactured in the United States increased from 5,555,818 in 2009 to 10,847,792 in 2013, the most recent year that gun manufacturing data is available. In other words, over the last five years, the number of guns produced annually in the United States has nearly doubled. See Matthew Speiser, "Gun Manufacturing in the US Is Exploding to New Records," *Business Insider,* July 23, 2015, http://www.businessinsider.com /us-gun-manufacturing-atf-report-2015–7.

9. See Rich Morin, "The Demographics and Politics of Gun-Owning Households" (Pew Research Center, July 15, 2014), http://www.pewresearch.org/fact-tank/2014/07/15 /the-demographics-and-politics-of-gun-owning-households. Gun ownership is greatest among Southerners, those who live in rural areas and small towns, Protestants, high income individuals, and individuals with high occupational status. In contrast, handgun owners constitute a more diverse group and are more likely than shotgun and rifle owners to live in cities. See James D. Wright and Linda L. Marston, "The Ownership of the Means of Destruction in the United States," *Social Problems* 23 (1975): 93–107. Robert Louis Young argues that rural WASPS buy guns out of an angry desire to retaliate against threatening criminals—and of course, to rural WASPS, the image of the threatening criminal is very often the image of a black man. Owning a gun is a means for protection, but also for immediate retribution. A person might look to a gun less for self-defense from future attack and more to enable revenge for some other misdeed. Young found that gun ownership positively correlates with both prejudice and punitive attitudes, making this explanation of gun ownership uncomfortably compelling. *Race, Sex, and Guns: A Social Psychology of Firearms Ownership* (Ann Arbor: University of Michigan Press, 1982).

10. Elizabeth Anker, "Mobile Sovereigns: Agency Panic and Gun Ownership" (unpublished manuscript, 2017). Guns also can make their owners feel powerful in a Freudian sense. The obvious source of power is in controlling a visually phallic object.

11. Ibid.

12. Edward Glaeser and Spencer Glendon, "Who Owns Guns? Criminals, Victims, and the Culture of Violence," *American Economic Review* 88 (1998): 458–62.

13. Anker, "Mobile Sovereigns: Agency Panic and Gun Ownership."

14. Ibid.

15. Ibid.

16. Arthur Schlesinger has said that the "men doubtful of their own virility cling to the gun as a symbolic phallus and unconsciously fear gun control as the equivalent of castration." Quoted in Bruce Briggs, "The Great American Gun War," *National Affairs* 45 (1976): 37–62.

17. See Walter Menninger, "Guns and Violence: An American Phenomenon," *American Journal of Social Psychiatry* 4 (1984): 37–40.

18. Anker, "Mobile Sovereigns: Agency Panic and Gun Ownership." On the most ostensible level, guns are tools designed to serve specific practical functions. A decent amount of research has been dedicated to assessing which functions of guns Americans seek when they purchase firearms. Different surveys have reached different conclusions. The 2004 national firearms survey asked respondents for the most important reason for their ownership of firearms. The most common response was self-defense (46%), followed by sport shooting (29%) and collecting (25%). For long gun owners specifically, however, the most common response is sport shooting (77%). See L. Hepburn, M. Miller, D. Azrael, and D. Hemenway, "The United States Gun Stock: Results from the 2004 National Firearms Survey," *Injury Prevention* 13 (2007): 15–19. A survey performed by Diener and Kerber found different results. Recreation was the most commonly cited reason for gun ownership: 81% say they own guns for target shooting, 70% say they own guns for hunting, 54% say they find guns to be interesting devices. Next was protection: 46% cite protection of home, 8% cite protection of self. "To avoid violence with trouble-makers" and "So others won't bother me" were the most infrequently checked boxes on the survey. Edward Diener and Kenneth Kerber, "Personality Characteristics of American Gun Owners," *Journal of Social Psychology* 107 (1979): 227–38.

19. Tabitha Fleming, "New Bill Would Make Gun Owners Protected Class under State Human rights Law," *Penn Forum*, June 2, 2017, http://pennrecord.com/stories/511118527 -new-bill-would-make-gun-owners-protected-class-under-state-human-rights.act.

20. Ibid.

21. Ibid.

22. What follows draws on material prepared for inclusion in this book by Lorenzo Villegas.

23. Robert Spitzer, *Gun Control: A Documentary and Reference Guide* (Westport, CT: Greenwood Press, 2009), 2.

24. Joyce Malcolm, *To Keep and Bear Arms: The Origins of an Anglo-American Right* (Cambridge, MA: Harvard University Press, 1996), 122.

25. Spitzer, *Gun Control*, xxiv.

26. Quoted in Craig Whitney, *Living with Guns: A Liberal's Case for the Second Amendment* (New York; Public Affairs, 2012), 75.

27. Ibid.

28. Constitution of Pennsylvania, 1776, chap. 1, "A Declaration of the Rights of the Inhabitants of the State of Pennsylvania" and "Vermont Declaration of Rights," 1777, XV (emphasis added).

29. Michael Waldman, *The Second Amendment: A Biography* (New York: Simon & Schuster, 2014), 62–63.

30. For example, the Uniform Militia Act of 1792 attempted to prepare militia-eligible men for service by requiring them to own arms. Several other laws—An Ordinance Respecting the Arms of Non-Associators (1776) and An Act Obliging the White Male Inhabitants of this State to Give Assurances of Allegiance (1777)—gave states the power to confiscate weapons from individuals who were not part of a militia service or refused to swear a loyalty oath to the revolutionary governments.

31. Waldman, *The Second Amendment: A Biography*, 32.

32. Saul Cornell, *A Well-Regulated Militia: The Founding Fathers and The Origins of Gun Control in America* (New York: Oxford University Press, 2006), 142.

33. Waldman, *The Second Amendment: A Biography*, 67. Complementing this individual rights theory, a more radical "Abolitionist Theory" of the right to bear arms gained traction. In this view the Second Amendment was seen not only to protect the right of personal self-defense, but also a right to revolt effected by an armed militia. See Cornell, *A Well-Regulated Militia*, 153.

34. *Bliss v. Commonwealth*, 12 KY (2 Litt.) 90, 13 Am. Dec. 251 (1822). The 1840 case of *Aymette v. State* was more representative of the prevailing sentiments of the time. A Tennessee court ruled that the right to bear arms referred to a collective right for local or national defense. *Aymette v. State*, 2 Humphreys 154 (Tenn 1840). This opinion was reaffirmed and refined in an Arkansas case, *State v. Buzzard. Buzzard* found that the right to bear arms was intended to foster an effective militia, not to enable individuals to defend themselves with guns. It also held that weapons regulation was both constitutionally legitimate and necessary for public protection. *State v. Buzzard*, 4 Ark (2 Pike) 18 (1842).

35. Cornell, *A Well-Regulated Militia*, 144.

36. Peter Duffy, "100 Years Ago the Shot That Spurred New York's Gun Control Law," *New York Times*, January 23, 2011, https://cityroom.blogs.nytimes.com/2011/01/23/100-years-ago-the-shot-that-spurred-new-yorks-gun-control-law/comment-page-2/?mcubz=0.

37. Waldman, *The Second Amendment: A Biography*, 80.

38. Cornell, *A Well-Regulated Militia*, 200.

39. Spitzer, *Gun Control*, 253.

40. Cornell, *A Well-Regulated Militia*, 202.

41. *United States v. Miller*, 307 U.S. 174 (1939).

42. Spitzer, *Gun Control*, 184.

43. Ibid.

44. The U.S. Supreme Court first reviewed the meaning of the right in 1875. In its decision in *U.S. v. Cruikshank*, 92 U.S. 542 (1876), the court rejected the view that the Second Amendment protects an individual's right to bear arms for their personal defense. Rather, the court held that the Second Amendment is a limitation on the federal government's ability to disarm state militias. This view was reaffirmed a short time later in *Presser v. Illinois*. Though the Second Amendment limited only the federal government, states could not pass laws that would deprive the people of their ability to maintain public security through militias. *Presser v. Illinois*, 116 U.S. 252 (1886).

45. Eugene Volokh, "Implementing the Right to Keep and Bear Arms for Self-Defense: An Analytical Framework and a Research Agenda," *UCLA Law Review* 56 (2009): 1450.

46. *McDonald v. Chicago*, 561 U.S. 742 (2010).

47. "Protecting Strong Gun Laws: The Supreme Court Leaves Lower Court Victories Untouched," Smartgunlaws.org, August 2, 2016, http://smartgunlaws.org/protecting-strong-gun-laws-the-supreme-court-leaves-lower-court-victories-untouched/.

48. James Lindgren, "Forward: The Past and Future of Guns," *Journal of Criminal Law & Criminology* 104 (2015): 705–16, 710.

49. "Protecting Strong Gun Laws."

50. "Judge Overturns D.C. Ban on Guns in Public," *New York Times*, July 26, 2014, https://www.nytimes.com/2014/07/27/us/judge-overturns-dc-ban-on-guns-in-public.html. Following *Heller,* the Third, Fourth, Fifth, Tenth, and D.C. Circuit Courts of Appeal adopted an intermediate level of scrutiny for Second Amendment challenges. A few courts have applied strict scrutiny—which demands that a law be narrowly and clearly tailored to achieve a stated policy goal—to select cases. However, this mainly applies to cases involving lifetime firearm prohibitions under federal law. Reviewing laws that do not directly affect the right to have a handgun in the home, lower courts have applied a rational basis test. See "Post-Heller Litigation Summary," *Law Center to Prevent Gun Violence* (April 2017), http://smartgunlaws.org/wp-content/uploads/2017/04/Post-Heller-Litigation-Summary-2017-April.pdf.

51. *Wrenn v. District of Columbia* (March 2016), http://www.dcd.uscourts.gov/sites/dcd/files/154_Wrenn_PI_MemOp_Order.pdf.

52. Ibid.

53. *Wrenn v. District of Columbia* No. 15–7057, http://caselaw.findlaw.com/us-dc-circuit/1720807.html.

54. *Grace v. District of Columbia* No. 15–2234, https://scholar.google.com/scholar_case?case=3875477547500283404&hl=en&as_sdt=6&as_vis=1&oi=scholarr.

55. See http://www.handgunlaw.us/states/dc.pdf.

56. In June 2017, the Supreme Court declined to hear a challenge to the constitutionality of a California statute that places strict limits on carrying guns in public. See *Peruta v. California,* No. 16–894 (June 26, 2017). Justice Thomas dissented, claiming that the denial of certiorari in this case "reflects a distressing trend: the treatment of the Second Amendment as a disfavored right" (7).

57. Waldman, *The Second Amendment: A Biography,* 151.

58. Joseph Blocher, "Good Cause Requirements for Carrying Guns in Public," *Harvard Law Review Forum* (April 2014), https://harvardlawreview.org/2014/04/good-cause-requirements-for-carrying-guns-in-public/.

59. "25 States Don't Test Your Shooting Skills Before Issuing a Concealed Carry Permit," *Huffington Post*, February 3, 2016, http://www.huffingtonpost.com/entry/25-states-dont-test-your-shooting-skills-before-issuing-a-concealed-carry-permit_us_56b24cfbe4b04f9b57d81de9.

60. Katie Zezima, "More States Are Allowing People to Carry Concealed Weapons Without a Permit," *Washington Post*, February 24, 2017, https://www.washingtonpost.com/news/post-nation/wp/2017/02/24/more-states-are-allowing-people-to-carry-concealed-handguns-without-a-permit/?utm_term=.37109690e5f4.

61. Waldman, *The Second Amendment: A Biography,* 52.

62. George Halek, "Does Your State Acknowledge 'Stand Your Ground,'" *Concealed Nation* (September 2015), http://concealednation.org/2015/09/does-your-state-acknowledge-stand-your-ground. Stand Your Ground laws are strongly criticized by those who believe they allow for vigilante-like behavior that puts everyone at risk but that disproportionately endangers African Americans. See "Missouri Lawmakers Pass Sweeping Gun Rights Expansion," *New York Times*, May 14, 2016, https://www.nytimes.com/2016/05/15/us/missouri-lawmakers-pass-sweeping-gun-rights-expansion.html?mcubz=0&_r=0.

63. See Cornell, *A Well-Regulated Militia,* 153.

64. "Gun Violence by the Numbers," *EverytownResearch*, November 30, 2015, https://everytownresearch.org/gun-violence-by-the-numbers.

65. Michael Drexler, "Guns & Suicide: The Hidden Toll," *Harvard Public Health* (n.d.), https://www.hsph.harvard.edu/magazine/magazine_article/guns-suicide/.

66. "Gun Violence by the Numbers."

67. "Guns in the US: The Statistics behind the Violence," *BBC News*, January 5, 2016, http://www.bbc.com/news/world-us-canada-34996604.

68. See Michael A. Cohen, "A Mass Shooting—Just Another Day in America," *Boston Globe*, June 15, 2017, http://www.bostonglobe.com/opinion/2017/06/14/mass-shooting -just-another-day-america/pJ5EWVuclFBWnfWmWYcB8O/story.html.

69. Dave Gilson, "10 Pro-Gun Myths, Shot Down: Fact-Checking Some of the Gun Lobby's Favorite Arguments Shows They're Full of Holes," *Mother Jones* (January 2013). Found at http://www.motherjones.com/politics/2013/01/pro-gun-myths-fact-check. See also Michael Siegel, Craig S. Ross, and Charles King, "The Relationship between Gun Ownership and Firearm Homicide Rates in the United States, 1981–2010," *American Journal of Public Health* 103 (2013): 2098–2105, http://ajph.aphapublications.org/do /abs/10.2105/AJPH.2013.301409?journalCode=ajph.

70. See Donohue, "How US Gun Control Compares to the Rest of the World."

71. Ibid.

72. Jonathan Masters, "U.S. Gun Policy: Global Comparisons," *Council on Foreign Relations*, January 12, 2016, https://www.cfr.org/backgrounder/us-gun-policy-global-comparisons.

73. A. J. Willingham, "A Visual Guide: Mass Shootings in America," *CNN*, June 21, 2016, http://www.cnn.com/2016/06/13/health/mass-shootings-in-america-in-charts -and-graphs-trnd/index.html. Also see Donohue, "How US Gun Control Compares to the Rest of the World."

74. What follows draws on material prepared for inclusion in this book by John Malague.

75. See https://www.washingtonpost.com/news/volokh-conspiracy/wp/2015/10/31 /wrenn-history/?utm_term=.64503dc324f4.

76. A recent NRA video contained the following divisive and polarizing claim: "They use their media to assassinate real news. They use their schools to teach children that their president is another Hitler. They use their movie stars and singers and comedy shows and award shows to repeat their narrative over and over again." See Peter Holley, "The NRA Recruitment Video That Is Even Upsetting Gun Owners," *Washington Post*, June 29, 2017, https://www.washingtonpost.com/news/post-nation/wp/2017/06/29 /the-nra-recruitment-video-that-is-even-upsetting-gun-owners/?hpid=hp_hp-more-top -stories_nra-935pm%3Ahomepage%2Fstory&utm_term=.7568904e0c01.

CHAPTER 1

The Changing Meaning of the Right to Keep and Bear Arms: 1688–1788

Neglected Common Law Contexts of the Second Amendment Debate

SAUL CORNELL

In *District of Columbia v. Heller*, a divided Supreme Court held that the "right of the people to keep and bear arms" was an individual right to possess a weapon for self-defense unconnected to service in a well-regulated militia.[1] The *Heller* decision unleashed a wave of litigation as challenges to local gun laws were filed across the United States, including one from Heller's attorneys targeting Chicago's restrictive gun laws.[2] Less than two years later, in *McDonald v. City of Chicago*, the Court once again affirmed 5–4 that the Second Amendment protected an individual right.[3] Here, the justices extended the reach of the right beyond Washington, D.C., to states and localities, effectively incorporating the Second Amendment.[4] Justice Scalia's majority opinion in *Heller* surveyed a multitude of historical sources, but his approach to the past was decidedly ahistorical.[5] According to Justice Scalia, the Second Amendment simply recognized a preexisting English right.[6] There are many problems with Scalia's interpretation of English legal history and its evolution in the centuries between the Glorious Revolution and the adoption of the Second Amendment. First, Scalia treats the preexisting right as static, when there is broad scholarly agreement that this was a period of revolutionary transformation.[7] Therefore, it would be odd if not astonishing for ideas about the right to keep and bear arms to remain frozen like a constitutional fly in amber during this tumultuous period.[8] Second, the most far-sighted American constitutional theorists did not view the right to bear arms as a treasured inheritance from Great Britain. In contrast to Justice Scalia, leading American constitutional thinkers such as St. George Tucker and William Rawle believed that the traditional English right to have arms was so anemic that it was virtually useless.[9] Still, despite *Heller's* radical historical revisionism, which effectively expunged the militia clause and the entire civic republican context of early American constitutionalism from the Amendment, history appears to be even more significant to the future Second Amendment jurisprudence.[10]

The roots of this historical paradox, rewriting history at the same time that it made history foundational to the future of Second Amendment law, can be traced to Justice Scalia's statement that "constitutional rights are enshrined with the scope they were understood to have when the people adopted them, whether or not future legislatures or (yes) even future judges think that scope too broad."[11] In another oft-quoted passage from *Heller*, the majority made another related assertion:

> Although we do not undertake an exhaustive historical analysis today of the full scope of the Second Amendment, nothing in our opinion should be taken to cast doubt on longstanding prohibitions on the possession of firearms by felons and the mentally ill, or laws forbidding the carrying of firearms in sensitive places such as schools and government buildings, or laws imposing conditions and qualifications on the commercial sale of arms.[12]

Heller clearly points to history for guidance in evaluating the constitutionality of gun regulation, but it offers little substantive insight or methodological guidance on how to ferret out that information. According to *Heller,* the legality of a particular gun law would seem to depend on whether it can be shown to be deeply rooted in some American legal or regulatory tradition.[13] An understanding of the evolving nature of the right to keep and carry arms is not only essential to correcting the historical record and implementing *Heller's* historical framework, but it may also aid in resolving some of the contradictions and jurisprudential problems created by the opinion.[14] In his dissent, Justice Breyer suggested a balancing model that Justice Scalia dismissed as incompatible with the original understanding of the right to keep and bear arms. Balancing was central to the way members of the founding generation approached issues related to firearms. In fact, balancing was indispensable to the Anglo-American law of firearms.[15] The liberty interest associated with the right to arms was always balanced against the concept of the king's peace.[16] If an individual's exercise of the right to bear arms threatened the peace and order of the realm, that individual could be disarmed, imprisoned, and forced to provide a surety, a type of peace bond.[17] Simply arming oneself was contrary to law and was by its nature a violation of the king's peace under English law. A complex framework had developed under English common law that determined if subjects could lawfully arm themselves in public. The American Revolution republicanized the concept of the king's peace by transmuting it into the people's peace, but this did not repudiate the centrality of the balancing process used to determine if armed travel violated the peace.[18] The Revolution did lead to an expansion in the number of circumstances in which traveling armed might be lawful, but it did not create a broad freestanding right to travel armed in public.[19]

"As Allowed by Law": The English Language of Rights in the Eighteenth Century

The English Declaration of Rights asserted "that the subjects which are Protestants may have arms for their defence suitable to their conditions and as allowed by law."[20] The plain meaning of the text would suggest that the right was not universal but limited by religion and class. Nor did this formulation do anything to restrain the Parliamentary power over arms. In *Heller*, Justice Scalia relies almost entirely on the work of gun rights scholar Joyce Lee Malcolm. In her view, the English enjoyed a broad right to keep and bear arms under the 1688 English Declaration of Rights. As Scalia notes, "By the time of the founding, the right to have arms had become fundamental for English subjects."[21] Although Blackstone described this as the fifth auxiliary right, a structural protection of English liberty, his discussion underscores the limited nature of this claim, which he described as "a public allowance, under due restrictions, of the natural right of resistance and self-preservation, when the sanctions of society and laws are found insufficient to restrain the violence of oppression."[22] Blackstone's elaboration of the right makes it clear that its inclusion in the Declaration of Rights did not limit Parliament's authority over arms in any way.[23] It is vital to recall the scope of Parliament's authority in this period. Commenting on the implausibility of Locke's political theory, Blackstone made it clear that there was no appeal beyond Parliamentary authority, which was final under British Law:

> It must be owned that Mr Locke, and other theoretical writers, have held, that "there remains still inherent in the people a supreme power to remove or alter the legislative, when they find the legislative act contrary to the trust reposed in them: for when such trust is abused, it is thereby forfeited, and devolves to those who gave it." But however just this conclusion may be in theory, we cannot adopt it, nor argue from it, under any dispensation of government at present actually existing. For this devolution of power, to the people at large,

includes in it a dissolution of the whole form of government established by that people, reduces all the members to their original state of equality, and by annihilating the sovereign power repeals all positive laws whatsoever before enacted. No human laws will therefore suppose a case, which at once must destroy all law, and compel men to build afresh upon a new foundation; nor will they make provision for so desperate an event, as must render all legal provisions ineffectual. So long therefore as the English constitution lasts, we may venture to affirm, that the power of parliament is absolute and without control.[24]

Scalia concedes the limits of English rights claims: "To be sure, it was an individual right not available to the whole population, given that it was restricted to Protestants, and like all written English rights it was held only against the Crown, not Parliament." Having made this concession that the right was virtually meaningless against Parliamentary power, he then notes: "But it was secured to them as individuals, according to 'libertarian political principles,' not as members of a fighting force." What is not clear is what it means to be an individual right when there is no legal remedy or legal claim against Parliamentary power over arms. Despite these facts, Scalia "cited the arms provision of the Bill of Rights as one of the fundamental rights of Englishmen." It is worth contrasting this account with Federalist William Rawle, who offered this account of the English right to have arms:

In most of the countries of Europe, this right does not seem to be denied, although it is allowed more or less sparingly, according to circumstances. In England, a country which boasts so much of its freedom, the right was secured to protestant subjects only, on the revolution of 1688; and it is cautiously described to be that of bearing arms for their defence, "suitable to their conditions, and as allowed by law." An arbitrary code for the preservation of game in that country has long disgraced them. A very small proportion of the people being permitted to kill it, though for their own subsistence; a gun or other instrument, used for that purpose by an unqualified person, may be seized and forfeited. Blackstone, in whom we regret that we cannot always trace the expanded principles of rational liberty, observes however, on this subject, that the prevention of popular insurrections and resistance to government by disarming the people, is oftener meant than avowed, by the makers of forest and game laws.[25]

Scalia actually quotes Rawle on several occasions in his opinion, but he seems to ignore his radically different interpretation of English history. Such contradictions are not important to Scalia, whose opinion is desperate to show that the right was individual, not collective in nature. Thus, after discussing the English inheritance he asserts firmly: "It cannot possibly be thought to tie it to militia or military service." Scalia's point is that the holder of the right was an individual, not a government-controlled militia. This critique was directed at the traditional collective rights argument about the Second Amendment. Yet this model of the Second Amendment as a collective right had virtually disappeared from the scholarly literature in the years prior to *Heller*. The *Heller* dissenters did not embrace the traditional collective rights view; rather, they asserted a new paradigm that had emerged in the scholarly literature a few years before *Heller* went to trial. This new historical paradigm variously described as a limited individual right, a militia-based right, or a civic right.[26] The point of the new alternative paradigm was not that the right belonged to the state or militia, but rather that the Amendment had to be read holistically.[27] According to the new model, the Amendment might be recast in the following terms: *Because a well regulated militia is necessary to the security of a free state, the right of individuals to keep and bear those arms needed to meet their civic obligation to participate in the militia are protected from unreasonable government regulation.* This was precisely how Rawle described the nature of the right:

> In the second article, it is declared, that a *well regulated militia is necessary to the security of a free state;* a proposition from which few will dissent. Although in actual war, the services of regular troops are confessedly more valuable; yet, while peace prevails, and in the commencement of a war before a regular force can be raised, the militia form the palladium of the country. They are ready to repel invasion, to suppress insurrection, and preserve the good order and peace of government. That they should be well regulated, is judiciously added. A disorderly militia is disgraceful to itself, and dangerous not to the enemy, but to its own country. The duty of the state government is, to adopt such regulations as will tend to make good soldiers with the least interruptions of the ordinary and useful occupations of civil life. In this all the Union has a strong and visible interest.

Rawle went on to state that "the corollary, from the first position, is, that *the right of the people to keep and bear arms shall not be infringed.*" Rawle expressly describes the right to bear arms as a corollary of the affirmation of the necessity of a well-regulated militia. This is almost the opposite of the modern gun rights view, which asserts that we have a basic right to bear arms which makes it possible to have a well-armed militia. It also challenges Justice Scalia's effort to treat the preamble as stating a purpose, but not the purpose of the Amendment. Rawle does not describe it as a corollary, but as *the* corollary.

Self-Defense and English Law in the Age of Blackstone

Part of the problem in *Heller* stems from its confusing treatment of the right of self-defense under English law. Most Americans today would argue that because there is a right of self-defense one must be able to own a firearm. This was decidedly not how English subjects in the seventeenth century would have understood the right of self-defense.[28] The scope of self-defense under English law was fairly narrow in scope. The right of self-defense described by Blackstone and other English writers was understood in radically different terms from its modern counterpart. Technically, a claim of self-defense was less a free-standing right and more of a contextually dependent claim to be exempt from prosecution should one need to defend oneself against an imminent deadly assault.[29] Thus, to effectuate this claim one might use any weapon legally possessed, but the right did not entail any positive right to keep or use any particular weapon to exercise this right.[30]

Giles Jacob, author of a popular legal dictionary and several general guides to the law,[31] summarized the general rule for self-defense concisely: "There must be an unavoidable Necessity for Self-preservation to making killing justifiable."[32] Individuals were obliged to retreat, not stand their ground.[33] William Blackstone endorsed this view later in the century:

> this right of preventive defence, but in sudden and violent cases; when certain and immediate suffering would be the consequence of waiting for the assistance of the law. Wherefore, to excuse homicide by the plea of self-defence, it must appear that the slayer had no other possible means of escaping from his assailant.[34]

Modern rights claims are typically not context-dependent in this way. Thus the right to assemble may be subject to reasonable time, place, and manner restrictions, but the right is general in nature.[35] The right of self-defense under English common law was almost the opposite of this type of modern rights claim. The right of self-defense could only be claimed under specific circumstances that were determined by the time, place, and manner of the threat.[36] The burden of proof was on the subject, to show that deadly force had been justified because neither retreat nor the opportunity to seek assistance was possible.[37]

Even the cherished common law "castle doctrine" was bounded and context sensitive. The Castle Doctrine was a well-established common law maxim: "The Law hath given to Dwelling Houses several privileges," treating "a man's Castle for his defence." Thus, a different set of rules applied to confrontations in the home, where there was no legal obligation to retreat. Yet deadly force was not justified in every case of trespass. For example, a mere trespass at night might justify deadly force while a similar act in the day would not.[38]

Parliament restricted access to firearms by the various Game Acts designed to prevent poaching. Preventing subjects from hunting not only reinforced the aristocratic privileges of England's land-owning classes, it deprived the lower sort of additional sources of food and fire wood that made them more dependent on wage labor. The effective disarmament of a large part of the population also served as a way of checking popular radicalism.[39] The property requirements for owning guns imposed by the Game Acts limited legal access to firearms for most English subjects. The British Game Laws not only limited who might keep arms, but also placed limits on who could travel armed and in what manner.[40]

One of the most important sources for understanding the original scope of the protections afforded by the English Declaration for arms is the revision of the game laws in the 1690s. Neither Scalia nor Malcolm effectively contextualizes the debates in Parliament over this question. The House of Commons considered and rejected by a 2–1 majority a rider to the revised game act that would have allowed "any Protestant to keep a Musquet in his House, notwithstanding this or any other act."[41] The reaction of the House of Lords was no less negative, quashing the idea as too radical because it tended to "arm the mob."[42] The fact that an effort was made to express a right to own firearms in the home for reasons of self-defense is significant. The assertion of such a right is certainly a significant milestone in the evolution of the right to keep and bear arms, but the fact that the proposal was resoundingly defeated in both the Commons and the House of Lords clearly demonstrates that in the 1690s, English law had not yet embraced the "pre-existing" right Malcolm and Scalia claim was rooted in the Declaration of Rights (1689).[43]

By ignoring the role of such moments, important steps in the historical evolution of ideas about arms, Scalia can cast his view of the Second Amendment as protecting a fixed "preexisting right" that was a direct inheritance from England's Glorious Revolution. Originalism's obsession with an ahistorical notion of fixed meaning does great violence to the historical record, and Scalia's *Heller* opinion is no exception.[44] It was not until the middle of the eighteenth century that a broader conception of a right to have a gun in the home emerged as courts reinterpreted the meaning of the game acts in a fashion that finally recognized that individuals might own firearms.[45] Nor was this right constitutional in any meaningful sense; it was a common law right elaborated by English judges who effectively recast existing law by using common law methods of interpretation. It was a classic exercise in what the distinguished legal historian John Phillip Reid calls "forensic history."[46] Judges concluded that the mere presence of a gun in a home was no longer per se evidence of an attempt to illegally hunt game.[47] Further, courts finally acknowledged that there might be other legitimate and legal uses for guns, most notably pest control and home defense.[48] Although English courts articulated this legal doctrine in a series of cases decided between the late 1730s and the middle of the 1750s, this new, more robust understanding of the law took some time to permeate English legal culture. Popular guides to the law did not start to reflect the new understanding until the late 1750s.[49] Prior to the reinterpretation of the game acts by English courts there was no right to have a firearm for reasons of self-defense. Subjects would have been limited to whatever weapons they were legally entitled to own and could use those weapons to defend themselves.

The Right to Travel Armed under English Law: The Myth of Peaceable Carry

The most contentious issue in the post-*Heller* jurisprudence is the scope of the right outside the home.[50] *Heller* seemed to suggest that such a right was implicit in the self-defense-based view of the Second Amendment, but it provided little guidance on the scope of that right. One of the most significant constraints on armed travel was the 1328 English Statute of Northampton, which declared that all individuals, regardless of their station, were bound to "bring no force in affray of the peace, nor to go nor ride armed by night nor by day."[51] The Statute of Northampton further explained,

> It is enacted, that no man great nor small, of what condition soever he be, except the king's servants in his presence, and his ministers in executing of the king's precepts, or of their office, and such as be in their company assisting them, and also [upon a cry made for arms to keep the peace, and the same in such places where such acts happen,] be so hardy to come before the King's justices, or other of the King's ministers doing their office, with force and arms, nor bring no force in affray of the peace, nor to go nor ride armed by night nor by day, in fairs, markets, nor in the presence of the justices or other ministers, nor in no part elsewhere, upon pain to forfeit their armour to the King, and their bodies to prison at the King's pleasure. And that the King's justices in their presence, sheriffs, and other ministers in their bailiwicks, lords of franchises, and their bailiffs in the same, and mayors and bailiffs of cities and boroughs, within the same cities and boroughs, and borough-holders, constables, and wardens of the peace within their wards, shall have power to execute this act. And that the justices assigned, at their coming down into the country, shall have power to enquire how such officers and lords have exercised their offices in this case, and to punish them whom they find that have not done that which pertained to their office.[52]

Two radically different interpretations of the Statute of Northampton have emerged in the recent scholarly literature.[53] Gun rights advocates such as Eugene Volokh claim that "only public carrying 'accompanied with such circumstances as are apt to terrify the people' was thus seen as prohibited; 'wearing common weapons' in 'the common fashion' was legal."⁵⁴ David Kopel, another gun rights advocate, also argues that a legal concept of peaceable carry had emerged under English law by the time of the Glorious Revolution.⁵⁵ The other interpretation of the Statute of Northampton advanced by historian Patrick Charles disputes the Volokh/Kopel gun rights model of peaceable carry. Charles explains that although there were certain circumstances in which English subjects might travel armed, these were exceptions, not the rule.⁵⁶ The most obvious examples of such exceptions were the duty to put down riots and assist with the other community efforts at policing, such as the "hue and cry."⁵⁷

It is hard to reconcile the gun rights reading of Statute of Northampton offered by Volokh and Kopel if one parses the text carefully; the statute plainly enacts several categorical bans on armed travel in public. For example, one may not come before the king's ministers armed, even with peaceable intent. Similarly, one may not attend fairs or markets whilst armed regardless of intentions. Joseph Keble, the author of a popular guide to the law published shortly after the Glorious Revolution, reminded readers that if a subject was so "bold as to go or ride Armed, by night or day, in Fairs, Markets, or any other places," constables could disarm him and "commit him to the gaol."⁵⁸ All the leading English legal commentators and popular legal guides written for justices of the peace in the period between 1688 and 1788 repeat these categorical bans on armed travel in public. The same texts also enumerate a clear list of exemptions to the general prohibition on traveling armed imposed by the Statute of Northampton.⁵⁹ It would not have been necessary for these texts to set out such a list of exemptions if there had been a broad general right to travel armed in public.⁶⁰ Among the most important exceptions was the right to arm oneself to assist in the lawful suppression of violence, crime, riot, or revolt.⁶¹ Hawkins's *Pleas to the Crown*, an influential eighteenth-century commentary on English law, made it clear that when an individual armed himself to "suppress rioters, rebels, and enemies" or assist officers of the crown, the individual was not subject to the restrictions imposed by the Statute of Northampton.⁶² Indeed, in this situation arming oneself was as much a civic obligation as it was a right. During the 1780 Gordon Riots in London, the Recorder of London, the city's chief lawyer, described this hybrid right/obligation in forceful terms:

> It seems, indeed, to be considered, by the ancient laws of this kingdom, not only a right, but as a duty; for all the subjects of the realm, who are able to bear arms, are bound to be ready, at all times, to assist the sheriff, and other civil magistrates, in the execution of the laws and the preservation of the public peace.⁶³

Joyce Lee Malcom cites this as evidence for a robust individual right to keep and bear arms, but the duty referred to was one of the exceptions to the Statute of Northampton. Thus, she effectively confuses the exception to the rule with the rule itself.[64] Although in extraordinary circumstances individuals were legally allowed to respond on their own to deal with one of these violations of the king's peace by arming themselves, contemporary guidebooks underscored that it was always better to await a summons by a representative of the law, if at all possible, before traveling armed to the scene of a riot to help restore the king's peace.[65] If there had been a general right to travel armed in public, such caution would have been needless. The fact that legal texts stressed that "the safest Way is to be armed in Assistance of the King's Officers or Ministers of Justice" only underscores the limited nature of the right to arm oneself in public.[66]

Another key source of confusion in the gun rights account of this history stems from the anachronistic interpretation of the English legal concept *in terrorem populi*, meaning "to the terror of the people." The common law crime of affray was premised on this concept: traveling armed in terror to the people was a crime against the public peace.[67] Legal dictionaries and guidebooks often repeated this definition: "*Effrayer*, which signifieth to terrifie, or bring fear; and which the Law understandeth to be a common wrong."[68] As with most crimes during this period of English history, proof of actual intent to do harm was not required to establish criminality. Instead, the necessary, evil intent could be inferred from the illegal act itself.[69] In the 1689 edition of his justice of the peace manual, Joseph Keble offered a lucid account of why armed travel violated the king's peace irrespective of any specific malicious intent:

> Yet may an Affray be, without word or blow given; as if a man shall shew himself furnished with Armour or Weapon which is not usually worn, it will strike a fear upon others that be not armed as he is; and therefore both the Statutes of Northampton made against wearing Armour, do speak of it. . . .[70]

In another justice of the peace manual written almost a century later, John Ward echoed Keble's view that the mere act of arming oneself created an asymmetry of power that was the source of the terror prohibited by law.[71] Like other commentators on the Statute of Northampton, John Ward reminded his readers that when a man travels with "weapons not usually worn, it may strike a fear into others unarmed."[72] Keble's and Ward's interpretations also accord with another vital context for interpreting armed travel in this period: the king's peace. "The common law," Blackstone observed, "hath ever had a special care and regard for the conservation of the peace; for peace is the very end and foundation of civil society."[73] Under English law, "all offenses are either against the King's Peace or his crown and dignity."[74] In addition, any "affront to that power, and breaches of those rights, are immediate offenses against him."[75] The mere traveling with arms impugned the majesty of the crown, implying that the king and his representatives were incapable of keeping the peace. In short, the notion of a general right to travel peaceably armed in public would have been legally incoherent under English common law in the eighteenth century.[76]

The most important judicial decision on the meaning of Statute of Northampton, *Sir John Knight's Case*, also underscores the broad nature of the prohibition on armed travel and the centrality of the concept of the king's peace to English criminal law in the era of the Glorious Revolution. The key figure in the case, Sir John Knight, was a militant Protestant, opposed to tolerance for Catholics and Protestant Dissenters. He was charged with violating the statute of Northampton by walking about the streets of Bristol "armed with blunderbusses, like an armadillo."[77] The trial took place in the fraught environment after the Exclusion Crisis and before the Glorious Revolution. England was filled with rumors of Catholic conspiracies, and the claims of the monarch James II to the throne were being disputed by Parliament, which feared his Catholic leanings would lead England to abandon Protestantism. Although Sir John avoided the full force of the law because a local jury of militant Protestants sympathetic with his virulent anti-Catholicism refused to convict him, he was still forced to post bond for surety of the peace. That Sir John Knight may have benefited from a sympathetic jury who shared his anti-Catholic sentiments provides scant support for claiming that his exoneration established the legality of peaceable armed travel in public. By ordering Sir John Knight to pay a peace bond despite the jury's verdict, the judges of the King's Bench made clear that armed travel without just cause was unlawful because it was an affront to the King by its very nature, implying that "King were not able or willing to protect his subjects."[78] Although the judges of the King's Bench could not reverse the jury's verdict, Sir John Knight was held legally accountable for his wrongful conduct by the only legal means available to the court.[79]

The Statute of Northampton in Colonial America

Popular legal guidebooks published in the colonies repeated the standard interpretations of the Statute of Northampton and the limits on armed travel found in earlier English legal texts. George Webb's *Virginian Justice of Peace* framed these issues in language drawn from English authority. "Justices of the Peace, upon their own View, or upon Complaint, may apprehend any Person who shall go or ride armed with unusual and offensive weapons, in an Affray, or among any great Concourse of People." Webb also recognized the continuing relevance of earlier categorical prohibitions, such as not coming armed before the king's legal representatives. He also included the traditional exceptions to this rule, such as arming oneself to put down riots and rebellions, which had been carried over into Virginia law. Webb's elaboration of the contextual factors that might determine if one were likely to run afoul of the concept of creating a "terror to the people" is instructive. According to Webb, traveling armed "among any great concourse of people" was by its nature a violation of the king's peace. Such a judgment makes sense given the earlier elaborations of the crime of affray and the notion of the king's peace. Webb also devoted some attention to the special status of slaves, Indians, mixed-race persons, and free blacks whose rights were very limited under Virginia law.[80]

One of the most pronounced differences between American colonial law and English law was the expansion of the number of situations in which individuals were required to carry arms to enforce the peace. For, example, under English common law, the raising of the "hue and cry" was one of the most important examples of an exception to the prohibition on armed travel. Constables and other representatives of the king's justice were empowered to raise the hue and cry, requiring subjects to apprehend felons and assist agents of the crown in preserving the peace. Once the hue and cry was raised, individuals could arm themselves with whatever weapons they were legally entitled to possess.[81] In America, by contrast, there were other specific cases in which colonists could be obligated to arm themselves outside the context of a militia muster. A 1619 Virginian law clearly expanded the scope of normal militia duties to require some colonists to bear arms during *mandatory* church attendance.[82] Yet it is important to recognize that this 1619 law applied only to the portion of the population liable to bear arms, a subset of white men, a fact that makes it a dubious precedent for a robust modern-style rights claim. The full statute declares:

> ALL men that are fittinge to beare armes, shall bringe their pieces to the church uppon payne for every effence, if the default be in the master, to pay 2lb. of tobacco, to be disposed by the church-wardens, who shall levy it by distresse, and the servants shall be punished commander.[83]

The law illustrates the extraordinary power early colonial governments exercised over inhabitants, but it does not vindicate a strong liberty interest that might be claimed against government authority. This was not an example of a permissive peaceable carry law, as it required a subset of colonists to arm themselves or face penalties for failing to arm. In 1770, Georgia enacted a similar law that required all white men "liable to bear arms in the militia" to bring arms to church. The preamble of Georgia's statute made clear that the purpose of the law was to promote the "necessary security and defense of this province from internal dangers and insurrections."[84] Rather than support the myth of lone colonists, gun in hand, fighting off threats, or the notion of an absent state with little power and no interest in regulating arms, these early laws demonstrate that individual colonies compelled subjects to arm themselves when public safety required it.

In colonial America the militia also came to play a much more prominent role than it had in England. It served as a first line of defense against external and internal threats and was one of the most important local institutions in many communities.[85] Most colonies, with the exception of Quaker Pennsylvania, typically required adult white men between the ages of sixteen and forty-five, who were not infirm or exempt because of their occupation, to equip themselves with a musket or rifle and participate in the militia.[86] Although, in the overheated rhetoric that developed in the context of the Imperial Crisis and the American Revolution, Americans often spoke as if the militia were literally the people in arms, the historical reality was far more complex. A substantial portion of the adult free male population was required to participate in the militia, but simply equating the militia with the people is a mistake. Americans understood the difference between an armed mob and a well-regulated militia. The former was a threat to liberty and the latter was one of liberty's most important defenses. In much the same way that individuals acting on their own accord could not constitute themselves as a jury, so too individuals acting without legal authority could not claim to be part of a well-regulated militia.[87]

One of the clearest expositions of how the concept of a militia had been transformed by the colonial experience can be found in a remarkable series of essays published by Samuel Adams as relations with Britain worsened prior to the American Revolution. Adams defended the Boston Town meeting's decision to call on residents to arms themselves, invoking English and local legal authority:

> "It is beyond human art and sophistry to prove that British subjects, to whom the privilege of possessing arms is expressly recognized by the Bill of Rights, and who live in a province where the law requires them to be equip'd with arms, &c. are guilty of an illegal act, in calling upon one another to be provided with them, as the law directs." How little do those persons attend to the rights

of the constitution, if they know anything about them, who find fault with a late vote of this town, calling upon the inhabitants to *provide themselves with arms for their defence* at any time; but more especially, when they had reason to fear, there would be a necessity of the means of self-preservation against the *violence of oppression.*—Everyone knows that the exercise of the military power is forever *dangerous* to civil rights.[88]

Adams did not base his claim on a preexisting British right; the liberty he claimed was distinctly American. It was certainly a claim that individuals, at least adult white men, might claim, but it was also clearly exercised collectively. The right Adams described does not easily fit into the simple dichotomies that have defined Second Amendment debate in the modern era. It was neither an individual right nor a collective right in the conventional sense in which these terms have been used in modern Second Amendment debate. The right was one exercised by individuals, but it was one effectuated by the Boston government acting through its collective legal authority. Individuals did not act on their own accord but acted in concert for a collective public purpose, the protection of constitutional liberty. Nor was the right claimed by Adams and other colonists a pure expression of natural rights. Bostonians had not entered the state of nature. The appeal was to law, not to natural rights.[89] The right they claimed was customary, but it was a right that had emerged in America and had no obvious parallel in England at the time. It was an expression of the idea of ordered liberty and only made sense within the context of the rule of law.[90]

A New Constitutional Right Emerges beside an Old Common Law Right

Even before Independence was declared, the Continental Congress instructed the states to draft new constitutions.[91] Most of the new state constitutions included a written declaration of rights. Although it is hard to imagine a modern American state constitution without a provision on the right to bear arms, most of the first state constitutions did not include one. As the table below shows, only two of the states drafting a constitution in 1776 had an arms-bearing provision. Interestingly, Virginia separated its militia provision from the assertion of a right of self-defense, one of the absolute rights described by Blackstone. Pennsylvania, the first state to affirm a right to bear arms, also separated this right from a separate provision on self-defense. It is remarkable that so many modern accounts of the meaning of the Second Amendment and its analogues among the early state bill of rights conflate the two rights, which clearly were originally treated as both separate and distinct in the first state constitutions. Yet even these venerated rights were less common than the affirmation of the need for a well-regulated militia in these first bills of rights. The right not to be compelled to bear arms for those religiously scrupulous was at least as important as the right to bear arms. Although most modern Americans could easily dispense with the militia clause of the Second Amendment, eighteenth-century Americans were of a different opinion on the primacy of this ideal. Indeed, the chart sheds new light on one of the most frequently invoked but most misunderstood early American commentators of the Second Amendment, William Rawle.[92] In *A View of the Constitution of the United States*, Rawle described the right to bear arms as a corollary of the need for a well-regulated militia, a fact borne out by the texts of the first state constitutions.

Provision	Virginia	Pennsylvania	Delaware	Maryland	North Carolina
Militia	X	X	X	X	X
No standing armies in peacetime	X	X	X	X	X
Civilian control of military	X	X	—	X	X
No quartering troops	—	—	—	X	—
Right to bear arms	—	X		—	X
Right not to be forced to bear arms	—	X	X	—	—
Life, Liberty, and Property	X	X	—	—	—
Protections of the Common law	—	—	X	X	—

Data from: The Constitutions of the Several Independent States of America *(London, 1783).*

Rawle also took up the limits of the common law right to travel armed, noting that

> an assemblage of persons with arms, for an unlawful purpose, is an indictable offence, and even the carrying of arms abroad by a single individual, attended with circumstances giving just reason to fear that he purposes to make an unlawful use of them, would be sufficient cause to require him to give surety of the peace. If he refused he would be liable to imprisonment.[93]

A few general points are worth making about these comments. He notes that in England an armed assembly gathered for unlawful purpose or even an individual armed could be subjected to arrest and placed under a peace bond. During the unrest of the 1790s, Rawle, a Federalist, had prosecuted western Pennsylvanians during both the Whiskey Rebellion and Fries Rebellion for precisely such actions.[94] Rawle invoked English common law restrictions on armed travel. The main disagreement between the prosecution and the defense in both cases did not turn on arguments about a right to travel armed in public. Both sides conceded that there was no broad, free-standing right to travel armed. The lawyers for the rebels insisted that their actions constituted a riot under common law but were not by themselves treasonous. Rawle disagreed and he eventually prevailed in the trial. Rawle's legal strategy and the decision of the Court prompted criticism from the ardent Jeffersonian St. George Tucker.[95] In contrast to Rawle and the Federalist judge in the trial, Samuel Chase, Tucker thought that the scope of the right to have arms in Virginia was broader and rendered aspects of English common law void, particularly the case of citizens traveling with their militia weapons:

> But ought that circumstances of itself to create any such presumption in America, where the right to bear arms is recognized and secured in the constitution itself. In many parts of the United States, a man no more thinks, of going out of his house on any occasion, without his rifle or musket in his hand, than an European fine gentleman without his sword by his side.[96]

Tucker was commenting on a federal case that he believed had been decided incorrectly, so it is odd that so many modern gun rights lawyers would treat his comment, and not the federal court decision, as the legally authoritative source. Furthermore, Tucker did not claim that the situation in Virginia was universally recognized in all parts of America, but he quite clearly stated that it was not the norm elsewhere. Finally, Tucker was talking about a musket, a militia-type weapon, and not about pistols or other nonmilitary weapons. Justice Chase certainly did not share Tucker's views, and the successful prosecution of the rebels in both the Whiskey Rebellion and later in Fries Rebellion suggests that Justice Chase's more narrow Federalist view, not Tucker's more expansive Jeffersonian view, was the dominant one in the 1790s.[97] Despite the obvious disagreement between Tucker and Rawle, virtually every gun rights–oriented scholar insists on treating their views as if they spoke with a single voice and were in accord with one another on the meaning of the right to keep and bear arms.[98]

The American Revolution represented both a break with and a continuation of earlier English law when it came to arms. Indeed, deciding how much of the common law and English legal theory had been absorbed in American law would prove to be one of the most complex and contentious issues in the early Republic. The American Revolution's impact on the common law, including the right to keep arms and restrictions on armed travel, was complicated. Rather than speak of the Americanization of the common law, it might be more accurate to discuss it in terms of a process of creolization, as new hybrid Anglo-American conceptions supplemented traditional English common law. Although there were some important areas in which English law remained stable, there were also many examples in which the law had evolved to reflect the different social and legal realities of different colonies, particularly with respect to the right to bear arms.[99]

No early American legal figure was more attuned to this issue than Virginia jurist St. George Tucker, who believed that "the adoption of the laws of England, we see was confined to such as had been theretofore adopted, used, and approved, within the colony, and usually practiced on, in the courts of law; with an exception as to such parts as were repugnant to the rights and liberties contained in the constitution." Moreover, Tucker noted that one might have recourse to "every law treatise from Bracton, and Glanville, to Coke, Hale, Hawkins, and Blackstone; or in every reporter from the year-books to the days of Lord Mansfield," but such authority mattered little if the law was not consistent with the new state constitutions. If that were the case, such a contrary law in the Constitution would "have no more force in Massachusetts, than an edict of the emperor of China."[100]

Some states absorbed the common law by constitutional means. Thus, Maryland's declaration of rights affirmed: "The Common Law of England, and the trial by Jury, according to the course of that law, and to the benefit of such of the English statutes as existed on the Fourth day of July, seventeen hundred and seventy-six; and which, by experience, have been found applicable to their local and other circumstances, and have been introduced, used and practiced by the Courts of Law or Equity."[101] Some states passed reception statutes, incorporating parts of the common law. Pennsylvania's statute affirmed:

> Each and every one of the laws or acts of general assembly that were in force and binding on the inhabitants of the said province on the fourteenth day of May last shall be in force and binding on the inhabitants of this state from and after the tenth day of February next . . . and the common law and such of the statute laws of England as have heretofore been in force in the said province, except as is hereafter excepted.[102]

Several states, including North Carolina, Virginia, and Massachusetts, expressly adopted their own versions of the Statute of Northampton.[103] North Carolina's formulation of the prohibition followed closely on its English predecessor. It declared that no person may "go nor ride armed by night nor by day, in fairs, markets." Virginia's statute also drew on the original English text, with one important change, noted by William Hennig, a leading lawyer in the state, who remarked that the legislature introduced additional due process protections for those accused of violating the law. "The act of assembly of Virginia materially differs from the act of parliament," he wrote, "being more favorable to liberty." In Virginia, a justice of the peace could not seize arms and imprison an individual for more than a month. To impose a stiffer penalty required a jury verdict, a higher due process standard, and hence a greater safeguard for liberty.[104]

In 1795, Massachusetts enacted its own version of the Statute of Northampton, borrowing heavily from the language used in popular justice of the peace manuals. The new law forbade anyone who "shall ride or go armed offensively, to the fear or terror of the good citizens of this Commonwealth."[105] This was a common gloss on the Statute of Northampton used in many of the popular English justice of the peace manuals of the previous century. It framed the prohibition in terms of traveling with offensive weapons. The criminal conduct did not require the demonstration of a modern style *mens rea*; the mere act of traveling armed with offensive weapons demonstrated the evil intent required by law.[106] Massachusetts's alternative formulation was drawn from prior English commentators.[107]

The transformation of the English legal concept of the king's peace into a post-Revolutionary legal concept consistent with republicanism had implications for understanding the limits on armed travel in public. For example, the notion of traveling armed as rebuke to the king's majesty and authority no longer had any legal significance. In a society in which the people were sovereign, the notion of the peace was effectively republicanized. Still, the primary function of the justice of the peace in the new American republic remained essentially unchanged: preserve the peace.[108] As a Connecticut guide for justices of the peace observed, "The term peace, denotes the condition of the body politic in which no person suffers, or has just cause to fear any injury."[109] The offense was now one that harmed the body politic, not the king's majesty. Disturbing the peace remained a serious legal matter, and justices of the peace continued to exercise considerable power and authority, including a power to preempt violence by imposing peace bonds, disarmament, or incarceration.

A New Jersey guide for constables discussed common law restrictions on the right to carry in terms similar to those in the Massachusetts statute. The New Jersey guide banned anyone from going "armed offensively."[110] The author of this guide elaborated: "So a Justice of the Peace may, in his own discretion, require sureties for the peace from one who shall go or ride armed offensively to the terror of the people, though he may not have threatened any person in particular, or committed any particular act of violence."[111]

Technology, Social Change, and the Common Law

Justice Breyer's dissent in *Heller* recommended that the Court employ a balancing methodology.[112] This suggestion prompted Justice Scalia to issue a sharp rebuke, deriding Breyer's approach as "judge-empowering." Moreover, Scalia opined, "We know of no other enumerated constitutional right whose core protection has been subjected to a freestanding 'interest-balancing' approach." In Scalia's view, "The very enumeration of the right takes out of the hands of government—even the Third Branch of Government—the power to decide on a case-by-case basis whether the right is *really worth* insisting upon. A constitutional guarantee subject to future judges' assessments of its usefulness is no constitutional guarantee at all."[113] Breyer pointed out that if the Second Amendment were treated as a fundamental individual right, as the majority claimed it was, the real jurisprudential task was to engage in precisely the type of balancing exercise that Scalia dismissed. Thus Breyer wrote: "Any attempt *in theory* to apply strict scrutiny to gun regulations will *in practice* turn into an interest-balancing inquiry, with the interests protected by the Second Amendment on one side and the governmental public-safety concerns on the other, the only question being whether the regulation at issue impermissibly burdens the former in the course of advancing the latter. I would simply adopt such an interest-balancing inquiry explicitly."[114]

A number of legal scholars, including Joseph Blocher, Allen Rostron, and Mark Tushnet, have persuasively argued that Scalia's critique of balancing may be misplaced.[115] The notion that the Second Amendment precludes balancing is neither supported by text, history, nor structure—the three modalities of constitutional interpretation so esteemed by originalists, including Justice Scalia. The assertion that applying an interest balancing test to the Second Amendment would render it a second-class right rests on a misreading of First Amendment doctrine and history.[116] Although Scalia did not clarify his jurisprudential logic, he clearly seems to have believed that founding-era legislatures, and legislatures almost a century later than the founding era, were entitled to engage in balancing exercises that are simply off-limits to modern legislatures. According to Justice Scalia:

> The First Amendment contains the freedom-of-speech guarantee that the people ratified, which included exceptions for obscenity, libel, and disclosure of state secrets, but not for the expression of extremely unpopular and wrong-headed views. The Second Amendment is no different. Like the First, it is the very *product* of an interest-balancing by the people—which Justice Breyer would now conduct for them anew. And whatever else it leaves to future evaluation, it surely elevates above all other interests the right of law-abiding, responsible citizens to use arms in defense of hearth and home.[117]

Given that the *Heller* majority conceded that the right protected by the Second Amendment was not absolute, then it seems to follow logically that there would have to be some fact pattern in which the government might have an interest that would need to be balanced against the liberty interest at stake. Indeed, *Heller*'s own abbreviated list of examples of "presumptively lawful" gun regulations are themselves indicative that legislatures sitting sometime after the adoption of the Second Amendment had the authority to engage in the types of balancing judgments that Scalia claimed were precluded by having enshrined the right as an amendment. In some cases the legislation could not even have been contemplated until a new technology had emerged. The founders could not have banned machine guns before they existed and had become sufficiently common to pose a serious problem requiring the legislature to act.[118]

By accepting the legitimacy of technological change, Scalia's originalism must also implicitly address the changes caused by technology as well. The development of new weapons and their proliferation in the market creates new problems requiring new legislation. The first genuinely modern-style gun control laws emerged in response to the market revolution and the proliferation of cheap, reliable hand guns for the first time. This techno-logical change generated the first great wave of early state test cases on the meaning of the scope of the right to bear arms. Given that Scalia treats these laws and the early judicial response to them as probative of the Second Amendment's meaning, it would seem to suggest that technology and its responses are fair game as sources for original meaning. Thus, despite his protestations to the contrary, the text of *Heller* appears to suggest that courts must not only acknowledge technological change, but the social consequences of those changes. Of course, this was precisely the genius of the common law to both preserve traditional rights but allow for enough growth and flexibility so that the law could adapt to changing times.

Conclusion

Although Justice Scalia invoked a static preexisting right to keep and bear arms in *Heller*, the actual history of the changing meaning of this right in the period between the Glorious Revolution and the Constitution is far more complex. The time period between 1688 and 1788 was a century of revolutionary transformation in Anglo-American law and politics. Few aspects of English law were left unchanged by these momentous developments, and the right to keep and bear arms was no exception. Prior to 1688, the English right to bear arms was narrowly limited, particularly by religion and class. The adoption of the English Declaration of Rights did little to change this fact in the years following its adoption. The right of Parliament to legislate in this area was not diminished in any way.

Although English constitutional law did not change to embrace a more robust view of the right to keep arms, English common law did. By the 1730s courts had begun to recognize that keeping a gun in the home was not by itself a violation of the game acts because there were other legal uses of firearms, including defense of home. The law regarding the public carry of arms was always much more complex because it contained both categorical prohibitions and a number of context sensitive exceptions. The built-in flexibility of the law in this area made it more resilient and adaptable to changing circumstances.

The relationship between the American Revolution and traditional English common law was complex. The first state constitutions included affirmations of a right of self-defense and separate provisions on the right to bear arms. In contrast to modern America, neither of these was considered important enough to prompt the majority of the first constitutional drafters to expressly protect these rights. These texts tend to underscore William Rawle's argument that the right to bear arms is the corollary of a well-regulated militia: the opposite of the view articulated in *Heller*.

The evolving history of Anglo-American law in these two centuries also suggests that Justice Breyer's balancing model was not alien to the founding era. The right to travel armed in public was always weighed against the potential threat to the peace that such actions posed. Balancing had been central to the way Anglo-American law had dealt with arms for more than three centuries by the time of the American Revolution.

Notes

1. *District of Columbia v. Heller*, 554 U.S. 570 (2008).

2. For an overview of this literature, see Saul A. Cornell and Nathan Kozuskanich, *The Second Amendment on Trial: Critical Essays on District of Columbia v. Heller* (Amherst: University of Massachusetts Press, 2013), and Joseph Blocher, "New Approaches to Old Questions in Gun Scholarship," *Tulsa Law Review* 50 (2014): 477–89.

3. *McDonald v. City of Chicago*, 561 U.S. 3025 (2010).

4. Ibid. The only legal issue of note in *McDonald* was the method of incorporation. The Court used the doctrine of substantive due process, prompting Justice Thomas to write a separate opinion arguing to revive the Fourteenth Amendment's privileges and immunities clause as a basis for incorporation. See generally *McDonald*, 561 U.S. at 806–58 (Thomas, J., concurring in part and concurring in judgment). Despite the significant increase in the number suits brought by gun rights advocates after *McDonald*, most gun laws have been upheld.

5. The Court had last dealt with the Second Amendment in *United States v. Miller*, 307 U.S. 174 (1939), in which it ruled that since shotguns with barrels less than eighteen inches in length had no relationship to a well-regulated militia, the Second Amendment did not guarantee a right to keep and bear such firearms. For a good sampling of scholarly reactions to *Heller*, see Cornell and Kozuskanich, *The Second Amendment on Trial*.

6. See *Heller*, 554 U.S. at 592.

7. 554 U.S. 570 (2008). Scalia's account rests largely on the work of Joyce Lee Malcolm, *To Keep and Bear Arms: The Origins of an Anglo-American Right* (Cambridge, MA: Harvard University Press, 1994). For studies that emphasize the profound changes in the Anglo-American world in this period, see T. H. Breen, "Ideology and Nationalism on the Eve of the American Revolution: Revisions Once More in Need of Revising," *Journal of American History* (1997): 13.

8. Most professional historians have been critical of *Heller*'s distorted account of the history of the Second Amendment. See, e.g., Pauline Maier, "Justice Breyer's Sharp Aim," *New York Times*, December 21, 2010.

9. See infra pp. 34–35.

10. 554 U.S. 570 (2008). On *Heller*'s relationship to civic republican constitutionalism, see Sanford Levinson, "United States: Assessing *Heller*," *International Journal of Constitutional Law* 7 (2009): 316–28.

11. Ibid.

12. Nelson Lund, "Promise and Perils in the Nascent Second Amendment Jurisprudence," *Georgetown Journal of Law and Public Policy* 14 (2016).

13. Justice Scalia developed a similar framework, in *Rutan v. Republican Party of Illinois*, 497 U.S. 62, 95–96 (1990) (Scalia, J., dissenting). For an exploration of this perspective, see Michael W. McConnell, "Tradition and Constitutionalism before the Constitution," *University of Illinois Law Review* 1998, no. 1 (1998): 174. For a critical discussion of this model in the Second Amendment context, see Allen Rostron, "Justice Breyer's Triumph in the Third Battle over the Second Amendment," *George Washington Law Review* 80, no. 3 (2012): 731–32.

14. Rostron, "Justice Breyer's Triumph" (explaining that lower courts have been applying a form of intermediate scrutiny that entails some aspects of balancing).

15. See infra p. 37.

16. Michael P. O'Shea, "Modeling the Second Amendment Right to Carry Arms (I): Judicial Tradition and the Scope of 'Bearing Arms' for Self-Defense," *American University Law Review* 61 (2012): 637 (employing a similarly ideologically distorted and ahistorical account of the scope of the right to travel armed in public).

17. See infra pp. 27–30.

18. On the centrality of the peace to early American law, see Laura F. Edwards, *The People and Their Peace: Legal Culture and the Transformation of Inequality in the Post-Revolutionary South* (Chapel Hill: University of North Carolina Press, 2009).

19. See infra pp. 33–37.

20. "William and Mary, 1688: An Act declaring the Rights and Liberties of the Subject and Settling the Succession of the Crowne. [Chapter II. Rot. Parl. pt. 3. nu. 1.]," in *Statutes of the Realm: Volume 6, 1685–94*, ed. John Raithby (s.l, 1819): 142–45. *British History Online* http://www.british-history.ac.uk/statutes-realm/vol6/pp142–145 (accessed January 28, 2017). William Blackstone, *Commentaries on the Laws of England* (London, 1753), 1:139.

21. 554 U.S. 570 (2008) at 593–94.

22. William Blackstone, *Commentaries on the Laws of England* (London, 1753), 1:139. In his *Commentaries*, Blackstone describes such rights as follows: "But in vain would these rights be declared, ascertained, and protected by the dead letter of the laws, if the constitution had provided no other method to secure their actual enjoyment. It has therefore established certain other auxiliary subordinate rights of the subject, which serve principally as barriers to protect and maintain inviolate the three great and primary rights, of personal security, personal liberty, and private property."

23. On the nearly unlimited scope of Parliamentary power in the eighteenth century, see David Liberman, *The Province of Legislation Determined: Legal Theory in Eighteenth Century Britain* (Cambridge: Cambridge University Press, 1989).

24. William Blackstone, *Commentaries* (1753), 1:237–38, 243–44.

25. Ibid.

26. See William Merkel, "A Cultural Turn: Reflections on Recent Historical and Legal Writing on the Second Amendment," *Stanford Law and Policy Review* 17 (2006):667, 672 (arguing that historical scholarship opposing the individual rights view is best seen in terms of a republican school focusing on a civic right and a traditional states' rights interpretation, sometimes described as a collective right).

27. For a useful overview of this concept and the related notion of civic human-ism, see Philip Pettit et al., "Republicanism," *The Stanford Encyclopedia of Philosophy* (ed. Edward N. Zalta, 2003), http://plato.stanford.edu/archives/spr2003/entries/republicanism/; Athanasios Moulaskis, Civic "Humanism," *The Stanford Encyclopedia of Philosophy* (ed. Edward N. Zalta, 2011), http://plato.stanford.edu/archives/win2011/entries/humanism-civic/.

28. For a useful summary of recent writing on the evolution of Anglo-American criminal law, particularly the law of homicide, see Guyora Binder, *Criminal Law* (Oxford: Oxford University Press, 2016).

29. For an elaboration of this point, see ibid.

30. Even the 1688 Declaration of Rights expressly limited the kinds of arms to those suitable to a subject's condition and further stipulated that Parliament could regulate the scope of that right as it saw fit. Although the maxim "when the law doth give anything to any man, it giveth also, impliedly, whatsoever is necessary for the taking and enjoying of the same" might seem to apply to specific arms, this rule must be read against the Declaration of Rights affirmation that subjects were only entitled to "arms suitable to their condition" and the game laws property requirements for owning firearms. For this and other relevant maxims, see A Gentleman of the Middle Temple, *The Grounds and Rudiments of Law* (London: T. Osborne, 1749), 321.

31. On Jacob's role in expanding the genre of popular legal writing, see Julia Rudolph, "That 'Blunderbuss of Law': Giles Jacob, Abridgement, and Print Culture," *Studies in Eighteenth Century Culture* 37 (2008).

32. On the limited scope of self-defense under English law at this moment in history, see Giles Jacob, *The Laws of Appeals and Murder* (London: Eliz. Nutt and R. Gosling (assigns of Edward Sayer, Esq.) for Bernard Lintot, 1719), 46. Accord William Hawkins, *A Treatise*

of the *Pleas of the Crown, or, A System of the Principal Matters Relating to That Subject: Digested under Their Proper Heads* (London: In the Savoy: Printed by Eliz. Nutt [executrix of J. Nutt, assignee of E. Sayer, Esq.] for J. Walthoe and J. Walthoe, June 1716); Matthew Hale, *Pleas to the Crown: Or, a Methodical Summary of the Principal Matters Relating to that Subject* (London: Richard and Edward Atkyns, Esqs. for D. Brown and J. Walthoe, 1707).

33. Blackstone, *Commentaries*, 4:184. See also Giles Jacob, *A Law Grammar, or Rudiments of the Law: Compiled from the Grounds, Principles, Maxims, Terms, Words of Art, Rules, and Moot-Points of Our Law* (London: In the Savoy: printed by Henry Lintot, [assignee of Edw. Sayer, Esq.] for Aaron Ward, at the King's Arms in Little-Britain, 1744): 22 (explaining that deadly force was justified in the case of sudden attack where there was no opportunity to retreat).

34. Blackstone, *Commentaries* 4:184.

35. "Legal Rights," Kenneth Campbell, *The Stanford Encyclopedia of Philosophy* (rev. Winter 2016), https://plato.stanford.edu/archives/win2016/entries/legal-rights/.

36. For a discussion of time, place, and manner restrictions in the context of modern First Amendment doctrine, see *Cox v. New Hampshire*, 312 U.S. 569 (1941). See also Joseph Blocher, "Firearm Localism," *Yale Law Journal* 123 (2013) (describing how the scope of rights maybe impacted by location but that is distinct from a right that only exists in specific locations).

37. Jacob, *The Laws of Appeals and Murder*, 46.

38. Hawkins, *A Treatise of the Pleas of the Crown*, 1:73, §25.

39. E. P. Thompson, *Whigs and Hunters: The Origin of the Black Acts* (New York: Pantheon, 1975).

40. For examples of the various game acts, see William Nelson, *The Laws of England Concerning the Game: Of Hunting, Hawking, Fishing, and Fowling*, 2nd ed. (London, 1727), 167–77; *The Game Law: Or, A Collection of the Laws and Statutes Made for the Preservation of the Game of This Kingdom*, 5th ed. (London: 1714), 13, 36.

41. *Journal of the House of Commons: Volume 10, 1688–1693* (London: His Majesty's Stationery Office 1802). British History Online, accessed January 26, 2017, http://www .british-history.ac.uk/commons-jrnl/vol10.

42. Malcolm, *To Keep and Bear Arms*, cited in 554 U.S. 570 (2008). For critiques of Malcolm, see Lois Schwoerer, *Gun Culture in Early Modern England* (Charlottesville: University of Virginia Press, 2016), 169.

43. Patrick J. Charles, "The Faces of the Second Amendment outside the Home, Take Two: How We Got Here and Why It Matters," *Cleveland State Law Review* 64 (2016): 373, for examples of historical errors in Malcolm's work.

44. On the role of the fixation thesis in originalism, see Lawrence B. Solum, "The Fixation Thesis: The Role of Historical Fact in Original Meaning," *Notre Dame Law Review* 91, no. 1 (2015). For critiques of the fixation thesis, see Jack M. Balkin, "The New Originalism and the Uses of History," *Fordham Law Review* 82 (2013): 641, 657; see generally Richard H. Fallon Jr., "The Many and Varied Roles of History in Constitutional Adjudication," *Notre Dame Law Review* 90 (2015): 1753; Saul Cornell, "Originalism As Thin Description: An Interdisciplinary Critique," *Fordham Law Review* 84 (2015): 1; Saul Cornell, "Meaning and Understanding in the History of Constitutional Ideas: The Intellectual History Alternative to Originalism," *Fordham Law Review* 82 (2013): 721; Jonathan Gienapp, "Historicism and Holism: Failures of Originalist Translation," *Fordham Law Review* 84 (2015): 935; Jack N. Rakove, "Tone Deaf to the Past: More Qualms about Public Meaning Originalism," *Fordham Law Review* 84 (2015): 3.

45. See *Rex v. Gardner*, 93 Eng. Rep. 1056, 1056 (K.B. 1738) (holding that simply possessing a gun is permissible because "a gun is necessary for defence of a house, or for a farmer to shoot crows"); *Wingfield v. Stratford*, 96 Eng. Rep. 787, 787 (K.B. 1752) (reinterpreting the game laws by concluding that the King's Bench was not supposed "to disarm all the people of England").

46. Malcolm erroneously accepts the court's historical conclusion at face value and reads the new conception of gun rights backward in time to 1688. See Malcolm, *To Keep and Bear Arms*. The Court's conclusion is better interpreted as an example of a style of common law legal reasoning that historian John Reid dubs forensic history; see John Phillip Reid, "Law and History," *Loyola of Los Angeles Law Review* 27, no. 1 (1993). English lawyers essentially constructed a new version of the past to justify legal change, preserving the appearance that the law was fixed.

47. Scalia's approach to constitutional meaning seems inconsistent with the common law methods familiar to many in the founding era; see Bernadette Meyler, "Towards a Common Law Originalism," *Stanford Law Review* 59 (2006).

48. *Gardner,* 93 Eng. Rep. at 1056.

49. The evidence also suggests that changes in case law did not immediately translate into new treatments in the standard guides to the law. See Richard Burn, *The Justice of the Peace, and Parish Officer,* 2nd ed. (London: Oxford University, 1756), 468 (demonstrating that there was a lag time between the cases and their incorporation in popular legal guidebooks).

50. For the gun rights view of this right, see Michael P. O'Shea, "Modeling the Second Amendment Right to Carry Arms (I): Judicial Tradition and the Scope of 'Bearing Arms' for Self-Defense," *American University Law Review* 61 (2012): 637. For a critique of O'Shea and the notion of a broad right to travel armed, see Saul Cornell, "The Right to Carry Firearms Outside of the Home: Separating Historical Myths from Historical Realities," *Fordham Urban Law Journal* 39 (2012): 1695.

51. Statute of Northampton 2 Edw. 3, c. 3 (1328).

52. Ibid.

53. Ibid.

54. Eugene Volokh, "The First and Second Amendments," *Columbia Law Review* 109 (2009): 101.

55. Ibid.

56. See Patrick J. Charles, "The Faces of the Second Amendment Outside the Home: History versus Ahistorical Standards of Review," *Cleveland State Law Review* 60 (2012): 8. For a legal scholar who argues in favor of the minimalist reading of Charles, see Darrell A. H. Miller, "Guns as Smut: Defending the Home-Bound Second Amendment," *Columbia Law Review* 109 (2009): 1317.

57. Ibid.

58. Joseph Keble, *An Assistance to Justices of the Peace, For the Easier Performance of Their Duty* (London: Printed by W. Rawlins, S. Roycroft, and H. Sawbridge, Assigns of R. and E. Atkins Esq; for Samuel Keble at the Turks Head over against Fetter Lane End in Fleet-street, MDCLXXXIII, 1683), 147, 224.

59. Michael Dalton, *The Country Justice, Containing the Practice of the Justices of the Peace out of Their Sessions* (1618), 30; Keble, *An Assistance to Justices of the Peace,* 224; Giles Jacob, *A New Law-Dictionary* (1729); John Ward, *The Law of a Justice of Peace and Parish Officer* (1769), 6–7; James Ewing, *A Treatise on the Office and Duty of the Justice of the Peace, Sheriff, Coroner, Constable* (1805) (demonstrating the continuity in English legal views on the limited nature of the right to travel armed in the period between the Glorious Revolution and the American Revolution).

60. For other examples of ahistorical originalist accounts asserting a broad right to carry, see Nicholas J. Johnson et al., *Firearms Law and the Second Amendment: Regulation, Rights, and Policy* (2012), 81–82; Eugene Volokh, "Implementing the Right to Keep and Bear Arms for Self-Defense: An Analytical Framework and a Research Agenda," *UCLA Law Review* 56 (2009): 1516–17, 1522–23 (all these works erroneously import aspects of modern criminal law's *mens rea* requirement into earlier period of English legal history

when such a requirement had not yet emerged). For a discussion of the earlier model of criminality, see infra note 29–30.

61. Hawkins, *Pleas to the Crown.*

62. Ibid.

63. William Blizard, *Desultory Reflections on Police: With an Essay on the Means of Preventing Crimes and Amending Criminals* (1785), 59–60.

64. Until the middle of the eighteenth century, the restrictions of the game laws would have prohibited firearms ownership to those who failed to meet the property requirement. Those individuals who failed to meet this requirement would have been expected to show up with appropriate weapons to the station, either edged weapons or clubs, but not guns.

65. Joseph Shaw, *The Practical Justice of the Peace* (1728), 81.

66. Ibid.

67. In his account of the Statute of Northampton, gun rights activist David Kopel casts Tyrell as a modern libertarian who defended an expansive right to travel armed, a characterization that is almost the mirror image of what Tyrrell actually argues. See David Kopel, "The First Century of Right to Arms Litigation," *Georgetown Journal of Law and Public Policy* 14 (2016). Contra Charles, "The Faces of the Second Amendment," (providing an extensive critique of Kopel's interpretation).

68. Dalton, *The Country Justice,* 30 (providing a similar account).

69. Simon Stern, "Blackstone's Criminal Law: Common-Law Harmonization and Legislative Reform," *Foundational Texts in Modern Criminal Law* (2014): 61; George Fletcher, *Rethinking Criminal Law* (1978); Guyora Binder and Robert Weisberg, "What Is Criminal Law About?" *Michigan Law Review* 114 (2016): 1173.

70. Keble, *An Assistance to the Justices,* 147. See Statute of Northampton, 2 Edw. 3, c. 3 (1328) (Eng.); 20 Rich. 2, c. 1 (1396–97) (Eng.) (explaining why the mere act of traveling with an arm triggered an affray irrespective of any particular threatening act or intent to commit a crime).

71. John Ward, *The Law of a Justice of Peace and Parish Officer* (1769), 6–7.

72. Gun rights advocates and libertarian scholars have turned this history on its head, arguing that riding armed was only criminal if it specifically triggered a terror in the people because of malicious intent. See infra pp. 29–30.

73. Blackstone, *Commentaries* 1:349.

74. Ibid., 1:258.

75. Ibid.

76. *Sir John Knight's Case,* 87 Eng. Rep. 75 K.B. (1686).

77. Narcissus Luttrell, *A Brief Historical Relation of State Affairs from September 1678 to April 1714* (1857), 389.

78. *Sir John Knight's Case,* 87 Eng. Rep. 75.

79. Patrick Charles, "The Statute of Northampton by the Late Eighteenth Century: Clarifying the Intellectual Legacy," *Fordham Urban Law Journal City Square* (December 2012).

80. George Webb, *The Office and Authority of a Justice of the Peace* (1736).

81. Sir John Comyns, *Digest of the Law of England,* 4th ed. (1793), 4:538 (mispaginated as 358).

82. William Walter Hening, *Act XLV 1 Statutes at Large 1619* (1823), 198.

83. Ibid.

84. Robert George Watkins, *A Digest of the Laws of the State of Georgia* (Philadelphia, 1800), 157.

85. Kevin Sweeney, "Firearms, Militias, and the Second Amendment," *The Second Amendment on Trial: Critical Essays on District of Columbia v. Heller* (2013), 310 (discussing the role of the militia in early American society).

86. Ibid.

87. Saul Cornell, *A Well-Regulated Militia: The Founding Fathers and the Origins of Gun Control in America* (Oxford: Oxford University Press, 2006).

88. Samuel Adams, "E.A.," *The Writings of Samuel Adams* (1904–8) 1:316.

89. On Anglo-American conceptions of liberty and rights in this era, see John Phillip Reid, *Constitutional History of the American Revolution: The Authority of Rights* (Madison: University of Wisconsin Press, 1986) and *The Concept of Liberty in the Age of the American Revolution* (Chicago: University of Chicago Press, 1988).

90. Cornell, *A Well Regulated Militia*.

91. G. Edward White, *Law in American History* (Oxford: Oxford University Press, 2012), 1:143.

92. William Rawle, *A View of the Constitution of the United States* (2nd ed., 1829), 125–26.

93. Ibid.

94. *United States v. Mitchell* 2 U.S. 348 (1795); *United States v. Vigol* 2 U.S. 346 (1795); *United States v. Fries*, 3 U.S. 3 Dall. 515 (1799).

95. O'Shea, "Modeling the Second Amendment."

96. St. George Tucker, Commentaries on Blackstone (1803), Appendix B, *On Treason*, 14.

97. Paul Douglas Newman, *Fries's Rebellion: The Enduring Struggle for the American Revolution* (Philadelphia: University of Pennsylvania Press, 2004).

98. David B. Kopel, "The Second Amendment in the Nineteenth Century," *BYU Law Review* 59 (1998); Malcolm, *To Keep and Bear Arms*.

99. Lauren Benton and Kathryn Walker, "Law for the Empire: The Common Law in Colonial America and the Problem of Legal Diversity," *Chicago-Kent Law Review* 89 (2014): 937; William E. Nelson, *The Common Law in Colonial America* (Oxford: Oxford University Press, 2008).

100. St. George Tucker, *View of the Constitution of the United States*, appendix to Blackstone's Commentaries.

101. M.D. Const. art. III, § 1 (1776); DE Const. art 25 (1776); William B. Stoebuck, "Reception of English Common Law in the American Colonies," *William and Mary Law Review* 10 (1968): 393.

102. Statutes at Large of Pennsylvania (1903), 9:29–30.

103. Francois Xavier Martin, *A Collection of Statutes of the Parliament of England in Force in the State Of North-Carolina* (1792), 60–61 (prohibiting conduct by individuals who "ride armed by night nor by day"); *A Collection of All Such Acts of the General Assembly of Virginia, of a Public and Permanent Nature, as Are Now in Force* (1794), 33 (prohibiting that an individual "go or ride armed by night or day").

104. William Waller Hening, *The New Virginia Justice Comprising the Office and Authority of a Justice of the Peace, in the Commonwealth of Virginia. Together with a Variety of Useful Precedents Adapted to the Laws Now in Force.* Hening went on to become the compiler of Virginia's *Statutes at Large*.

105. *The Perpetual laws, of the Commonwealth of Massachusetts, from the Establishment of its Constitution to the Second Session of the General Court*, in 1798 (Isaiah Thomas Worcester 1799), 2:259.

106. Binder, *Criminal Law*.

107. *The Perpetual Laws, Of The Commonwealth of Massachusetts*, 2:259 (prohibiting individuals who "shall ride or go armed offensively, to the fear or terror of the good citizens of this Commonwealth").

108. As Laura Edwards demonstrates, the traditional English practice of using private prosecutions for assault and similar crimes gradually gave way to a focus on public prosecution as an affront to the people's peace in the South. See Edwards, *The People and Their Peace*.

109. Joseph Backus, *The Justice of the Peace* . . . (Hartford, 1816), 23.

110. Francois Xavier Martin, *A Treatise on the Power and Duties of a Constable According to the Law of North Carolina* (1806), 9.

111. James Ewing, *A Treatise on the Office and Duty of the Justice of the Peace, Sheriff, Coroner, Constable* (1805).

112. 554 U.S. 570 (2008).

113. Ibid.

114. Ibid.

115. Rostron, "Justice Breyer's Triumph," 803; Joseph Blocher, "Categoricalism and Balancing in First and Second Amendment Analysis," *New York University Law Review* 84 (2009): 375–434; Mark Tushnet, "Heller and the Perils of Compromise," *Lewis & Clark Law Review* 13 (2009): 419.

116. In the view of Mark Tushnet, there is little difference between Scalia and Breyer's view once one digs beneath the rhetoric; see Tushnet, "Heller and the Perils of Compromise" ("Despite the tone of Justice Scalia's opinion, he is on the same methodological page as Justice Breyer, though he cannot admit the fact").

117. 554 U.S. 570 (2008).

118. For a discussion of modern gun control, see Robert J. Spitzer, *Guns across America: Reconciling Gun Rules and Rights* (Oxford: Oxford University Press, 2016).

CHAPTER 2

The Expressive Second Amendment

DARRELL A. H. MILLER

In *The Secret Agent,* Joseph Conrad's masterpiece about anarchists in late Victorian England, the most arresting character is called simply the "Professor." The Professor is a bespectacled, "dingy little man": physically weak, sullen, prideful, smarting from a thousand imagined injustices.[1] Ordinarily, he would be a target of ridicule, or an object of indifference—a figure to ignore or harass. But nobody does. Because the Professor has strapped a bomb to his chest and holds the detonator constantly in his hand. Everybody knows the Professor, and nobody bothers him. Not the criminal element who would prey on him, not the government agents who would tyrannize him.

Now, imagine an honest, intrepid law enforcement official takes the Professor unawares, seizes his bomb, and charges him with possession of a weapon of mass destruction.[2] What if the Professor claims he has a Second Amendment right to carry such a weapon? Doubtless the weapon has made him secure, despite the great risk to himself and to others. But imagine the Professor goes further. Imagine the Professor claims that the bomb not only makes him safe, it makes him *feel* safe; that it makes him feel respected and powerful; that it makes him feel independent; that it affirms his self-image as an outsider and nonconformist; that it exhibits his contempt for ordinary morality and for corrupting government. How should a court address these Second Amendment arguments?

People keep and carry weapons for all sorts of reasons. What kind of reasons should the law respect? Governments regulate the keeping and carrying of weapons for all sorts of reasons. What kind of reasons should the law reject?

At first, the question seems trivial. In *District of Columbia v. Heller,* the Supreme Court identified self-defense as the "core" of the Second

Amendment right to keep and bear arms.[3] Hence, the law of the Second Amendment should respect reasons and reject regulations to optimize self-defense. We may disagree over who should make those decisions, in what manner, and with what evidence, but we don't disagree over the ultimate goal.

But the Second Amendment described in *Heller* and discussed in American culture and politics doesn't neatly converge on self-defense as the sole—or even the primary—purpose of the Second Amendment. Consider a convicted felon who has served his time and is now free. To make it more pointed, imagine that the felon had committed a particularly heinous crime, like murder or rape. Almost nobody believes that the felon, once released, has forever surrendered a right to defend himself from attack. The felon may bear the stigma of conviction, but he is not a true "outlaw"—a person placed outside the protection of the law and vulnerable to anyone's private violence at any time. Yet most people would be outraged if a court held that convicted rapists have a constitutional right to own a gun.

Or consider short-barreled shotguns. The federal government has heavily regulated these weapons since at least 1934.[4] For some persons, a short-barreled shotgun would be an ideal weapon. It is easily handled, it has a broad spread of fire, and it requires little marksmanship to be lethal.[5] But the very features that make a short-barreled shotgun useful for self-defense also make it attractive to criminals.[6] Indeed, one reason the national government regulated short-barreled shotguns was because they had become popular among Jazz Era bootleggers.[7] *Heller* held that "dangerous and unusual weapons"[8] could be prohibited regardless of their utility, and what makes a weapon like a short-barreled shotgun dangerous and unusual appears to be its association with criminals rather than with law-abiding citizens. Clearly, some element other than the costs and benefits of armed self-defense influences decisions about gun rights and policy. I think that additional element is the expressive component of the Second Amendment.

This essay attempts to chart some features of the expressive Second Amendment. Of necessity, it will be schematic. This essay cannot supply a comprehensive sociology of gun rights, gun control, or the Second Amendment. Instead, it offers guideposts for a more searching exploration of the relationship between expressive theories of law and the persistent issues that surround Second Amendment adjudication.

The first part of this essay isolates those strands of gun rights and regulations that, when unwound, seem tethered to something other than an instrumental concern for self-defense or safety. The second part fits gun rights and regulation within a larger framework of expressive theories of law. This is a vast and contested literature. My objective in this second part is largely descriptive: to explain how expressive theories model the inter-action between law and norms and to describe how law can shape norms. It relies on assumptions about norms and behavior that those with more time, space, and empirical skills are attempting to prove.[9] The third part is more prescriptive, but also more speculative: having isolated how gun rights and regulations incorporate factors that diverge from self-protection, and having identified how law can shape norms and vice-versa, what is the role of constitutional law, in particular the Second Amendment, with respect to these expressions? Specifically, what kind of norm-shaping activity does the Second Amendment prohibit, and what kind of legal expression does the Second Amendment forbid, irrespective of its effect on human behavior?

Weapons are symbols as well as instruments.[10] Yes, a gun is a tool of self-defense, and that is now the chief reason people give for owning one.[11] But it is misleading to believe that guns are only about self-defense. A focus solely on protection ignores a far more complicated set of issues about the right to keep and bear arms. It is the "social meanings [of guns] . . . and not just . . . the consequences" imposed by gun ownership that animate our most contentious debates over the Second Amendment and gun policy.[12]

People own and carry guns for a number of reasons besides personal protection. A person may carry a gun to express her independence. In North Dakota and Iowa, legally blind citizens have obtained permits to carry concealed handguns.[13] A New Jersey man, rendered a quadriplegic following a football injury, sued authorities to obtain a permit to buy a shotgun, altered to fire with a breathing tube, so that he could hunt. A National Rifle Association representative lauded the disabled man for pursuing his Second Amendment rights.[14]

A person may carry guns to show that he is powerful, respected, or mature, even if the perception is illusory or fleeting. Jeffery Fagan and Deanna Wilkinson have explored how "guns became symbols of respect, power, and manhood"[15] among urban youth during the late twentieth century. As one interviewee remarked, "Ain't no more manhood it's gunhood."[16]

Carrying a gun may betoken membership in a select and self-conscious social or cultural group. The Black Panthers and the Deacons for Defense armed themselves expressly as an act of racial pride and as defenders against threatened and actual racist aggression.[17] The sociologist Jennifer Carlson has documented how many concealed-carry holders consider themselves members of a brotherhood of community protectors.[18]

Gun ownership can symbolize integration into the larger national political community. Guns have historically been a symbol of who can be a citizen, who can "partake in the imagined life of the nation . . . [and] enter into [its] mythologies."[19] Laws that limited the ability of African Americans, Native Americans, or immigrants to purchase or carry firearms prove this point.[20]

Conversely, people may carry guns to express their contempt for a political, economic, or social system that they consider corrupt or ineffective. A German labor group in the nineteenth century, called the "Lehr und Wehr Verein," marched in an armed parade in Illinois as an act of worker solidarity and to protest what its members perceived was a corrupt management-friendly political system.[21]

Doubtless, individuals may keep and carry arms for more than one of these reasons. A blind person may want a rifle because he loves hunting and to demonstrate his independence. A young African American may want a pistol to reject the existing political order and to protect himself.

Assume that one could demonstrate a near-zero probability that a severely disabled person could successfully use a firearm to defend himself from attack. Or assume one could prove, thorough expert testimony, that no amount of small arms could ever prevent the military from imposing despotism on the nation. I wager that the gun owner would still desire a weapon—and not just because he disbelieves the evidence.[22] If pressed, he likely would argue that it is his right to possess a weapon, whatever the likely cost to himself or to others, and no matter how ineffective it may be. If that is true, possessing the gun only incidentally relates to its use in defending against a burglar or a military junta. Owning and carrying a gun expresses some other value, whether we understand that value to be something like independence, belonging, self-esteem, or defiance.

On the other side of the ledger, society may regulate guns for reasons that appear only tenuously related to safety. Currently, federal regulations prohibit most felons from possessing firearms, no matter how old the conviction and no matter the type of crime.[23] Barring a statutory rapist from possessing a firearm may have little to do with the danger posed by that person, or even the deterrent effect of the penalty, and have everything to do with the opprobrium society wants to express toward persons who commit crimes against children.[24]

A number of historical and modern regulations prohibit carrying weapons into churches, schools, or polling places. These places are not necessarily rendered safer as a result. Indeed, gun rights advocates strenuously claim it makes such places *less* safe. Instead, some other value—religious devotion, education, democratic participation—seems frustrated by the presence of lethal implements.[25]

Similarly, many laws prohibit firearms in government buildings or punish assaults against government officers more severely than assaults on civilians.[26] Governments regulate firearms differently in government-controlled facilities, in the presence of government officials, or in public areas for reasons that may be about asserting the state's authority over violence as much as it is about protection of the public and public servants.[27]

I suspect that defenders of these kinds of regulations would reject evidence that more guns in more places makes everyone safer. But their rejection may not be due to confirmation bias—the tendency to accept data that confirm your prejudice and reject data that contradict it. Instead, I wager that persons defending these types of regulations would support them even *if* more guns in more places were to make everyone safer and even *if* they believed the data supporting that view. These defenders may not be motivated by the consequences of firearms on safety, as much as they want firearm policy to express outrage, faith, respect, or republican virtue, in a way that mirrors the reasons a gun owner may want to carry a weapon in the first place.

Guns have social meaning; so does law.[28] Law communicates. It expresses. In the past thirty years, scholars from various disciplines have generated a prodigious literature on the expressive function of law. This literature falls roughly into two categories: descriptive and prescriptive.[29] The descriptive account of law's expressive function focuses on the economic, psychological, sociological, or anthropological issues surrounding law. How does law affect human behavior? How do individuals or groups come to understand law as an obligation? How do individuals or groups distinguish law from other kinds of norms? Which comes first, norms or law? What does a culture's law say about how that culture understands itself? These are descriptive questions.

By contrast, scholars also have generated prescriptive accounts of law's expressive function. This is largely a philosophical exercise, and, like most prescriptive accounts, generally separate into consequentialist and deontological approaches. The consequentialist assumes that law's expression influences human behavior in predictable and measurable ways. Given this assumption, the consequentialist asks what the law should express to generate optimal outcomes (however defined). Alternatively, the deontologist is less concerned with consequences and is more concerned with the morality of the law's expression itself.[30]

Equal protection, establishment clause jurisprudence, voting rights, and much of criminal law becomes tractable when we understand law's expression along both of these dimensions—law's ability to reflect, shape, or coordinate behavior as well as the moral evaluation of that expression.[31] This isn't to say there's no force to law. Law coerces, without doubt. Law involves the deployment of force by persons invested with that power.[32] Law can confine bodies, seize property, and extinguish life.[33]

But law also communicates. It *means* something to punish assault on a police officer more harshly than assault on a civilian. It *means* something to say that a battery motivated by racial hatred is a crime to be distinguished from ordinary battery. It *means* something to single out Islamic law as alien to American law. The law communicates something about people and about society both in what the law regulates and what it says about that regulation.[34] Justice Jackson and (more recently) Justice Kennedy, in their rhetorical flights, may insist the state has no power to designate what is orthodox in public or private life[35]—but frankly, that's nonsense.[36] By definition, law tells us something about good and bad, orthodox and unorthodox.[37] And, by design, law expresses messages to affect behavior and shape norms.

Laws are entangled with social meanings, and laws affect social meanings.[38] Law can entrench preexisting social norms. For example, exchanging money for body parts, or votes, or babies is widely considered taboo.[39] Law confirms these social understandings. It also prevents market norms from attaching to these kinds of exchanges by fixing the stigma of criminal sanction on those who would offer or accept payment in these transactions.[40]

Law can also change social meanings. It can do so directly, by functioning as a normative counterweight, undermining or destroying other kinds of norms that already exist. The Civil Rights Act of 1964 is an example. The anti-discrimination norm of the Civil Rights Act helped suppress the norm of racial discrimination in private businesses by raising the costs for engaging in such discrimination.[41] Even regulations with low chances at effective enforcement—like stopping at a red light—can function in this way by associating a breach of a social norm with illegality.

Law can also change social meanings by "ambiguating" the social understating of a behavior.[42] Lawrence Lessig offers the example of dueling. Southern gentlemen abided by social norms that deplored cowardice and extolled public service. Simply proscribing dueling would not make a person less of a coward if the challenged individual refused to duel. But banning dueling, and barring from public office those who did duel, could make ambiguous the meaning of a refusal to duel. Cowards refuse to duel, but so do honorable men who want to preserve their ability to serve the public.[43]

Law can also coordinate behavior through its expression. The classic example is a law that designates which side of the road to drive on. People could arbitrarily choose a side anytime they got into their car, but that would make everyone worse off, both in the form of accidents and in the precautions necessary to avoid accidents. As a result, legal prescriptions that drivers must drive on the right side of the road (in America) act as a signal to coordinate behavior and reduce inefficiency. Those who insist on driving on the left side are tortfeasors or criminals; those who drive on the right side are law-abiding citizens.[44] A similar example is the ability of law, even when unaccompanied by sanctions, to "nudge" persons onto a particular normative track.[45] Prohibitions on smoking or laws concerning recycling, for example, can serve this function.[46] The object of law is to elicit a "norm cascade," in which the expression of the law (whether to protect or to condemn) acts as a signal that can swiftly change social norms.[47]

Prohibitions on concealed weapons is an example of law used in this fashion. Concealed weapons were historically associated with assassination, criminality, and unmanliness.[48] Therefore, many regulations on carrying concealed weapons entrench this social attitude despite the potential utility of carrying them hidden. Conversely, efforts to normalize concealed carry through law are calculated to remove any stigma associated with such behavior, and perhaps trigger what gun rights proponents feel is a positive norm cascade in favor of more guns in more places.[49]

It is still common in some parts of the country for people to shoot guns into the air on New Year's Day or the Fourth of July, with fatal results. Arizona responded to a particularly tragic event when Shannon Smith, a fourteen-year-old girl talking on the phone in her backyard, was killed by a falling bullet. "Shannon's Law" elevated the penalty for so-called celebratory gunfire from a misdemeanor to a felony.[50] Virginia enacted a similar law in 2014 after a seven-year-old boy was killed walking to an Independence Day celebration the previous year. A physician writing about the Virginia law said that "[the] law sends the right message, [but] in too many jurisdictions . . . celebratory gunfire is considered a misdemeanor."[51] These laws seem to be particularly expressive, given the difficulty of identifying perpetrators.[52]

Until a federal district court judge struck down the law, North Carolina prohibited anyone from carrying a firearm off her property during a government-declared state of emergency.[53] The coordinating function of this law is obvious. During a state of emergency, such as the aftermath of a hurricane, the tendency for each person to adopt an "every man for himself" attitude can be overwhelming. The law is an expressive signal, designed to prevent an avalanche of otherwise rational self-preserving behavior—everyone taking a gun to the only working gas station, for example—so that the government can provide orderly procedures for disaster relief.[54]

As noted above, the Constitution's role in regulating the law's expressive function can be consequentialist or deontological. That is, the Constitution could prohibit laws designed to shape or reinforce norms because the law is likely to lead to sub-optimal results; or it could prohibit laws because of some moral imperative about the law's expression itself.

The law of obscenity provides an example at the consequentialist end of the spectrum. The First Amendment does not cover obscenity, and pandering obscenity is a crime that can carry harsh penalties as well as social stigma. But the definition of unprotected obscenity encodes a naked cost-benefit matrix. A work is obscene, and hence unprotected, only when "the average person, applying contemporary community standards would find . . . the work . . . appeals to the prurient interest . . . [second] . . . the work depicts or describes, in a patently offensive way, sexual conduct specifically defined by the applicable state law; and [third] . . . the work, taken as a whole, lacks serious literary, artistic, political, or scientific value."[55] In this way, the First Amendment incorporates norms (an average person, applying contemporary community standards), shapes norms (the work must lack serious value), and does so in a way that is attentive to consequences (punishing speech without value without over-deterring speech that has value).

At the more deontological end of the spectrum, it is well established that if the government picks out one religion for ridicule or, conversely, for special veneration, the government has violated the First Amendment. As Justice O'Connor wrote, when government "sends a message to nonadherents [of a particular religion] that they are outsiders, not full members of the political community, and an accompanying message to adherents that they are insiders, favored members of the political community," then government has run afoul of the Constitution.[56] This kind of expressive harm could occur even if the individual or group's material welfare remained unchanged. Oklahoma's ban on Sharia law and San Francisco's resolution condemning a Catholic priest's adoption policy present deontological questions about constitutional prohibitions, in addition to whatever negative effects those government actions produce.[57] Similarly, when race is the only factor used to draw certain distinctions, it violates the Equal Protection Clause, even if those affected could not possibly understand the law's expression. A race-segregated cemetery for orphans or a race-segregated nursery for infants would both violate the Constitution, for example.[58]

What does the Second Amendment have to say about such expressive uses of the law when they concern firearms? As an initial matter, it is apparent that there is nothing per se unconstitutional under the Second Amendment or almost any constitutional provision about government using law for expressive purposes. Constitutional rights are often regarded as "trumps," in the words of Ronald Dworkin.[59] People treat rights as personal vetoes against majoritarian sentiments, including majoritarian efforts to confirm or change social meanings. As Justice Jackson put it: "The very purpose of a Bill of Rights was to withdraw certain subjects from the vicissitudes of political controversy, to place them beyond the reach of majorities and officials."[60] But, as a number of scholars have noted, this conception of rights does not accurately reflect American constitutional practice.[61]

An anti-burning law designed to punish disrespect for the American flag may violate the First Amendment, but an anti-burning law designed to prevent release of toxic pollutants does not.[62] A municipality may violate the First Amendment when it wants to stifle racist or anti-racist protest, but not when it wants to control noise or avoid traffic congestion.[63]

Constitutional rights, including the Second Amendment right to keep and bear arms, then, are not blanket prohibitions on the government's use of law to confirm or alter social meanings. Nor are they trumps that insulate individuals from reputational or material harm when they violate a norm. Instead, constitutional rights are mechanisms for regulating "the kinds of reasons" that the government may offer for its rules.[64] In this conception of rights, a constitutional right is a right to be sanctioned by a rule laid down for the right reasons and subject to some minimum quantity of proof. It is not a right to engage in some primary conduct simpliciter.[65] As Matt Adler says, "Constitutional rights . . . are structured, not as shields *around* particular actions, but as shields *against* particular rules."[66]

If rights are not shields around actions, if the Second Amendment right to keep and bear arms does not protect the mere *act* of keeping and bearing arms, then what does it protect? A partial answer is that the Second Amendment, like other constitutional rights, allows individuals to produce "common goods" or "public goods," broadly conceived, and facilitates development and maintenance of institutions to supply these goods.[67] The right shields individuals from rules designed to prevent development of these kinds of public goods, or from rules whose effects are so severe that society cannot organize to produce these kinds of goods.[68] Put another way, the expressions the Second Amendment is meant to forbid, and the expressions the Second Amendment is meant to protect, are inextricably linked with the kinds of common goods the Second Amendment is meant to provide.

Freedom of speech and of the press is a liberty designed to produce an informed, engaged, educated electorate, and the institutions necessary to facilitate self-government. Unconstitutional reasons are those aimed at the public good that freedom is supposed to supply.[69] Laws that proscribe posting billboards advocating a political candidate violate the First Amendment, because the freedom of speech is supposed to foster a vibrant and engaged political culture. Choosing to prohibit speech on behalf of a candidate is almost certain to frustrate this purpose. However, these kinds of public goods—like an engaged and informed political culture—develop in an environment where other social norms and rights also supply common goods. Our justice system is supposed to be impartial, and due process requires it to be impartial, and for it to function, our justice system must possess the trust and confidence of the people. So some kinds of regulations that facilitate development of other kinds of common goods may impinge upon rights on other margins, and the courts must take heed of these conflicts. The Supreme Court's recent decision that permits states to prohibit direct campaign solicitations by judicial candidates, notwithstanding the First Amendment, is an example of this dynamic.[70]

What kind of reasons may government offer for rules that would punish someone like the Professor from carrying his bomb? This question may be addressed in three steps. The first step requires some notion of what the right to keep and bear arms is *for*—what kind of public good, broadly conceived, the Second Amendment helps supply. If the regulation is not aimed at the public good the right is supposed to supply, then it would not facially violate the Constitution. The second step considers the purpose or effect of the regulation with respect to other kinds of public goods, protected by rights in the same or another institution.[71] The third step looks at whether there is some consequence of sufficient urgency or some aggregation of consequences of such force to justify an inhibition of the right.[72]

What public good is the right to keep and bear arms meant to supply? That is a difficult question to answer, because, beyond an unhelpfully broad statement of "self-defense," the common good supplied by a right to keep and bear arms is as contested as the social meaning of guns themselves. One could look to the ethos of the nation, to contemporary political morality, or to the intentions of the framers. I do not have the space in this short essay to discuss how, when, why or whether the Constitution (or the justices) can designate—or "fix"—the public good supplied by a constitutional right.[73] As a provisional matter, I look to both *Heller* and its sequel *McDonald v. City of Chicago*[74] for guidance, recognizing that these cases are often opaque and contingent.

As my colleague Joseph Blocher and I have written elsewhere, *Heller* and *McDonald* suggest the Second Amendment is meant to supply at least three kinds of public goods.[75] First, the right could provide some form of tyranny prevention; second, the right could provide—not self-defense per se—but *safety*; third, the right could provide some social benefit like respect for human dignity or autonomy.

The tyranny-preventing role is the notion, advanced by Justice Scalia in *Heller*, that when people are trained in arms, "they are better able to resist tyranny."[76] Therefore, the right to keep and bear arms is a right to have arms so that government preserves democratic institutions. This is the "doomsday" understanding of the Amendment, and it commands an intense following in some circles.[77] It is also probably the closest to what may have been in the original justification for the Amendment, although the framers likely believed the anti-tyranny impulse would be channeled through intermediary institutions—chief among them the states, their elected leaders, and their militias.

The tyranny-preventing interpretation of the Amendment, however, is limited. It is limited, first, because the public good supplied by the right, a government that is not tyrannical, makes the right always nascent. A democracy that is functioning, even functioning poorly, is not a despotism. So long as the structural features of a functioning democracy are in place—respect for the rule of law, orderly transfer of power, operation of the procedures of political dynamics—the anti-tyranny notion of the right to keep and bear arms shouldn't be ripe.[78] Second, and relatedly, the anti-tyranny feature of the right to keep and bear arms is itself the product of a political process. The deterrent effects of private arms are not individual rights to threaten government with weapons, any more than the person who votes against the president may exit from the social compact on the basis of his vote. The entire Lockean notion of a right to dissolve the social compact and return to the state of nature is not an activity that occurs in some atomized individual sense. It is a collective decision that cannot be adjudicated in any sense beforehand.[79] Third, the mechanism for this public good is incidental and not direct. *Heller* itself remarks that one reason for the right is to suppress rebellion, which casts serious doubt on the proposition that the *kinds* of weapons that any one individual can possess must be effective against a standing army. Instead, the ability to possess arms for private protection is only indirectly related to checking a potentially despotic government. In sum, the public good conceived by the Second Amendment is not a cowed and dysfunctional government, but an appropriately cautious one.

The right to keep and bear arms could be designed, not to supply self-defense per se, but to supply a more general public good of safety. *Heller* itself seems to acknowledge this goal. On the one hand, it reduces the right to a "core" of self-defense. On the other, it offers a litany of regulations concerning felons, the mentally ill, and guns in sensitive places that are "presumptively lawful."[80] The structure of offering rights plus some kinds of regulations suggests that the Court acknowledges a Second Amendment equilibrium that provides optimum safety for everyone.

The safety interpretation sounds in what Professor Blocher and I have referred to as the "marketplace of violence" theory of the Amendment. That is, the Amendment contemplates a marketplace—much as the marketplace of speech—where society provides an optimum amount of safety for every-one, because, in the aggregate, those persons with bad or neutral motives for having firearms will be overwhelmed by those with good motives.[81] This is what Wayne LaPierre, executive director of the NRA, suggests when he says that "the only thing that stops a bad guy with a gun is a good guy with a gun."[82]

This theory also has limits, and those limits help to evaluate the consti-tutionality of the reasons for, and effects of, a regulation. The "marketplace of violence" does not have to mean a libertarian marketplace, in which the total number of guns is maximized, bad gun use is eclipsed by good gun use, and the invisible hand ineluctably leads to ideal safety. The very notion of a marketplace designed to produce some public good, called safety, also presumes that government can enter to avoid market failures, reduce negative externalities, or assist in coordinating market participants. Government cannot supply safety by proscribing all private arms—that would negate the Second Amendment altogether—but it can regulate in ways that minimize certain familiar collective action problems. For example, it may be that good guys with sawed-off shotguns are useful to counter threats by bad guys with sawed-off shotguns. But it may be that the proliferation of sawed-off shotguns actually produces worse safety outcomes overall. By making sawed-off shotguns illegal—even for persons who would use them for good purposes—the law acts to solve a collective action problem in which everyone acting in his own best interest makes everyone less well off.

The final theory doesn't look much like a public good at all, and it has to do with individual autonomy. Not autonomy in the atomistic sense of truly being a law unto one's self—instead, the Second Amendment may protect autonomy as a kind of second-best allocation of decision-making authority that leads to an optimal supply of public goods like security or respect for life. In other words, by allowing each individual to make personal decisions within the broadest range of choices, the aggregated effect will be optimal for everyone. In this case, the government's burden would not be to prove that the individual has made a poor personal decision, but that the system-wide effect of his decision is a net negative.

How would we evaluate the Professor's claims for Second Amendment protection under this three-step process? Working in reverse order, if we think that a sufficiently catastrophic consequence is likely to follow from an otherwise constitutionally protected choice, that reason may be enough in itself to limit the right. Even if the Second Amendment claim is in some sense deontological or dignitary, consequences are still relevant. Indeed, generating consequences can and is an important role in the expressive function of law.[83] The debate then transposes to questions of institutional competence, candor, and trust in the regulator. Putting these difficult issues aside, most moral theories of law leave some space for a sufficiently serious consequentialist analysis of a rule. Whether the consequence must be "catastrophic" or merely "very serious" is an issue I cannot address here.[84] It is sufficient to say, for now, that even if we were to concede that seizing the Professor's bomb compromised his feelings of security, pride, independence, or contempt, there should be space in Second Amendment theory to consider the consequences of permitting him to travel armed in his preferred manner.

Second, assume the state could not prove a calamitous consequence for allowing the Professor to carry his bomb. Even then, there should be an opportunity to show that the regulations advance other kinds of rights and public goods along other dimensions, and not just on the axis of self-defense and safety. As Adrian Vermeule has written, one defect of focusing too closely on one dimension of risk when adjudicating constitutional rights is that courts may be less attentive to risks along other margins. A court that polices structural rights too vigorously in protection of political minorities can lead to gridlock, which leads to popular dissatisfaction with government, which gives rise to populist authoritarians.[85] Similarly, a government that protects gun rights too vigorously can lead to net losses in other areas, like political participation, voting, education, religious exercise, or other kind of public goods supplied by other kinds of rights in other kinds of institutions.[86] Even if the Professor traveling about with his weapon of choice didn't threaten catastrophic consequences, the risk along other margins is significant. Knowing that there is a weapon in a lecture hall or a polling booth can have a negative impact on the political culture that rights like the freedom of speech and the right to vote are designed to provide.[87]

Finally, what if—either directly through the law's enactment, or revealed through litigation—it was conceded that government's reason for the rule against destructive devices was to keep the Professor and people like him from feeling independent, to undermine his sense of self as an anarchist, or to disapprove of his form of protest against ordinary morality and corrupting government? In other words, what if the reasons for the regulation targeted precisely the expressive, non-instrumental reasons the Professor wants his bomb? Would *those* kinds of reasons violate the Second Amendment?

The question seems somewhat fanciful, for, as Joseph Blocher has written, under what circumstances would the state concede that its *only* purpose is to oppress?[88] That said, some common regulations clearly express hostility to self-help and self-reliance, and express instead a preference for deference to government authority. Prohibitions on resistance to an unlawful arrest, laws against forcible repossession of chattels, anti-terrorism legislation,[89] and even the common law of self-defense (which requires that an individual retreat as far as possible before using deadly force), all express disapproval of the independence, pride, clannishness, or government hostility that may motivate someone like the Professor to carry his weapon.

My strong sense is that these kinds of reasons still would not violate the Second Amendment. As Bernard Brown has written, "The first business of a ruler is the elimination of all forms of self-help."[90] His summary simply confirms the Lockean notion that in return for the security of the state, each person surrenders his right to execute his own judgments of natural right on every other person.[91] Hence, if the reason for the law is to foster respect for democratic institutions, to exhibit the state's authority in choice and use of violence, and to reaffirm that the Professor in fact operates within a society, then it seems those reasons cannot be constitutionally suspect under the Second Amendment.

If those reasons don't violate the Second Amendment, what kind of reasons would? As discussed before, a bare declaration that a law is intended to disarm the entire population would violate the Second Amendment, because expressive theories of the law operate on the assumption that words have meaning, and the Second Amendment guarantees a right of the people to keep and bear arms. Even though such a feat of universal disarmament would be impossible, the expressed negation of a constitutional right through law could be the very kind of expressive injury to the rule of law that the Second Amendment recognizes.

A wish to disarm some identifiable segment of the population—such as African Americans or Muslims—may violate equality norms within the Second Amendment, as well as those norms within the First and Fourteenth Amendments. This does not mean, for example, that persons who want to protect themselves with bombs or some other preferred weapon constitute some kind of "discrete and insular minority" within the Second Amendment. It means simply that, as between otherwise equal rights claimants, there is nothing about the Second Amendment that would permit distinctions between groups that would otherwise violate equality values in other constitutional domains. The analogy would be to the First Amendment. Obscenity is not protected speech, but the state cannot outlaw obscenity only when it disparages Christians or Hispanics.[92] In a similar way, as between otherwise indistinguishable law-abiding adult citizens, the state could not make distinctions, even as to unprotected arms, based on the bare desire to disadvantage or stigmatize a population, as opposed to promote some other value like safety.

Finally, this idea may apply to individuals. A naked desire to denigrate the Professor's right to self-protection—not with any particular implement, but his right to self-defense alone—or, worse, a public signal that the state will not protect the Professor and will not protect him when he protects himself, may well be the kind of regulatory motive the Second Amendment would prohibit.[93] Whether this kind of expressive harm is a null set, because it would never occur, or because no regulation could ever work this way, because due process and necessity exceptions are implicit in nearly every rule, is a matter I leave to other writers.[94]

Notes

1. Joseph Conrad, *The Secret Agent* (1907; reprint, New York: Anchor Books 1953), 62.
2. We will assume for the hypothetical that the Professor is now in America.
3. *District of Columbia v. Heller*, 554 U.S. 570, 630 (2008).
4. National Firearms Act, 73rd Congress, Sess. 2, 48 Stat. 1236 (June 26, 1934).
5. Nelson Lund, "The Second Amendment, *Heller*, and Originalist Jurisprudence," *University of California Los Angeles Law Review* 56 (2009): 1367n73 ("short-barreled shotguns may be optimal weapons for home defense in many circumstances").

6. Justice Breyer says something very similar to this in his dissent in *Heller* concerning handguns. *District of Columbia v. Heller,* 554 U.S. 570, 711 (2008) (Breyer, J., dissenting) ("the very attributes that make handguns particularly useful for self-defense are also what make them particularly dangerous").

7. Brian L. Frye, "The Peculiar Story of *United States v. Miller,*" *NYU Journal of Law & Liberty* 3 (2008): 67–68.

8. *Heller,* 627.

9. For some examples of empirical tests of expressive law, see Yuval Feldman, "The Expressive Function of Trade Secret Law: Legality, Cost, Intrinsic Motivation and Consensus," *Journal of Empirical Studies* 6 (2009), and Patricia Funk, "Is There An Expressive Function of Law?: An Empirical Analysis of Voting Laws With Symbolic Fines," *American Law & Economics Review* 9 (2007).

10. Dan M. Kahan and Donald Braman, "More Statistics, Less Persuasion: A Cultural Theory of Gun-Risk Perceptions," *University of Pennsylvania Law Review* 151 (2003): 1294.

11. Gallup Poll, "Guns," October 3–6 (2013), http://www.gallup.com/poll/1645/guns .aspx (showing 60 percent of responders chose "Personal Safety/Protection" as the reason for owning a gun); Pew Research Center, "Why Own a Gun? Protection Is Now Top Reason," March 12, 2013 (showing 48 percent of gun owners say they own guns for protection), http://www.people-press.org/2013/03/12/why-own-a-gun-protection-is-now-top-reason/.

12. Kahan and Braman, "More Statistics, Less Persuasion," 1294.

13. Jason Clayworth, "Iowa Grants Permits for Blind Residents To Carry Guns in Public," *Des Moines Register,* September 8, 2013; "Blind Man Gets Concealed-arms Permit in N.D.," January 3, 2001, http://www.deseretnews.com/article/817321/Blind-man-gets -concealed-arms-permit-in-ND.html?pg=all.

14. Jennifer Golson, "Quadriplegic Sues Manville, Police Chief for Denying Him a Firearms ID," *The Star Ledger,* May 27, 2009, https://www.nj.com/news/index.ssf /2009/05/quadriplegic_sues_town_police.html; Associated Press, "Quadriplegic Hunter Wins Legal Fight, Takes Aim," December 9, 2009, http://www.nbcnews.com/id/34348491 /ns/us_news-life/t/quadriplegic-hunter-wins-legal-fight-takes-aim/.

15. Jeffrey Fagan and Deanna L. Wilkinson, "Gun Youth Violence and Social Identity in Inner Cities," *Crime & Justice* 24 (1998): 179.

16. Deanna L. Wilkinson and Jeffrey Fagan, "The Role of Firearms in Violence 'Scripts': The Dynamics of Gun Events among Adolescent Males," *Law & Contemporary Problems* 59 (1996): 81.

17. Nicholas Johnson, *Negroes and the Gun* (New York: Prometheus 2014), 265, 287.

18. Jennifer Carlson, *Citizen-Protectors* (New York: Oxford University Press, 2015), 106–7.

19. Laura Browder, *Her Best Shot: Women and Guns in America* (Chapel Hill: University of North Carolina Press, 2006), 19.

20. Pratheepan Gulasekaram, "Guns and Membership in the American Polity," *William & Mary Bill of Rights Journal* 21 (2012).

21. *Presser v. Illinois,* 116 U.S. 252 (1886).

22. Kahan and Braman, "More Statistics, Less Persuasion," 1314.

23. 18 U.S.C. § 922(g)(1).

24. *Binderup v. United States,* 836 F.3d 336 (3d Cir. 2016) (allowing a Second Amendment as-applied challenge to the felon-in-possession law by a person convicted of misdemeanor corruption of a minor).

25. Darrell A. H. Miller, "Institutions and the Second Amendment," *Duke Law Journal* 66 (2016): 92, 101–3.

26. New York Penal Law § 125.27(1)(a)(i); Markus Dirk Dubber, "Policing Possession: The War on Crime and the End of Criminal Law," *Journal of Criminal Law & Criminology* 91

(2001): 959 ("The protection of state officials is achieved through a variety of status-based provisions, sprinkled throughout modern American criminal codes").

27.　One interpretation of the seventeenth-century *Sir John Knight's Case* suggests that certain kinds of public carriage of weapons was illegal because it conveyed the impression that the king was not willing or was unable to maintain the public peace. *Sir John Knight's Case* (1686) 87 Eng. Rep. 75, 76 (K.B.)

28.　Cass R. Sunstein, "On the Expressive Function of Law," *University of Pennsylvania Law Review* 144 (1996): 2022.

29.　Maggie Wittlin, "Buckling Under Pressure: An Empirical Test of the Expressive Effects of Law," *Yale Journal on Regulation* 28 (2011): 423–28.

30.　Ibid., 428. Matthew Adler questions whether such a moral theory of expressive law is possible. Matthew Adler, "Expressive Theories of Law: A Skeptical Overview," *University of Pennsylvania Law Review* 148 (2000).

31.　Elizabeth Anderson and Richard H. Pildes, "Expressive Theories of Law: A General Restatement," *University of Pennsylvania Law Review* 148 (2000): 1533–56; Adler, "Expressive Theories of Law," 148; Sunstein, "On the Expressive Function of Law," *University of Pennsylvania Law Review* 144 (1996): 2021 ("Actions are expressive; they carry meanings"); Avlana Eisenberg, "Expressive Enforcement," *UCLA Law Review* 61 (2014): 860 ("Laws send messages").

32.　Frederick Schauer, *The Force of the Law* (Cambridge, MA: Harvard University Press, 2015), 1–2.

33.　Ibid.

34.　As Murray Edleman wrote, a full understanding of law, like politics, must recognize both the "instrumental and expressive" aspects of this human activity. Murray Edelman, *The Symbolic Uses of Politics* (Urbana: University of Illinois Press, 1964), 12.

35.　*West Virginia State Board of Education v. Barnette*, 319 U.S. 624 (1943); *Lawrence v. Texas*, 539 U.S. 558 (2003).

36.　Lawrence Lessig, "The Regulation of Social Meaning," *University of Chicago Law Review* 62 (1995): 946.

37.　Ibid.

38.　Cass Sunstein, "Social Norms and Social Roles," *Columbia Law Review* 96 (1996): 913 ("A good deal of governmental action is self-consciously designed to change norms, meanings, or roles, and in that way to increase the individual benefits or decrease the individual costs associated with certain acts").

39.　Sunstein, "Expressive Function," 2038.

40.　Ibid.

41.　Ibid.; Lessig, "Social Meaning," 965, 971–72.

42.　Lessig, "Social Meaning," 971.

43.　Ibid. Lessig does concede that southern legislatures frustrated the effectiveness of the regulation through "grandfathering" provisions. Lessig, "Social Meaning," 972.

44.　A similar illustration appears in Richard H. McAdams, *Expressive Powers of Law* (Cambridge, MA: Harvard University Press, 2015), 5–6.

45.　Sunstein, "Expressive Function," 2033.

46.　Richard H. McAdams, "The Origin, Development, and Regulation of Norms," *Michigan Law Review* 96 (1997): 400–406; Richard Thaler and Cass Sunstein, *Nudge* (New Haven, CT: Yale University Press, 2008).

47.　Sunstein, "Social Norms and Social Roles," 912.

48.　*State v. Atkinson*, 141 N.C. 734, 734 (1906) ("Firing a pistol concealed in the pocket of a coat, through the cloth, without the risk of first taking it out of the pocket, is a most cowardly and unfair advantage "); *State v. Chandler*, 5 La. Ann. 489, 490 (1850) (disparaging concealed weapons as tools for "unmanly assassinations" and their regulation necessary to "counteract a vicious state of society").

49. Scottie Lee Meyers, "Fight over Gun Rights at Universities Is about More Than Public Safety, Says Professor," *Wisconsin Public Radio* (October 13, 2015), http://www.wpr.org/fight-over-gun-rights-universities-about-more-public-safety-says-professor (stating that "many gun advocates . . . want to see guns everywhere, they want to see guns normalized") (quotation of Adam Winkler).

50. Amy B. Wang, "Out of Tragedy Father Led Crusade for 'Shannon's Law,' " January 29, 2015, https://www.azcentral.com/story/news/local/phoenix/2015/01/30/tragedy-father-led-crusade-shannons-law/22570107/; "Teen Killed by Stray Bullet in Back Yard," October 15, 2004, http://archive.azcentral.com/specials/special14/articles/1015coldcase15.html.

51. Ford Vox, "Enough with the Celebratory Gunfire," August 21, 2015, http://www.cnn.com/2015/07/03/opinions/vox-celebratory-gunfire-danger/.

52. Sunstein, "Expressive Function," 2032.

53. *Bateman v. Perdue*, 881 F. Supp. 2d 709 (E.D.N.C. 2012).

54. Michael Steven Green, "Why Protect Private Arms Possession? Nine Theories of the Second Amendment," *Notre Dame Law Review* 84, no. 1 (2008): 138 (suggesting the prisoner's dilemma presented by carrying firearms).

55. *Miller v. California*, 413 U.S. 15, 24 (1973).

56. *Lynch v. Donnelly*, 465 U.S. 668, 688 (1984) (O'Connor, J., concurring).

57. *Awad v. Ziriax*, 670 F.3d 1111 (10th Cir. 2016); *Catholic League for Religious and Civil Rights v. City and County of San Francisco*, 624 F.3d 1043 (9th Cir. 2010).

58. Debora Hellman uses this latter example. Deborah Hellman, "The Expressive Dimension of Equal Protection," *Minnesota Law Review* 85 (2000): 55.

59. Richard Pildes, "Why Rights Are Not Trumps: Social Meanings, Expressive Harms, and Constitutionalism," *Journal of Legal Studies* 27 (June 1988): 727 (quoting Ronald Dworkin, *Taking Rights Seriously*, 184–205 [Cambridge, MA: Harvard University Press, 1977]).

60. *West Virginia Board of Education v. Barnette*, 319 U.S. 624, 638 (1943).

61. Richard Pildes, "Why Rights Are Not Trumps," 725; Adler, "Rights against Rules: The Moral Structure of American Constitutional Law," *Michigan Law Review* 97 (1998): 3, 4. Frederick Schauer, "A Comment on the Structure of Rights," *Georgia Law Review* 27 (1993).

62. Matt Adler uses this example. Adler, "Rights against Rules," 3, 4; Pildes, "Why Rights Are Not Trumps," 729, 730.

63. *Ward v. Rock Against Racism*, 491 U.S. 781 (1989).

64. Pildes, "Why Rights Are Not Trumps," 725; Adler, "Rights against Rules," 3, 4.; Schauer, "A Comment on the Structure of Rights," 429–31.

65. Adler, "Rights against Rules," 13.

66. Ibid.

67. Pildes, "Why Rights Are Not Trumps," 730, 731. Pildes goes on to say: "An intended and justifying consequence of rights is that through protecting the interests of specific plaintiffs, rights also realize the interest of others, including construction of a political culture with a specific kind of character." Ibid., 731.

68. This description makes explicit the kinds of consequential considerations that Pildes seems to acknowledge. Pildes, "Why Rights Are Not Trumps," 734 ("Government can infringe on rights for reasons consistent with the norms that characterize the common goods that those rights are meant to realize" but not for "reasons inconsistent with those common goods").

69. Pildes, "Why Rights Are Not Trumps," 734.

70. *Williams-Yulee v. Florida Bar*, 135 S. Ct. 1656 (2015).

71.   Pildes, "Why Rights Are Not Trumps," 750.

72.   Schauer, "Comment on the Structure of Rights," 431; Sunstein, "Expressive Theory,"
2045–47.

73.   For discussion of the "fixation" thesis in constitutional thought, see Lawrence
B. Solum, "The Fixation Thesis: The Role of Historical Fact in Original Meaning," *Notre
Dame Law Review* 91 (2015).

74.   561 U.S. 742 (2010).

75.   Joseph Blocher and Darrell A. H. Miller, "What Is Gun Control? Direct Burdens,
Incidental Burdens, and the Boundaries of the Second Amendment," *University of Chicago
Law Review* 83 (2016): 347–54. For additional reading, Michael Steven Green—who influ-
enced our thinking on this point—identifies nine reasons. Michael Steven Green, "Why
Protect Private Arms Possession? Nine Theories of the Second Amendment," *Notre Dame
Law Review* 84, no. 1 (2008).

76.   *Heller*, at 598.

77.   The terminology comes from Judge Kozinski's dissent in *Silveira v. Lockyer*, 328
F.3d 567, 570 (9th Cir. 2003).

78.   Firmin DeBrabander, *Do Guns Make Us Free? Democracy and the Armed Society*
(New Haven, CT: Yale University Press, 2015), 192–93.

79.   See Green, "Nine Theories," 180; DeBrabander, *Do Guns Make Us Free?*, 74–75.

80.   *Heller*, 627n26.

81.   My colleague discusses the marketplace metaphor in the context of the First
Amendment in Joseph Blocher, "Institutions in the Marketplace of Ideas," *Duke Law
Journal* 57, no. 4 (2008).

82.   Eric Lichtblau and Motoko Rich, "N.R.A. Envisions 'a Good Guy with a Gun' in
Every School," *New York Times*, December 21, 2012.

83.   Sunstein, "Expressive Function of Law," 2047.

84.   Schauer, "Structure of Rights," 423; Robert Nozick, *Anarchy, State, and Utopia*
(New York: Basic Books, 1974), 29n.

85.   Adrian Vermeule, *The Constitution of Risk* (New York: Cambridge University
Press, 2014), 58.

86.   Miller, "Institutions and the Second Amendment," 101–2.

87.   Ibid.; DeBrabander, *Do Guns Make Us Free?*, 160–62.

88.   Joseph Blocher, "Categoricalism and Balancing in the First and Second Amendments," *New York University Law Review* 84 (2009): 428

89.   David M. Herszenhorn, "Bipartisan Senate Group Proposes 'No Fly, No Buy' Gun
Measure," *New York Times*, June 21, 2016.

90.   Bernard Brown, "Self-Defence in Homicide from Strict Liability to Complete
Exculpation," *Criminal Law Review* 1958 (1958): 583.

91.   Green, "Nine Theories," 160.

92.   *R.A.V. v. City of St. Paul*, 505 U.S. 377, 384 (1992).

93.   This could amount to something like "outlawry" and render the Professor vulnerable to anyone's private violence. *Autry v. Mitchell*, 420 F. Supp. 967, 970 (E.D.N.C.
1976) (outlawry "license[d] the public to kill the [outlaw] if he runs after being called on
to surrender"). It could violate other kinds of constitutional norms such as due process,
but I will leave that aside.

94.   Blocher, "Categoricalism and Balancing," 428.

CHAPTER 3

Guns, Interpretation, and Executive Branch Constitutionalism

KATHERINE SHAW

When it comes to guns and the law, the development of constitutional *doctrine* has been largely driven by self-conscious strategies of constitutional *practice*. That is, the recent transformation in the constitutional status of guns has been shaped by processes of constitutional mobilization, in a wide variety of arenas. This mobilization has involved litigation, to be sure—but it has also unfolded in scholarship, organizing, and advocacy, much of it aimed at forging new understandings of guns and the Constitution.

Much of this story has been well told.[1] But in this chapter I want to focus on a relatively unnoticed group of actors in this constitutional drama: state and local government officials. These ground-level actors—police officers and sheriffs, mayors, even attorneys general and governors—are important players in the ongoing, iterative story of development, contestation, and mobilization around guns and the Constitution. And a focus on these officials and the sites at which they encounter, respond to, and help shape the meaning of the Second Amendment—from amicus briefs in affirmative litigation to claims of interpretive autonomy paired with non-enforcement of state or federal gun laws, to advocacy of federal legislation that would allow states to export their visions of the Second Amendment's scope outside the boundaries of their own states—can shed new light on how constitutional meaning is forged.

The analysis therefore employs the lens of popular or democratic constitutionalism[2]—that is, a focus on non-judicial actors as important players in the elaboration of constitutional meaning—as well as administrative constitutionalism,[3] a subset of popular constitutionalism that focuses on administrative agencies and officials as key participants in that process. And it trains those lenses on state and local executive-branch officials. While the role of the federal executive branch in shaping Second Amendment understandings and arguments has been to some degree explored,[4] there has to date been only limited analysis of the role of state and local officials.[5]

Popular Constitutionalism and the Road to Heller

The Supreme Court's 2008 decision in *District of Columbia v. Heller*,[6] which for the first time identified an individual gun right in the Constitution's Second Amendment, represented the culmination of a decades-long campaign for constitutional change. *Heller* is in many ways a case study in constitutional mobilization;[7] and much of its story unfolded outside the courts.

A number of scholars, in particular Reva Siegel, have masterfully demonstrated both the degree to which *Heller* represented the culmination of a campaign of "mobilization, countermobilization, coalition, and compromise"[8] in the decades leading up to the case, and the strain of democratic constitutionalism that ultimately "helped shape the right" *Heller* announced.[9] So, Siegel argues, although *Heller* purports to be an originalist opinion, in many ways it is equally or even more the product of understandings of the Second Amendment that emerged long after the framing of the Constitution. On Siegel's account, the "originalism" in *Heller* is really the result of the "constitutional politics of the late twentieth century."[10]

Of the many passages in *Heller* that speak in the register of popular or democratic constitutionalism, perhaps the most important appears in a footnote responding to Justice Stevens's dissent. The passage from the dissent criticizes the majority for rejecting the accumulated wisdom of "hundreds of judges" who "relied on the view of the Amendment we endorsed [in the 1939 case *United States v. Miller*—i.e., that it protected a militia-linked right, rather than an individual right]."[11] Justice Scalia's majority opinion responds dismissively:

> As for the "hundreds of judges," who have relied on the view of the Second Amendment Justice Stevens claims we endorsed in *Miller*: If so, they overread *Miller*. And their erroneous reliance upon an uncontested and virtually unreasoned case cannot nullify the reliance of millions of Americans (as our historical analysis has shown) upon the true meaning of the right to keep and bear arms.[12]

As Professor Siegel argues, this passage articulates "the amendment's 'true meaning' in a full-throated populist voice,"[13] elevating this popular understanding of the Second Amendment above not just the wisdom of "hundreds of judges," but also above the eighteenth- and nineteenth-century understandings the opinion elsewhere suggests should be controlling.

In addition to announcing that the *nature* of the right secured by the Second Amendment is an individual one, the *Heller* majority opinion says several things about the *scope* of the right, in ways that courts and commentators still struggle to apply, over a decade after the opinion. In one significant passage, the Court writes:

> Like most rights, the right secured by the Second Amendment is not unlimited. From Blackstone through the 19th-century cases, commentators and courts routinely explained that the right was not a right to keep and carry any weapon whatsoever in any manner whatsoever and for whatever purpose. . . . Nothing in our opinion should be taken to cast doubt on longstanding prohibitions on the possession of firearms by felons and the mentally ill, or laws forbidding the carrying of firearms in sensitive places such as schools and government buildings, or laws imposing conditions and qualifications on the commercial sale of arms.[14]

This passage seems to single out a list of particular types of restrictions and to identify them as presumptively constitutionally permissible—with a passing reference to the historical understandings of "commentators and courts," but nothing beyond that by way of explanation.

In addition to the passage above regarding "longstanding prohibitions," the opinion's next passage identifies another important limitation on the Second Amendment right it announces—a limitation to weapons in common use. That is, the Court sees *no* Second Amendment right to own "dangerous and unusual weapons." The full passage reads:

> We also recognize another important limitation on the right to keep and carry arms. *Miller* said, as we have explained, that the sorts of weapons protected were those "in common use at the time." We think that limitation is fairly supported by the historical tradition of prohibiting the carrying of "dangerous and unusual weapons."[15]

Based largely on these two passages, a number of scholars have discerned in *Heller* something of a divide between the *nature* and the *scope* of the Second Amendment right. That is, the *existence* of an individual right to gun ownership under the Constitution as identified by the *Heller* majority has much to do with the popular imagination and popular understandings of the Constitution, both during the founding era and in the much more recent past; but the precise nature, shape, and contours of that right—and by extension permissible regulation of that right—left mostly unanswered in *Heller*,[16] are subject to a somewhat distinct, and quite historically inflected, analysis. Some have described this analysis as a "historical-categorical approach"[17]—a historically based inquiry grounded in the existence of positive law restrictions on gun use and ownership over time.

Heller was followed, two years later, by *McDonald v. City of Chicago,* in which the Court concluded that the right identified in *Heller* was incorporated against the states through the Fourteenth Amendment.[18] *McDonald,* like *Heller,* relied on both founding-era materials and many that were more recent, in particular from the Civil War era, to conclude that the individual right "to keep and bear arms for purposes of self-defense"[19] was fully applicable to the states. And it provided additional guidance regarding state and local firearms regulations,[20] engaging in a lengthy discussion of Civil War and Reconstruction-era practices; a number of lower courts have read this discussion to suggest that historical evidence from those eras is especially relevant when it comes to evaluating state and local gun laws.[21]

Following *Heller* and *McDonald,* lower courts have faced challenges to a wide range of state and local gun laws, with most courts concluding that the challenged laws are constitutionally permissible. Upheld regulations have ranged from bans on assault weapons,[22] to "good cause" requirements for the carrying of concealed weapons,[23] to state-level background check requirements,[24] among others.[25]

At the same time, outside the courts, competing voices—including state and local government actors—have worked to give form and shape to the right the Court announced in *Heller* and incorporated in *McDonald.*

The Post-*Heller* Landscape: Local Officials, Firearms Nationalism

In recent years, a number of local officials, primarily sheriffs, as well as some state-level officials, have emerged as supporters of an almost boundless reading of the scope of the Second Amendment—even where such a reading would seem to cut against their interests as law enforcement actors.

In their appearances in the arenas of action I describe here—amicus briefing, the actual enforcement (or non-enforcement) of gun laws, and advocacy for concealed-carry reciprocity—several interesting threads emerge. First, local officials regularly appear to invite courts to tie the hands of states and localities, encouraging courts to adopt a broad interpretation of the Second Amendment that would prevent states and localities from enacting robust gun regulations, even where their populations (as is the case with many urban populations) would prefer such regulation. Second, and related, much of the rhetoric deployed by such officials is distinctly nationalist in tone. Rather than embrace diversity and federalism, the vision of the Second Amendment advanced by such officials seems to disavow basic precepts of federalist experimentation.[26] This skepticism presents not only in a diminished vision of federalism, but equally a rejection of variety and experimentation *within* individual states—a disavowal of localism as well as federalism.

State and Local Officials and Amicus Briefs

State and local government officials played a perhaps surprising role in both *Heller* and *McDonald*. First, in *Heller,* over thirty state attorneys general filed an amicus brief on the side of the challengers. They argued that the lower court had correctly concluded that the Second Amendment secures an individual right to keep and bear arms, and that D.C.'s handgun ban was unconstitutional.[27] Their brief also argued that the individual right protected by the Second Amendment applied not just against the federal government and in federal enclaves like D.C., but against the states as well.[28] A group of states also filed a brief in support of D.C., but their number was much smaller—just five states, with New York in the lead, as well as Puerto Rico.[29] A number of cities also weighed in on D.C.'s side; and each side had one brief from a group of law enforcement associations. So the picture of state and local officials was mixed. But their presence was significantly greater on the side of the case challenging—rather than defending—the D.C. handgun ban.

State and local officials had an even larger footprint as amicus filers in *McDonald v. City of Chicago.*[30] The respondents, the cities of Chicago and Oak Park, defended their challenged ordinances, which effectively banned handguns within their respective city limits. Both cities argued that neither due process nor the Court's incorporation precedents mandated the incorporation of the Second Amendment against the states. But fully *thirty-eight* state attorneys general joined a brief in support of the challengers, with a full-throated argument that the Second Amendment should be incorporated. Although the states' brief reiterated a commitment to basic precepts of federalism, the brief contended that "the discretion of state and local governments to explore legislative and regulatory initiatives does not include the power to experiment with the fundamental liberties of citizens safeguarded by the Bill of Rights."[31]

The majority opinion cited this brief, in an apparent attempt to quell any federalism concerns about the ruling: "As noted by the 38 States that have appeared in this case as *amici* supporting petitioners, '[s]tate and local experimentation with reasonable firearms regulations will continue under the Second Amendment.' "[32] Another group of amici filed a similar brief, though this one was not cited by the Court; this group was composed of district attorneys and several police organizations "concerned with protecting the public safety benefits of citizens possessing firearms for defense."[33] Their brief argued that the logic of *Heller* mandated incorporation, that the Constitution protected a "natural right" to self-defense, and that federalism interests did not "militate against ruling in favor of Second Amendment incorporation."[34]

As Justice Stevens noted, there was something exceedingly strange about these filings: the positions they advocated seemed to run almost directly contrary to the interests of the state and local filers. As Justice Stevens wrote, "It is puzzling that so many state lawmakers have asked us to limit their *option* to regulate a dangerous item."[35] These states, of course, were free under existing law to impose no restrictions on gun purchases or ownership beyond those imposed by federal law; but, as the Stevens dissent suggested, under normal circumstances states typically wish to limit the degree of judicial interference with state operations. In this filing, as in others in cases to follow, a commitment to a particular vision of the Second Amendment superseded these largely pragmatic considerations about guns and the community, and about federalism and local self-determination. And the position was framed in constitutional terms—not merely as political opposition to the efficacy or desirability of gun regulations, but an explicit request for a pronouncement that the Constitution did not permit such regulations even by states or municipalities in which the majority of citizens supported them.[36]

Recent litigation has focused on the scope of the right identified in *Heller* and extended to the states in *McDonald*, with questions of scope falling generally into three categories: the sorts of weapons that may be limited; the categories of individuals whose gun rights may be subject to limitations, beyond those applicable to the general population; and the other sorts of restrictions the amendment will permit.[37]

In 2015, the Supreme Court denied a certiorari petition asking the Court to invalidate a gun ordinance banning semiautomatic weapons and large-capacity magazines in the Chicago suburb of Highland Park.[38] The Seventh Circuit, in an opinion by Judge Frank Easterbrook, had concluded that the restriction left citizens with ample alternative means of self-defense and was justified by several substantial potential benefits, and thus survived constitutional scrutiny under *Heller* and *McDonald*.[39] When the Supreme

Court denied certiorari,[40] Justice Thomas penned a searing dissent from that denial; in fact, one of Justice Scalia's last official public acts as a Supreme Court Justice was to join Thomas's opinion. The Thomas/Scalia dissent from the denial of certiorari accused the majority of adopting a "crabbed reading" of *Heller* "that eviscerate[d] many of the protections recognized in *Heller* and *McDonald*."[41]

One of the most interesting aspects of this case was the identity of the amicus filers. A group of law enforcement associations—the New York State Sheriffs' Association, Western States Sheriffs' Association, Law Enforcement Legal Defense Fund, and a number of others—joined a brief urging the Court to grant certiorari and overturn the ban.[42]

The brief largely tracked the key arguments made by the challengers. It contended that the banned weapons were commonly possessed by law-abiding citizens for lawful purposes; that semiautomatic rifles, shotguns, and handguns have been in common use by civilians and law enforcement for more than a century; and that the prohibition undermined the core holding of *Heller*, which the brief characterized as a determination that the Second Amendment protected weapons that are "commonly possessed by law-abiding citizens for lawful purposes."[43] The brief argued that both law enforcement officers and civilians wished to be able to lawfully possess some of the banned firearms because of their superior characteristics for defensive use.

But the rhetoric in the brief was far more heated than the rhetoric of the amicus briefs in *Heller* and *McDonald*. The brief claimed: "the term 'assault weapon' is a political device for restricting firearm ownership" and further maintained that it "does not describe any class of firearms function-ally, but consists of firearms chosen for political purposes by anti-Second Amendment activists."[44] Heated and even overwrought rhetoric is in no way new to debates about gun rights,[45] but its appearance in briefs before the Supreme Court did seem to be a significant development.

A number of cases in the lower courts have involved similar filings. And some of those filings have begun to gesture toward the argument that law enforcement officials, by virtue of their offices and the oaths they take, possess a special relationship to the Constitution, giving them a privileged position when it comes to interpreting the Second Amendment. A brief filed in the Ninth Circuit case *Fyock v. Sunnyvale* made this argument:

> Sheriffs and other peace officers in the State of California take an oath in which they solemnly swear or affirm that they will "support and defend the Constitution of the United States and the Constitution of the State of Califor-nia" and "will bear true faith and allegiance to the Constitution of the United

States and the Constitution of the State of California. . . ." Cal. Const. art. XX, § 3. Thus, they are honor-bound not just to enforce state and local laws, but also to protect the constitutional rights of citizens. That includes the Second Amendment rights of those citizens.[46]

Many government officials, of course, take oaths of office, so it's not entirely clear what claims of authority this oath gives rise to. In any event, this sort of rhetoric by law enforcement, and activities that reflect this vision in particular of *sheriffs'* relationship to the Constitution, are the focus of the next section.

Affirmative Challenges and Non-Enforcement of State and Federal Law

In addition to their active participation as amici in gun-related litigation brought by others, several local law enforcement officers have either filed their own challenges to the constitutionality of state gun laws, or indicated that they will refuse to enforce or participate in the defense of particular state or federal gun laws. A sequence of events in Weld County, Colorado, supplies an illustrative example.

In 2013, in the wake of the mass shooting in a movie theater in Aurora, Colorado, the state enacted a new gun law. The most important provisions of the new law created mandatory state background checks and banned magazines containing over fifteen rounds of ammunition.[47]

Immediately following the passage of the bill, the sheriff in Colorado's Weld County, John Cooke, announced that he would not enforce the law.[48] A number of other sheriffs around the state followed suit.[49] Other local sheriffs criticized this stance, offering a competing understanding of the constitutional authority possessed by local sheriffs in this sphere. The Boulder County sheriff told a *New York Times* reporter: "A lot of sheriffs are claiming the Constitution, saying that they're not going to enforce this because they personally believe it violates the Second Amendment. . . . But that stance in and of itself violates the Constitution."[50]

Soon after the wave of non-enforcement announcements, fifty-four local sheriffs (of a total of sixty-two across the state), including Cooke, sued Colorado governor John Hickenlooper, seeking a declaratory judgment that the new state law violated the Constitution's Second Amendment.[51] The court determined that Cooke lacked standing (as a law enforcement officer, he was not subject to the prohibition) and dismissed him, along with the other sheriff plaintiffs, from the case.[52] On appeal, the Tenth Circuit agreed that the sheriffs lacked standing, and affirmed the district court decision dismissing them.[53] But the sheriffs' very attempt to pursue the litigation is notable.

Some of Cooke's rhetoric, both around the lawsuit and after it was dismissed, sounded in considerations merely of resources and priorities; following his dismissal from the case in the district court, for example, he told one reporter: "It's not [the judge's] job to tell me what I can and can't enforce. . . . I'm still the one that has to say where do I put my priorities and resources? And it's not going to be there."[54] This statement of enforcement priorities seems entirely within the discretionary domain of an ordinary executive official, and has no real constitutional dimensions. But at other times his rhetoric more clearly asserted authority not only over resource allocation and enforcement priorities, but also over the proper meaning of the Constitution. He told another reporter, for example: "These laws are unconstitutional and unenforceable due to the way they are written."[55] Coming *after* the district court decision, this was a startling claim of apparent interpretive primacy.

Similar non-enforcement announcements and efforts have unfolded in other states—including those outside areas such as the rural West and South, where the local gun culture has long been strong.[56] A Maryland sheriff made headlines when he told a reporter: "I made a vow and a commitment that as long as I'm the sheriff of this county I will not allow the federal government to come in here and strip my law-abiding citizens of the right to bear arms. . . . If they attempt to do that it will be an all-out civil war."[57] And in the wake of the mass shooting at Sandy Hook Elementary in Newtown, Connecticut, the neighboring state of New York passed a gun law that expanded an earlier definition of "assault weapon" and made it a felony to possess, transfer, or manufacture such a weapon in the state.[58] A subset of the state's local sheriffs voiced a range of objections to the bill. Some remained in the register of priorities and resources, indicating that they would de-prioritize enforcement of the law but would not defy it outright. Otsego County sheriff Richard Devlin, for example, explained that "I feel as an elected official and a chief law enforcement officer of the county it would be irresponsible for me to say, 'I'm not going to enforce a law I personally disagree with,' [but] . . . We're not checking out registrations. People that are lawfully using a firearm for target shooting, we're not bothering those people."[59] But another state sheriff, Schoharie County's Tony Desmond, did seem to assert a sort of interpretive authority: "If you have an [assault] weapon, which under the SAFE Act is considered illegal, I don't look at it as being illegal just because someone said it was."[60]

Some of these disputes not only feature local officials, but pit such officials against statewide officials. *Peruta v. San Diego County*, a recent case involving the constitutionality of a California law restricting the availability of "concealed carry" permits, had the potential to bring out such intra-executive dynamics, although a recent certiorari denial means that such dynamics will not play out before the Supreme Court. The California law in question requires a showing of "good cause" by any member of the public who wishes to carry a concealed weapon,[61] and it leaves to individual counties the task of promulgating and publishing their own "good cause" policies.[62]

Sheriffs in San Diego County and Yolo County issued such policies under the statute, and those policies were challenged by individuals who had unsuccessfully sought licenses in the counties. In both cases the counties prevailed in the district court,[63] but a divided panel of the Ninth Circuit reversed in both cases.[64] When the state of California moved to intervene in the suit to help defend the county's policy, the Ninth Circuit denied the requested permission.[65] The Yolo County sheriff petitioned for rehearing en banc, but the San Diego County sheriff announced that he would not seek rehearing. He did not cite any Second Amendment concerns with the county's standard, which required a showing of some sort of specific threat; rather, he explained to the press, "I don't make laws, I carry them out."[66] But the full Ninth Circuit, after permitting California to intervene, reversed the panel opinions and reinstated the district court opinions.[67] The Supreme Court then denied certiorari over the dissents of Justice Thomas and Justice Gorsuch, so that the good cause standards remain in effect in California.[68]

Both the state of California and the counties of San Diego and Yolo filed briefs in opposition to certiorari in the case. They differed somewhat, but the fact that the Court declined to take up the case means that we don't know what differences would have emerged between the two players in the merits briefing and argument before the Court. But other such cases—involving divergent positions between local and state-level officials—are bound to arise in the future.

Beyond the isolated incidents of local non-enforcement or non-defense, there have been calls for more such acts. At the center of such calls is an organization called the "Constitutional Sheriffs and Peace Officers Association" (CSPOA), founded in 2011 by former Arizona county sheriff and political activist Richard Mack.[69] The organization takes an almost unbounded view of the power of local sheriffs. Central to the organization's vision is the idea that the sheriff is a critical constitutional actor; its website explains that "in addition to upholding the law, the sheriff is also charged with upholding the supreme law, the Constitution."[70] But it also goes significantly further, suggesting a sort of supremacy enjoyed by local sheriffs that is essentially unlimited within their jurisdictions: "The law enforcement powers held by the sheriff supersede those of any agent, officer, elected official or employee from any level of government when in the jurisdiction of the county. The vertical separation of powers in the Constitution makes it clear that the power of the sheriff even supersedes the powers of the President."[71] The group openly "encourage[s] law enforcement officers to defy laws they decide themselves are illegal,"[72] and links defiance of gun laws to civil rights–era civil disobedience, like that of Rosa Parks. Mack is reported to have told audiences, "If there had been a true constitutional sheriff in Montgomery, Alabama, back in 1955 . . . that sheriff would have defied the segregation laws and protected Rosa Parks. . . . Today the constitutional sheriff does the same for Rosa Parks the gun owner."[73]

Mack has a long history of activism around guns and the law, and the transformation in Mack's rhetoric, strategies, and constitutional claims in recent decades represents something of a microcosm of the larger constitutional trajectory of debates about guns and the law.

In 1993 Congress enacted the Brady Bill, which amended the 1968 Gun Control Act, notably creating a new background-check scheme that involved participation by state and local officials. Mack, together with a second sheriff, Jay Printz, challenged the law's constitutionality on the grounds that it exceeded Congress's constitutional authority, invading the powers reserved to the states under the Constitution's Tenth Amendment. Mack and Printz prevailed in what became the 1997 case *Printz v. United States* (though the lower court litigation bore Mack's name).[74] The *Printz* Court held that provisions of the Brady Act requiring state and local officials to run background checks on prospective buyers of handguns represented impermissible federal "commandeering" of state officials in violation of the Tenth Amendment.[75]

In the 1990s, then, Mack's arguments centered on the protection of state prerogatives against an overreaching federal government. But Mack has shifted his advocacy substantially in recent years. He has begun encouraging local law enforcement officials to refuse to enforce gun regulations, rather than (or in addition to) challenging them in the courts. His focus has turned toward the Second Amendment, and away from structural constitutional provisions like the Tenth Amendment. And, as I discuss in the next part, he has embraced a set of arguments whose logical conclusion is a thoroughly national gun policy, without any real latitude at all for local tastes, preferences, and conditions.

Although the high-profile non-enforcement moves advocated by Mack and discussed above are somewhat isolated and generally viewed as controversial, a recent survey—which has been cited in a number of amicus briefs in gun-related cases—suggests that they may enjoy a surprising amount of support in law enforcement circles. Conducted in 2013 among law enforcement officials, this survey found that fully seventy percent of respondents viewed "favorably" or "very favorably" law enforcement officials who chose not to enforce gun laws.[76] When asked, "If you were Sheriff or Chief, how would you respond to more restrictive gun laws?" sixty-two percent of respondents reported that they would either "not enforce and join in the public, vocal opposition effort" or "not enforce and quietly lead agency in opposite direction."[77] The general approach of either overt or quiet non-enforcement, then, may enjoy broader support than the isolated instances to date reflect.[78] It should be noted, though, that this study has been roundly criticized: it did not use a random sample, but rather drew on a self-selecting group of Internet users affiliated with the group "PoliceOne. com."[79] Moreover, without additional information about the locations of the surveyed officials, it is impossible to know whether respondents' views represent something genuinely unique, or whether they simply track the views of the public at large in particular regions of the country.[80]

Most sheriffs are elected, so they certainly have a claim to a sort of popularly derived authority when it comes to the interpretation of the Constitution, including the Second Amendment. And under a strong version of popular constitutionalism, it might seem appropriate for such elected officials to engage in constitutional interpretation, especially where they are channeling views of the Constitution widely held within the body of the electorate.

But there are certain challenges entailed by the assumption that the popularly elected status of sheriffs confers on them the authority to engage in autonomous constitutional interpretation, particularly where that interpretation departs from that of the courts. Most state judges, for example, are popularly elected, but, as David Pozen has convincingly demonstrated, "judges are not actually authorized to 'represent' constituents in any formal sense, nor do they engage in the sorts of dialogic interactions that help make that representation meaningful."[81] The same is in many ways true of elected sheriffs and other local law enforcement officials: their claims to interpretive authority, where they are grounded in their status as *representatives*, may be weaker than the claims of members of legislative bodies, or even popularly elected officials like mayors, governors, and attorneys general, who actually engage, legislatively and administratively, in law- and policymaking of quite a different sort. Many states have staggering numbers of elected officials—from banking officials to election administrators[82]—and, though a full discussion of the application of theories of representation to unbundled or plural executives is outside the scope of this discussion,[83] it seems fair to say that empowering each such elected official to give expression to his or her own constitutional convictions, even where those views depart from those of courts or statewide elected officials, could lead to a high degree of instability and even chaos.

Reciprocity and Horizontal Federalism

Finally, I briefly consider the implications of a piece of federal legislation that has been introduced in several iterations in recent years: the Concealed Carry Reciprocity Act.

At present, a patchwork of state laws means that the right to carry a concealed weapon varies significantly between the states. A number of recent attempts at the federal level would allow holders of concealed-carry licenses to carry their weapons concealed not just in their home states, but elsewhere as well.[84] Versions of the bill have varied, from more modest versions that would require all "concealed carry" states to recognize licenses issued in sister states, to stronger versions that would require *all* states, regardless of their own gun policies, to permit individuals who may lawfully carry in their home states to lawfully carry in any other state.[85] This would include residents of the twelve so-called permitless concealed carry states—often referred to by proponents as "constitutional carry" states—which allow any adult not prohibited by law to carry concealed weapons, without any sort of permit or license requirement.[86]

The most recent version of the bill did not explicitly impose a substantive federal standard, and in that sense appears at first blush to comport with federalism principles, eschewing any top-down imposition of uniform federal law. But it is deeply concerning from the perspective of *horizontal* federalism. That is, the scheme would allow states to export their own understandings of the Second Amendment across state lines, in ways that could be profoundly inconsistent with the understandings that obtain in, and the enacted preferences of citizens in, those other states.[87]

If some version of this bill actually does achieve passage, it will no doubt face swift constitutional challenges.[88] But more important for purposes of this discussion are two notable features of the debate around the bill. First, proponents of concealed carry reciprocity seem to suggest that there exists some special relationship between a largely limitless concealed carry regime and the Constitution, evident in the use of the phrase "constitutional carry."

Second, the debate around the bill features an exceedingly strange proponent (though by this point familiar from similar advocacy in other venues): the local official who advocates a vision of guns and the law that would displace local preferences in a significant number of states. To be sure, some individual law enforcement officers and associations have expressed doubts about a federal concealed carry reciprocity requirement.[89] But many law enforcement players have voiced their support for some version of this bill,[90] and will doubtless continue to do so as the bill moves forward.[91]

Conclusion

Over the past three decades, the evolution of the constitutional doctrine that governs the legal regulation of guns has been inextricably linked to, and in many ways driven by, popular understandings of the constitution, and in particular the Second Amendment—what some scholars have termed constitutional culture.[92]

This general observation has been made—though with less sustained attention in recent years—but there remain pockets of this strain of extrajudicial constitutionalism that have not been the focus of this sort of scholarly inquiry. I hope this discussion has shown that a focus on state and local government officials' interactions with, and articulation of, constitutional norms and principles as they consider different modes of gun regulation can offer a concrete illustration of the dynamics of guns and the law outside the courts in 2018, a decade after the Supreme Court's decision in *District of Columbia v. Heller*.

The profoundly nationalist bent to much of the rhetoric now emanating from state and local officials feels particularly misplaced in the context of the Second Amendment. As scholars ranging from Joseph Blocher to Michael O'Shea have argued, though in different terms, the Second Amendment *should* allow a degree of local variation, albeit with some limits. And yet the claims made by the local officials discussed in this chapter would largely eviscerate such variation.[93] As Judge Easterbrook wrote in his majority opinion in *Friedman v. Highland Park*:

> The Constitution establishes a federal republic where local differences are cherished as elements of liberty, rather than eliminated in a search for national uniformity. *McDonald* circumscribes the scope of permissible experimentation by state and local governments, but it does not foreclose *all* possibility of

experimentation. Within the limits established by the Justices in *Heller* and *McDonald*, federalism and diversity still have a claim.[94]

There are, to be sure, other groups making claims and representations about the meaning of the Second Amendment—in particular, victims of gun violence and their family members, many of whom argue for additional restrictions on the availability or capacity of firearms. The politics of those movements and the Constitution involve another story that very much warrants telling. To date, however, their arguments have not always been presented in self-consciously constitutional terms. Perhaps recasting their claims in terms that are explicitly constitutional—regarding both the limits of the Second Amendment right secured in *Heller* and *McDonald*, and perhaps the affirmative constitutional interests in a degree of governmental protection from gun violence—would constructively impact the development of the debate about the meaning of the Constitution.[95]

Notes

My thanks to participants in a workshop at Amherst College and to Joseph Blocher for enormously helpful feedback, and to Benjamin Dynkin and Phil Ensler for terrific research assistance.

1. See Reva B. Siegel, "Dead or Alive: Originalism as Popular Constitutionalism in *Heller,*" *Harvard Law Review* 122 (2008): 191; Michael Waldman, *The Second Amendment: A Biography* (New York: Simon & Schuster, 2014), xiii; Jack Rakove, " 'A Well Regulated Militia': The Second Amendment in Historical Perspective," in *The Second Amendment in Law and History*, ed. Carl Bogus (New York: New Press, 2000).

2. Important sources include Larry D. Kramer, *The People Themselves: Popular Constitutionalism and Judicial Review* (New York: Oxford University Press, 2004); Mark Tushnet, *Taking the Constitution Away from the Courts* (Princeton, NJ: Princeton University Press, 1999); Robert Post and Reva Siegel, "*Roe* Rage: Democratic Constitutionalism and Backlash," *Harvard Civil Rights-Civil Liberties Law Review* 42 (2007): 374 (discussing democratic constitutionalism). On popular constitutionalism in the *state* context, see Katherine Shaw, "Constitutional Nondefense in the States," *Columbia Law Review* 113 (2014): 213; David E. Pozen, "Judicial Elections as Popular Constitutionalism," *Columbia Law Review* 110 (2010): 2047; Joseph Blocher, "Popular Constitutionalism and the State Attorneys General," *Harvard Law Review F.* 122 (2008): 108; Douglas S. Reed, "Popular Constitutionalism: Toward a Theory of State Constitutional Meanings," *Rutgers Law Journal* 30 (1999): 871.

3. By "administrative constitutionalism," I mean administrative agencies' and actors' interactions with the Constitution in the course of legal interpretation and implementation. See Gillian E. Metzger, "Administrative Constitutionalism," *Texas Law Review* 91 (2013): 1897 (describing cases involving "actions by federal administrative agencies to interpret and implement the U.S. Constitution," as "relatively straightforward instances of administrative constitutionalism"); see also Michael Herz, "*Chevron* Is Dead; Long Live *Chevron,*" *Columbia Law Review* 115 (2015): 1896–97 (describing administrative constitutionalism as the "various ways in which administrative agencies interpret, implement, and help define the meaning of the U.S. Constitution"); Sophia Z. Lee, "Race, Sex, and Rulemaking: Administrative Constitutionalism and the Workplace, 1960 to the

Present," *Virginia Law Review* 96 (2010): 801 (defining administrative constitutionalism as "regulatory agencies' interpretation and implementation of constitutional law").

4. See Office of the Attorney General John Ashcroft, *Memorandum to all United States Attorneys*, November 9, 2001; Opinions of the Office of Legal Counsel, *Whether the Second Amendment Secures an Individual Right: Memorandum Opinion for the Attorney General*, by Steven G. Bradbury, Howard C. Neilson, Jr., and C. Kevin Marshall, August 24, 2004, https://www.justice.gov/file/18831/download; Jennifer Ray, "The Department of Justice's Position on the Second Amendment," *University of Pittsburgh Law Review* 65 (2003): 103.

5. The one exception of which I am aware is Joseph Blocher's excellent short piece "Popular Constitutionalism and the State Attorneys General," *Harvard Law Review Forum* 122 (2008): 109.

6. 554 U.S. 570 (2008).

7. See generally Siegel, "Dead or Alive"; Blocher, "Popular Constitutionalism and the State Attorneys General," 109.

8. Siegel, "Dead or Alive," 193.

9. Ibid., 194. See also Blocher, "Popular Constitutionalism and the State Attorneys General," 109 ("some form of popular constitutionalism played an important—if uncredited—role in *Heller*").

10. Siegel, "Dead or Alive," 192.

11. *Heller*, 554 U.S. at 638.

12. *Heller*, 554 U.S. at 624n24.

13. Siegel, "Dead or Alive," 201.

14. *Heller*, 554 U.S. at 626 (internal quotation marks omitted).

15. *Heller*, 554 U.S. at 628–29.

16. J. Harvie Wilkinson III, "Of Guns, Abortions, and the Unraveling Rule of Law," *Virginia Law Review* 95 (2009): 280.

17. See Joseph Blocher, "Firearm Localism," *Yale Law Journal* 123 (2013): 87 ("the majorities in *Heller* and *McDonald* endorsed a historical-categorical approach that evaluates contemporary gun control measures based on whether they have 'longstanding' historical analogues"); *United States v. Masciandro*, 638 F.3d 458, 470 (4th Cir. 2011); *Moore v. Madigan*, 702 F.3d 933 (7th Cir. 2011).

18. 561 U.S. 742 (2010).

19. 561 U.S. at 750.

20. See *Ezell v. City of Chicago*, 651 F. 3d 684 (7th Cir. 2011) ("*Heller* suggests that some federal gun laws will survive Second Amendment challenge because they regulate activity falling outside the terms of the right as publicly understood when the Bill of Rights was ratified; *McDonald* confirms that if the claim concerns a state or local law, the 'scope' question asks how the right was publicly understood when the Fourteenth Amendment was proposed and ratified").

21. *McDonald v. City of Chicago*, 561 U.S. 742, 770–78 (2010).

22. *Kolbe v. Hogan*, 813 F.3d 160 (4th Cir. 2017) (en banc); *Friedman v. City of Highland Park*, 784 F. 3d 406 (7th Cir. 2015).

23. *Peruta v. San Diego County*, 824 F.3d 919 (9th Cir. 2016) (en banc). See also Darrell A. H. Miller, "Peruta, the Home-Bound Second Amendment, and Fractal Originalism," *Harvard Law Review Forum* 127 (2014): 238.

24. *Colorado Outfitters Association v. Hickenlooper*, 823 F.3d 537 (10th Cir. 2016).

25. See, e.g., *Nat'l Rifle Ass'n v. Bureau of Alcohol, Tobacco, Firearms & Explosives*, 700 F.3d 185, 195–98 (5th Cir. 2012) (upholding federal law prohibiting firearms sale to those under the age of 21); *Wade v. University of Michigan*, 905 N.W. 2d 439 (Mich. Ct. App. June 6, 2017) (affirming state university's power to ban firearms on campus).

26. Cf. Joseph Blocher, "Firearm Localism," *Yale Law Journal* 123 (2013): 85 ("This Article argues that future Second Amendment cases can and should incorporate the longstanding and sensible differences regarding guns and gun control in rural and urban areas, giving more protection to gun rights in rural areas and more leeway to gun regulation in cities").

27. See Brief of the States of Texas et al. as *Amici Curiae* in support of Respondent at 23n.6, *District of Columbia v. Heller*, 554 U.S. 570 (2008) (No. 07–290). See also generally Margaret H. Lemos and Kevin Quinn, "Litigating State Interests: State Attorneys General as Amici," *New York University Law Review* 90 (2015): 1263–64 (discussing *Heller*).

28. Brief of the States of Texas et al., at 23n6, *District of Columbia v. Heller*, 554 U.S. 570 (2008) (No. 07–290) ("Although the Court need not reach the issue of incorporation in this case, amici States submit that the right to keep and bear arms is fundamental and so is properly subject to incorporation").

29. See Brief of the States of New York et al. as *Amici Curiae* in support of Petition, *District of Columbia v. Heller*, 128 S. Ct. 2783 (2008) (No. 07–290).

30. 561 U.S. 742 (2010).

31. Brief of Texas et al, supra note 27, at 22 (internal quotations omitted).

32. 561 U.S. 742, 785 (2010). See also Lemos & Quinn, "Litigating State Interests: State Attorneys General as Amici."

33. Brief for 34 California District Attorneys et al. as Amici Curiae, *McDonald v. City of Chicago*, 561 U.S. 742 (2010) (No. 08–1521), available at http://www.americanbar.org /content/dam/aba/publishing/preview/publiced_preview_briefs_pdfs_09_10_08_1521 _PetitionerAmCuThirty_FourCaliforniaDistrictAttorneys.authcheckdam.pdf.

34. Ibid.

35. *McDonald*, 561 U.S. at 903n.47 (Stevens, J., dissenting).

36. There is an interesting parallel here to an amicus brief filed by a group of twenty-three state attorneys general in support of criminal defendant Clarence Gideon in *Gideon v. Wainwright*. See Brief for the State Government Amici, *Gideon v. Wainwright*, 1962 WL 115122. See generally Bruce A. Green, "Gideon's Amici: Why Do Prosecutors so Rarely Defend the Rights of the Accused?," *Yale Law Journal* 122 (2013): 2336; see also Anthony Lewis, *Gideon's Trumpet* (New York: Vintage Books, 1964), 141–48 (describing efforts of two state attorneys general, including Minnesota's Walter Mondale, to enlist support of other state AGs in advancing the argument that the Constitution required the provision of counsel for all individuals charged with felonies).

37. See generally Jamal Greene, "*Heller* High Water," *Harvard Law and Policy Review* 3 (2009): 325.

38. 136 S.Ct. 447 (denying certiorari).

39. *Friedman v. City of Highland Park*, 784 F. 3d 406 (7th Cir. 2015).

40. 136 S.Ct. 447 (denying certiorari).

41. 136 S.Ct. 447, 449 (2015) (Thomas, J., dissenting from denial of certiorari).

42. Other groups included the Law Enforcement Action Network, Law Enforcement Alliance of America, International Law Enforcement Educators and Trainers Association.

43. Brief of Amici Curiae New York State Sheriffs' Association, Western States Sheriffs' Association, Law Enforcement Legal Defense Fund, Law Enforcement Action Network, Gun Owners of California, Law Enforcement Alliance of America, and International Law Enforcement Educators and Trainers Association in Support of Petitioners at 6–7, *Friedman v. City of Highland Park*, 136 U.S. 147 (2015) (No. 15–133).

44. Ibid.

45. See Joseph Blocher, "Gun Rights Talk," *Boston University Law Review* 94 (2014): 821 ("Apocalyptic rhetoric has long been a common ingredient in gun rights talk—each gun-control bill is the worst, and every debate is the last chance to save the right to keep and bear arms").

46. Brief of Amici Curiae Law Enforcement Trainers and Educators Association, *Fyock v. Sunnyvale,* 779 F.3d 991 (9th Cir. 2015) (No. 14–15408).

47. C.R.S.A. § 18–12–302, 312 (2013).

48. Amanda Paulson, "Sheriff Vows Not to Enforce Colorado's New Gun Control Laws," *Christian Science Monitor,* March 18, 2013, http://www.csmonitor.com/USA/2013/0318/Sheriff-vows-not-to-enforce-Colorado-s-tough-new-gun-control-bills ("They're feel-good, knee-jerk reactions that are unenforceable").

49. Erica Goode, "Sheriffs Refuse to Enforce Laws on Gun Control," *New York Times,* December 16, 2013, A1; Rebecca D. Maller, "Intrastate Interventions: The State Executive's Response to Local Nonenforcement," *Cardozo Law Review* 36 (2015): 1560–61.

50. Goode, "Sheriffs Refuse to Enforce Laws on Gun Control."

51. Complaint for Declaratory and Injunctive Relief, *Colorado Outfitters Association v. Hickenlooper,* 24 F.Supp.3d 1050 (D. Co. 2014) (No. 13–cv–01300–MSK–MJW), at 2013 WL 2149997.

52. *Colorado Outfitters Association v. Hickenlooper,* 24 F.Supp.3d 1050, 1059 (D. Co. 2014).

53. *Colorado Outfitters Association v. Hickenlooper,* 823 F.3d 537 (10th Cir. 2016).

54. Marlena Chertock et al., "'No' Sheriff in Town: Some Lawmen Refuse to Enforce Federal Gun Laws," *NBC News,* August 21, 2014, https://www.nbcnews.com/news/investigations/no-sheriff-town-some-lawmen-refuse-enforce-federal-gun-laws-n185426; see also Associated Press, "Weld County Sheriff Refuses to Enforce Gun Bills," *Denver Post,* March 17, 2013, https://www.denverpost.com/2013/03/17/weld-county-sheriff-refuses-to-enforce-gun-bills/.

55. "Cooke Vows to Continue Gun Fight to the Supremes," *Northern Colorado Gazette,* June 30, 2014, http://www.greeleygazette.com/press/?p=24082.

56. See Joseph Blocher, "Firearm Localism," *Yale Law Journal* 123 (2013): 117–19; Adam Winkler, *Gunfight: The Battle over the Right to Bear Arms in America* (New York: W.W. Norton & Company, 2011), 13.

57. Chertock, supra note 54.

58. Act of January 15, 2013, chap. 1, 2013 N.Y. Laws 1, amended by Act of March 29, 2013, chap. 57, pt. FF, 2013 N.Y. Laws 290, 389; *New York Rifle & Pistol Association v. Cuomo,* 804 F.3d 242 (2d Cir. 2015).

59. Chertock et al., "Enforcement of Gun Laws Hinges on Sheriffs' Interpretation of the Second Amendment," *Center for Public Integrity,* August 29, 2014, https://www.publicintegrity.org/2014/08/29/15423/enforcement-gun-laws-hinges-local-sheriffs-interpretation-second-amendment.

60. Ibid.

61. Cal. Penal Code §§ 26150.

62. Ibid., § 261610. See generally Nestor M. Davidson, "Localist Administrative Law," *Yale Law Journal* 126 (forthcoming 2017); Aaron Saiger, "Local Government as a Choice of Agency Form," *Ohio St. Law Journal* 77 (2016): 433; Joseph Blocher, "Good Cause Requirements for Carrying Guns in Public," *Harvard Law Review Forum* 127 (2014): 218.

63. *Peruta v. San Diego,* 758 F.Supp.2d 1106 (S.D. Cal. 2010).

64. *Peruta v. San Diego,* 742 F.3d 1144 (9th Cir. 2014).

65. *Peruta v. San Diego,* 771 F.3d 570 (9th Cir. 2014).

66. Kristina Davis, "Gun Carry Suit Back to 'Square One," *San Diego Union-Tribune,* April 12, 2015, http://www.sandiegouniontribune.com/sdut-concealed-gun-9th-circuit-en-banc-2015apr12-story.html.

67. *Peruta v. San Diego,* 824 F.3d 919 (9th Cir. 2016) (en banc).

68. *Peruta v. California,* 137 S.Ct. 1995 (2017).

69. Mack and his organization have been linked to the "Oath Keepers" organization and have been the subject of investigative reporting by the Southern Center for Poverty

Law. See "Intelligence Report: 'Constitutional Sheriffs' Movement Spreads, Promotes Defiance of Federal Laws," *Southern Poverty Law Center*, August 3, 2016, https://www .splcenter.org/news/2016/08/03/intelligence-report-constitutional-sheriffs-movement-spreads -promotes-defiance-federal-laws.

70. "About Constitutional Sheriffs and Peace Officers Association," Constitutional Sheriffs and Peace Officers Association, accessed December 27, 2017, http://cspoa.org /about/.

71. Ibid.; see also Jonathan Thompson, "The Rise of the Sagebrush Sheriffs," *High Country News*, February 2, 2016, http://www.hcn.org/issues/48.2/the-rise-of-the-sagebrush-sheriffs (describing "a growing cadre of county sheriffs, many of them from the rural West, who believe themselves above the reach of federal government, constitutionally empowered as the supreme law of the land").

72. Julia Harte and R. Jeffrey Smith, "The 'Army to Set our Nation Free,'" *Center for Public Integrity*, April 18, 2016, https://www.publicintegrity.org/2016/04/18/19568 /army-set-our-nation-free.

73. Thompson, "The Rise of the Sagebrush Sheriffs."

74. *Mack v. United States*, 66 F.3d 1025 (9th Cir. 1995).

75. 521 U.S. 898 (1997). Justice Scalia's majority opinion explained that the federal government lacked the power to "command the States' officers, or those of their political subdivisions, to administer or enforce a federal regulatory program."

76. "Gun Policy & Law Enforcement: Survey Results," *PoliceOne.com*, 2013, http:// police-praetorian.netdna-ssl.com/p1_gunsurveysummary_2013.pdf, at 7 (question 14).

77. Ibid., at 8 (question 15).

78. See, e.g., Martin Kaste, "Gun Debate Divides Nation's Police Officers, Too," *NPR*, October 9, 2015, https://www.npr.org/2015/10/09/446866939/gun-debate-divides-nations-police-officers-too (quoting Professor Jennifer Carlson, describing a "major shift" from "[a] generation ago," when "police chiefs made a common cause of legislation such as the Assault Weapons Ban and the Brady bill").

79. See Lori Robertson, "NRA Misrepresents Police Survey, Legislation," *FactCheck. org*, April 18, 2013, http://www.factcheck.org/2013/04/nra-misrepresents-police-survey-legislation/; Glenn Kessler, "NRA ad claims that poll data reflect views of 'America's policy,'" *Washington Post*, April 18, 2013, https://www.washingtonpost.com/blogs/fact-checker/post/nra-ad-claims-that-poll-data-reflects-views-of-americas-police/2013/04/17 /f32b82f6-a7ae-11e2-8302-3c7e0ea97057_blog.html?utm_term=.b2d0e8379fd8 (thorough critique of survey methodology).

80. And some law enforcement officials certainly remain supporters of robust firearm regulation. See, e.g., Campbell Robertson and Timothy Williams, "As States Expand Gun Rights, the Police Object," *New York Times*, May 3, 2016, https://www.nytimes. com/2016/05/04/us/as-states-expand-gun-rights-police-join-opposition.html.

81. David E. Pozen, "Judicial Elections as Popular Constitutionalism," *Colum. Law Review* 110 (2010): 2116; cf. Ethan Leib and Aaron-Andrew Bruhl, "Elected Judges and Statutory Interpretation," *University of Chicago Law Review* 79 (2012): 1215.

82. Christopher R. Berry and Jacob E. Gersen, "The Unbundled Executive," *University of Chicago Law Review* 75 (2008): 1400 (noting that "As of 1992 . . . , four . . . states— Texas, Pennsylvania, New York, and Florida—each had over six hundred nonlegislative elected officials").

83. Cf. ibid., at 1387 ("Unbundling executive authority enhances democratic accountabil-ity and government performance"), and William P. Marshall, "Break Up the Presidency? Governors, State Attorneys General, and Lessons from the Divided Executive," *Yale Law Journal* 115 (2006): 2446 (similarly defending state plural executive models), with Lawrence Lessig and Cass R. Sunstein, "The President and the Administration," *Columbia Law*

Review 94 (1994): 93 ("The framers believed that unitariness advanced the interests of coordination, accountability, and efficiency in the execution of the laws"), and Stephen G. Calabresi and Nicholas Terrell, "The Fatally Flawed Theory of the Unbundled Executive," *Minnesota Law Review* 93 (2009): 1740 ("A plural executive . . . neither promotes nor protects democracy to the degree that a unitary executive system does").

84. Darrell A. H. Miller, "Self Defense, Defense of Others, And the State," *Law & Contemporary Problems* 80 (2017): 101–2.

85. See Concealed Carry Reciprocity Act of 2017, S. 446, 115th Cong. (2017), https://www.congress.gov/bill/115th-congress/senate-bill/446/text. See also G. M. Filisko, "Gun War," *ABA Journal* 103 (May 2017): 54, http://www.abajournal.com/magazine/article/gun_war_state_legislation.

86. Michele Gorman, "Guns in America: North Dakota Latest to Allow Permitless Carry of Concealed Weapons," *Newsweek*, March 24, 2017, http://www.newsweek.com/guns-america-north-dakota-latest-state-legalize-permitless-carry-hidden-guns-573927.

87. Heather K. Gerken and Ari Holtzblatt, "The Political Safeguards of Horizontal Federalism," *Michigan Law Review* 113 (2014): 108; Samuel Issacharoff and Catherine M. Sharkey, "Backdoor Federalization," *UCLA Law Review* 53 (2006): 1371; Katherine Shaw and Alex Stein, "Abortion, Informed Consent, and Regulatory Spillover," *Indiana Law Journal* 91 (2016): 1.

88. See Joseph Blocher, "Constitutional Hurdles for Concealed Carry Reciprocity," *TakeCareBlog*, March 16, 2017, https://takecareblog.com/blog/constitutional-hurdles-for-concealed-carry-reciprocity; Will Baude, "A Better Constitutional Basis for the Concealed Carry Reciprocity Act of 2017," *Washington Post*, March 23, 2017, https://www.washington-post.com/news/volokh-conspiracy/wp/2017/03/23/a-better-constitutional-basis-for-the-concealed-carry-reciprocity-act-of-2017/?utm_term=.3235297ced86.

89. The gun safety group "Everytown" indicates in a lengthy policy discussion on its website, "A broad and impressive array of law enforcement organizations have spoken out against automatic concealed carry reciprocity." "Federally Mandated Concealed Carry Reciprocity," *Everytown*, 2015, https://everytownresearch.org/reports/federally-mandated-concealed-carry-reciprocity/. See also Michele Gorman, "How South Carolina Police Are Taking on the NRA and Constitutional Carry Legislation," *Newsweek*, May 1, 2017, http://www.newsweek.com/charleston-police-challenge-south-carolina-lawmakers-constitutional-carry-592522.

90. See, e.g., J. D. "Danny" Diggs, "Concealed Carry Measure Should Become Law," *Virginia Gazette*, May 20, 2017, http://www.vagazette.com/opinion/va-vg-edit-diggs-0520-20170520-story.html; Michele Gorman, "Guns in America: What Is National Concealed Carry Reciprocity?" *Newsweek*, March 3, 2017, http://www.newsweek.com/what-national-concealed-carry-reciprocity-563075.

91. These dynamics are in many ways replicated in state-level gun preemption laws, in which state laws operate to displace local laws that impose stricter gun regulations. See Eric Gorovitz, "California Dreamin: The Myth of State Preemption of Local Firearm Regulation," *University of San Francisco Law Review* 30 (1996): 395.

92. Reva B. Siegel, "Constitutional Culture, Social Movement Conflict and Constitutional Change: The Case of the De Facto ERA," *California Law Review* 94 (2006): 1323.

93. Joseph Blocher, "Firearm Localism," *Yale Law Journal* 123 (2013): 86–87; Michael O'Shea, "Federalism and the Implementation of the Right to Arms," *Syracuse Law Review* 59 (2008): 201. See also Allen Rostron, "A New State Ice Age for Gun Policy," *Harvard Law and Policy Review* 10 (2016): 327.

94. *Friedman v. City of Highland Park*, 784 F.3d 406, 412 (7th Cir. 2015).

95. Jamal Greene, "*Heller* High Water," *Harvard Law and Policy Review* 3 (2009): 344–45 (arguing that progressives should "glorify our Constitution's impressive ability to adapt to a changing world—to embrace its future rather than its past. . . . Why not ride an ethical wave away from naked individualism and toward mutual responsibility? Why not emphasize that our Constitution is limited not by the historical understandings of its framers and ratifiers but by our own generation's ambition, energy, and imagination?").

CHAPTER 4

The Hard, Simple Truth about Gun Control

CARL T. BOGUS

There are two kinds of people: those who divide the world into two kinds of people and those who don't. That old joke gets at the heart of the hard, simple truth about gun control. The consensus today is that society is divided into two kinds of people: those who can be trusted with guns and those who cannot. The goal is to devise a system of firearm regulation that allows responsible people to own guns and denies them to irresponsible people. Both gun control advocates and opponents implicitly accept that basic approach, even though they passionately disagree about how to implement it. Elected officials, who have little time to study the issue and rely on what advocacy groups on their side of the ideological divide tell them, also accept the consensus model. The problem with that model, however, is that it stems from fantasy. Society is not divided into two kinds of people; things are far more complicated than that. Moreover, even to the extent that there may be some kind of division between the trustworthy and the untrustworthy, it is not possible to devise a regulatory scheme that can effectively distinguish between the two. Nor will that ever be possible. The implacable obstacle to the consensus model is human nature, and that is not going to change.

That does not mean effective gun control is impossible. It is possible and, in fact, it has long existed in other affluent nations. Rhetoric about American exceptionalism notwithstanding, human beings in America are not different from human beings elsewhere. As we shall see, what makes the United States different from other affluent nations is not its level of violence, but its level of lethal violence—and that difference is due to the prevalence of guns. Other nations are horrified by the level of lethal violence we tolerate. If we regulated guns the way other countries do, we would save more lives and avoid more injuries than the U.S. Armed Forces experience in wars.

Why do Americans accept so much unnecessary carnage? For some Americans, the choice is a conscious one. They are willing to pay the price of living in a society with more gun-related homicides, injuries, robberies, assaults, and suicides in order to have what they perceive to be freedom. The founders, they believe, bequeathed us a sacred Second Amendment right. But for most Americans, the choice is largely unexamined. Because they don't hear people advocating for a different model, they assume that no other model is possible. They are not sure whether it is unavailable as a matter of constitutional law, politics, or sociology. They haven't thought it through far enough to ask whether another model is possible. Quite understandably, what they consider is framed by what they hear, and what they hear from all sides involves some variation of the good guy/bad guy model.

Gun control advocates routinely say that we must adopt "common sense" measures that keep guns out of the hands of criminals, the dangerously mentally ill, and potential terrorists while allowing responsible citizens to own guns.[1] That, pretty much, is what everyone believes. The principal difference is that gun control supporters stress keeping guns out of the hands of the irresponsible while gun control opponents stress allowing the responsible to own and carry guns. For example, Hillary Clinton's official presidential campaign platform stated that she "has a record of advocating for commonsense approaches to reduce gun violence," and favored keeping "guns out of the hands of domestic abusers, other violent criminals, and the severely mentally ill."[2] Meanwhile, in his official presidential campaign platform Donald Trump said:

> Here's another important way to fight crime—empower law-abiding gun owners to defend themselves. Law enforcement is great, they do a tremendous job, but they can't be everywhere all of the time. Our personal protection is ultimately up to us. That's why I'm a gun owner, that's why I have a concealed carry permit, and that's why tens of millions of Americans have concealed carry permits as well. It's just common sense. To make America great again, we're going to go after criminals and put the law back on the side of the law-abiding.[3]

To say that both sides agree on the same basic model is not to say that both sides are in basic agreement. They are not. Gun control advocates want more rigorous restrictions on gun ownership, and gun control opponents want either no more restrictions or want to relax existing restrictions. The issue that Trump mentioned—concealed carry permits—is a particular case in point: gun-rights organizations want private citizens to be able to carry concealed weapons on the public streets while gun control opponents do not want them to. This may be a significant detail, but it is a detail nonetheless. Whether or not citizens should be able to carry concealed handguns on the streets, both sides implicitly accept the same fundamental model that good guys should be able to possess handguns and bad guys should not.

What other model is possible? While it isn't possible to meaningfully divide people into two clear categories, it is possible to do that with gun control models. The two fundamental models are these: (1) everyone may possess a handgun except those who cannot; and (2) no one may possess a handgun except those who can. Note, first, that I have focused on handguns, not all guns. I shall, in due course, explain why the difference between handguns and long guns—that is, rifles and shotguns—is so important. The second thing to note is that despite the symmetry in descriptions, these are two fundamentally different models. The first model allows anyone to possess a handgun unless he or she demonstrably falls into a prohibited category, such as being a convicted felon, mentally ill, on a terrorist watch list, or the like. The second model allows no one to possess a handgun unless he or she falls into an exempted category, such as being a law enforcement officer, a member of the military, a security guard, or having a special need to own a handgun. Who among the general public has a special need to own a handgun? Although it may be a bit dated, my favorite example is Salman Rushdie, following the fatwa issued by the Ayatollah Khomeini calling for Rushdie's execution.[4] A more pedestrian example might be women who reasonably fear attack from a stalker.[5] Once again, while the details are not unimportant, they are details nonetheless. The basic difference between the two models is that the first presumptively grants a right to own a handgun to everyone, except those who demonstrably fit into special categories. The second model presumptively grants a right to own a handgun to no one, except those who demonstrably fit into special categories. The most consequential difference between the two models is that there will be far fewer handguns in general circulation under the second model than the first. That, as we shall see, makes all the difference in the world, for there is one kind of gun control that works—and only one kind that works—and it is this: anything that significantly reduces the number of handguns in general circulation.

That last sentence may bring some readers up short, for they immediately realize the terrible implications of my argument. In 2008, the U.S. Supreme Court held that the Second Amendment of the United States Constitution grants individuals a right to keep handguns in their homes.[6] Would a gun control program specifically designed to reduce the number of handguns in general circulation be unconstitutional? And am I arguing that only a program designed to accomplish that objective would be effective? The answers to both questions, broadly speaking, are yes. That is the hard, simple truth about gun control.

Why, then, read on? Do you really want to learn that the only kind of gun control that will be effective cannot be enacted into law? Suffice it say, for now, that I think you should read on. To reduce the gun carnage in America, we need to be clear-eyed about the facts. And, ultimately, we can in fact reduce the gun carnage.

Donald Trump mentioned concealed carry because it is currently a hot political issue, so let's start with the ability to carry handguns in public places. There are two different modes of handgun carry—open carry and concealed carry, depending upon whether one is carrying a visibly displayed handgun, most commonly in a holster on one's hip, or whether one is carrying a handgun concealed somewhere on one's person, often in a pocket or in a holster under a jacket. Only five states and the District of Columbia absolutely prohibit the open carrying of handguns.[7] Of the remaining forty-five states, about one-third require a license or permit to openly carry a handgun and two-thirds do not require a license or permit.[8]

Open carry has long been legally permitted in most states. It has never been much of an issue because so few people do it. Legal restrictions on open carry have been largely unnecessary because there is a strong cultural deterrent to openly carrying handguns: people are afraid of other people who they see walking around in public places with a handgun strapped to their waist. Restaurants, stores, and office buildings will ask gun-toting individuals to leave their premises. Those that don't do so are likely to see patrons quickly depart. Some people call the police when they see someone carrying a gun in a public place, and some police forces actively discourage open carry of weapons, even where law permits it. A spokesperson for the Philadelphia police department declared that someone openly carrying a handgun should expect to be "inconvenienced" by being ordered to lie on the ground while police check his permit, a process that might take some time as the first police officer on the scene might not approach the person he has—at gunpoint—ordered to the ground until backup arrives.[9] An organization named OpenCarry.org is dedicated to trying to make open carry socially acceptable by encouraging gun owners to carry guns openly more often.[10] Its motto is "A Right Unexercised is a Right Lost." A visit to its website suggests OpenCarry.org is struggling. Its events draw few participants, and its website complains that even Utah police find ways to charge people who are openly carrying firearms with disorderly conduct.[11]

However, even if these activists persuade police departments not to deliberately inconvenience people who are openly carrying handguns in jurisdictions where that is legally allowed, the public is not likely to be blasé about gun-toting people mingling with them in supermarkets, movie theaters, libraries, and the like, and social pressure will continue to stop open carry from becoming more common.

Because of the cultural impediments to open carry, the National Rifle Association (NRA) and other pro-gun groups have focused on expanding concealed carry.[12] In the past, most states either prohibited concealed carry entirely or had restrictive permitting systems.[13] Many states had "may issue" permit laws that gave the chief of police or other law enforcement official the discretion to issue a concealed carry permit to individuals who had special reasons to be armed. Chiefs of police typically granted few permits. The NRA, therefore, started lobbying states to enact "shall issue" permit laws that require the chief of police to issue a concealed carry permit to all applicants who do not fit into specified categories, such as having a record of criminal convictions or mental illness. The NRA lobbying effort for shall-issue permits got a big assist in 1997 when two economists, John R. Lott and David B. Mustard, published a paper in which, using complex econometric models, they claimed to have found an inverse statistical correlation between shall-issue concealed carry laws and violent crimes.[14] The following year Lott expanded his thesis into a book titled *More Guns, Less Crime*.[15] Lott wrote: "Allowing citizens to carry concealed handguns reduces violent crimes, and the reductions coincide very closely with the number of concealed-handgun permits issued. Mass shootings in public places are reduced when law-abiding citizens are allowed to carry concealed handguns."[16]

Notice the term "law-abiding citizens." It is the good guy/bad guy model that implicitly explains Lott's findings. The idea is that we can indeed sort out the good guys. Most obviously, police run a criminal-record check on people applying for concealed carry permits, and criminals have criminal records. But, of course, that last statement cannot be completely true, if only because some criminals have not yet been caught. There is another assumption lurking here, albeit unexamined: only good guys apply for concealed carry permits. That is not how bad guys behave (even bad guys without rap sheets).

Lott argued that concealed carry effectively deters violent crime because criminals are hesitant to rob or attack people who may be armed. When criminals realize that some significant fraction of potential victims are armed, but they cannot tell who is armed and who is not, they make a rational decision to change their behavior. The Lott-Mustard model showed that concealed carry laws were associated with a rise in property crime; Lott suggested this was because criminals, finding it more risky to rob people who may turn out to be armed, turned to safer alternatives such as auto theft and other nonviolent property crimes.[17]

The Lott-Mustard paper, and Lott's book, created a sensation.[18] They supercharged NRA lobbying efforts for right-to-carry laws, that is, laws that either have shall-issue permit systems or that allow people to carry concealed firearms without a permit or license of any kind. By 2014, forty-two states had right-to-carry laws.[19] In 1999, 2.7 million Americans had concealed carry permits. By mid-2014, that had increased to 11.1 million people.[20]

There are, however, big problems with Lott's "more guns, less crime" thesis. First, other researchers discredited his econometric analysis. Lott compared change in crime during the period 1985 to 1991 between states that adopted shall-issue laws and those that did not; he claimed to find smaller increases in crime in the first group. Crime was rising nationally during this time. Criminologists believed that, in at least significant part, the rise was due to a skyrocketing use of crack cocaine, especially in poor neighborhoods of large cities.[21] However, the two groups of states were very different in this regard. For example, states that enacted right-to-carry laws included Maine, Idaho, and Montana, while those that did not enact such laws included New York, California, and New Jersey. John J. Donohue and Ian Ayres, researchers at Stanford University and Yale University, respectively, extended the Lott-Mustard analysis through 1997. Donohue explained their dramatic findings as follows: "When the Lott and Mustard statistical model is run for the period in the 1990s when the spikes in crime reversed themselves, suddenly shall-issue laws are associated with uniform *increases* in crime."[22]

Later, Donohue and Ayres extended their analysis still further to 2006, a period of continuing decline in crime generally, and got similar findings.[23] Donohue and Ayres also found coding errors in the Mustard-Lott model that, when corrected, eliminated the claimed effect of concealed carry laws on robbery.[24] Meanwhile, Dan A. Black, an economist at the University of Chicago, and Daniel S. Nagin, an economist at Carnegie Mellon University, found that if the single state of Florida, where crime statistics were usually volatile, was removed from the Lott-Mustard econometric model, all the claimed effects of right-to-carry laws on violent crime disappeared.[25] A host of other researchers, including the most prominent pro-gun criminologist, found serious problems with Lott and Mustard's work. Their consensus was that one could not reliably draw conclusions from the Lott-Mustard econometric analysis.[26]

More recent studies that benefit from years of data after the crack cocaine epidemic ended support for the view that right-to-carry laws actually increase violent crime.[27] One study found that right-to-carry laws increase firearm homicides by about 9 percent over states with stringent concealed carry systems, while having no effect whatsoever on homicides committed with other weapons.[28]

One does not have to resort to econometrics to grasp the fallacy of the arm-the-good-guys approach. Consider, for example, this incident: in September 2013, one car tailgating another in Michigan led to a road rage incident in which both drivers drove to a parking lot, got out of their cars, pulled out handguns, and shot each other dead.[29] Both men had valid concealed carry permits. Aside from being a reciprocal-murder, this incident was not unusual. The Violence Policy Center (VPC) has been trying to track the number of people who were killed by someone with a concealed carry permit since May 2007. This is a difficult undertaking because there is no official database of such killings. In fact, some states make it unlawful for law enforcement to reveal such information. VPC must, therefore, rely principally on news accounts, and its count includes only a fraction of the actual total. As of this writing, VPC identified 1,119 people who have been killed by concealed carry permit holders.[30] That number includes homicides, suicides, and accidents but excludes the very small number of shootings made in self-defense. These killings occurred in forty states and the District of Columbia. Twenty-one victims were law enforcement officers. The incidents include thirty-one mass shootings that took the lives of 147 victims. It is also worth noting that except for suicides, where the lethality rate is very high with guns, there are many more shootings than killings because some wounded victims survive.

One might think that the NRA would be satisfied with persuading forty-two states to pass right-to-carry laws.[31] Not so. It is currently lobbying for passage of federal legislation known as the Concealed Carry Reciprocity Act of 2017, which would require every state to honor a concealed carry permit issued by another state, even if that state does not allow concealed carry by its own citizens.[32] In December 2017, that bill passed the House by 231–198 on a largely party-line vote, and is, as of this writing, awaiting action in the Senate.[33]

. . .

Let us next turn to mass shootings. Although mass shootings are not responsible for the largest share of gun carnage in America—casualties from more prosaic shootings involving one or a few victims far exceed those from mass shootings—mass shootings receive a great deal of news coverage and are especially terrorizing.

We can begin on August 1, 1966, the day that an engineering student and former U.S. Marine named Charles Whitman killed his wife and mother, and then, armed with rifles and other guns, climbed to the top of The Tower at the center of campus of the University of Texas at Austin, and from that perch shot students and others traversing the campus. Before he was killed by Austin police, Whitman murdered a total of eighteen people and wounded thirty-two more.[34] I have vivid memories of that event. I was then eighteen years old and going off to college in a month. You might think the Whitman massacre would have made someone like me and my family anxious, but I don't remember it creating anxiety. This was then the worst shooting massacre in U.S. history.[35] Mass shootings before this time were, in fact, rare in America.[36] The entire nation was stunned and horrified, of course, but we assumed that it was a bizarre event, an anomaly. No one realized that Charles Whitman was the harbinger of a new normal.

Here is an abbreviated list of some of the more memorable mass shootings:

McDonald's, San Ysidro, CA	1984:	22 dead, 19 wounded
Cleveland Elementary School, Stockton, CA	1989	6 dead, 30 wounded
Luby's Cafeteria, Killeen, TX	1991	24 dead, 20 wounded
Columbine High School, Littleton, CO	1999	15 dead, 23 wounded
Virginia Tech, Blacksburg, VA	2007	33 dead, 17 wounded
Safeway Parking Lot, Tucson, AZ	2011	6 dead, 13 wounded
Sandy Hook Elementary School, Newtown, CT	2012	28 dead
Inland Regional Center, San Bernardino, CA	2015	14 dead, 14 wounded
Emanuel A.M.E. Church, Charleston, SC	2015	9 dead
Pulse Nightclub, Orlando, FL	2016	50 dead, 53 wounded
Harvest Music Festival, Las Vegas, NV	2017	59 dead, 441 wounded
Sutherland Springs, TX	2017	26 dead, 20 wounded
Parkland, FL	2018	17 dead, 17 wounded[37]

There is plenty of national anxiety now. My wife and I work in different settings—she in a government agency and I in a university—but we have both been required to undergo active-shooter training by our employers, and surely this has become routine nearly everywhere. Americans feel very much at risk of finding themselves in a massacre. The general feeling, I

believe, is not only that no place is safe, but that eventually there will be
a mass shooting just about everywhere. Because some of the worst massacres have occurred in elementary schools, even small children are not
spared worry. Reminders of vulnerability are ever-present. My university,
for example, has just installed on all classroom doors fancy new locks with
a red button on the inside side of the door that, when depressed, locks the
door without need of a key. No one has explained why the new locks have
been installed—no one needs to—and those red buttons will remind us
constantly of potential threat. In case you are wondering, no shooting has
occurred at my university, though a former student sent menacing emails
to a dean and several faculty members (including me), and refused to open
his apartment door to talk to police who came to have a chat with him,
making it clear he was armed. No weapon was ever fired, but there was a
standoff that lasted awhile, an arrest, and after some weeks, a release. It
feels part of a new normal.

There is no universally accepted definition of "mass shooting."[38] How
many victims does it take to qualify as a mass shooting? Should we count
the total number of casualties, both killed and wounded, or just fatalities?
Should shooters who die at the scene be included in the number of fatalities?
Researchers and news organizations use different definitions, which often
makes apple-to-apple comparisons difficult. Gun Violence Archive (GVA),
an organization that defines its mission as providing independent, verified
data about gun violence to researchers and the public-at-large through its
website, defines mass shooting as a single event resulting in four or more
people being shot, not including the shooter.[39]

Depending upon how one defines the term, mass shootings may now
occur at a rate of one per day in the United States. The *New York Times*
counted 358 mass shootings with four or more casualties (including killed
and wounded) in 2015. GVA counted 275 mass shootings in 2014 and 333
in 2015. At the time I happen to be writing this, Sunday morning, January
22, 2017, GVA has already counted twenty mass shootings this year.

Near the end of 2015, the *Washington Post* looked at mass shootings in
the United States over the past fifty years.[40] For this purpose, it defined
mass shooting as an event in which four or more people were killed. It
excluded gang killings and killings stemming from other crimes such as
robberies but included the perpetrator in the number of fatalities. The *Post*
identified 124 such events, in which a total of 814 people were killed, an
average of seven fatalities per event. These mass shootings occurred in forty
states. With only three exceptions, all the shooters were male. The most

common venues for the massacres were, in declining order, workplaces, retail stores and restaurants, and schools. Shooters brought an average of three guns apiece to each shooting, for a total of 243 guns in all incidents. Most of the weapons were handguns. It was possible to determine how the shooters acquired 180 of the guns used, and of those 141—78.3 percent— were acquired legally. We also know that most mass shooters kill a former or current intimate partner, often at the beginning of their rampage.[41]

Can we create a system that will keep guns out of the hands of potential mass shooters while still allowing them to trustworthy individuals? The conventional wisdom is that mass shooters suffer from serious mental illnesses, and that we might be able to drastically reduce these events by making improvements in the mental health system.[42] However, according to Michael Stone, a forensic psychiatrist at Columbia University, only 20 percent of mass shooters are suffering from serious mental illnesses such as schizophrenia, delusions, or psychoses.[43] The rest of them may have personality or sociopathic disorders, and while they may exhibit rage, an extreme lack of empathy, humiliation, or paranoia, they know what they are doing. According to Stone, this second group can neither be reliably identified nor helped by the mental health system, no matter how well the system is improved. Other researchers agree. James Alan Fox, a criminologist at Northeastern University, says that most mass killers are depressed, not delusional.[44] A group of three psychiatrists, a social worker specializing in mental health, and a sociologist-economist specializing in gun violence who together studied gun violence and mental health note that epidemiological research shows that people with mental illness are responsible for only a small proportion of violence in America. They go on to write:

> The very small proportion of people with mental illnesses who are inclined to be dangerous often do not seek treatment before they do something harmful; they therefore do not acquire a gun-disqualifying record of mental health adjudication (or criminal record, either) that would show up in a background check. Psychiatrists, using clinical judgment, cannot accurately foresee which patients will be violent.[45]

Mass murderers, of course, are not the average guys. Experts tell us mass murderers are often socially isolated. They don't fit in and often come from communities where fitting is considered very important. They are often frustrated and externalize blame, says James Alan Fox. "Nothing is ever their fault. . . . They see themselves as good guys mistreated by others."[46] Those who commit family massacres, says Fox, are typically "vengeful" but not mentally ill.[47] But risk factors such as anger, frustration, alienation, and even some degree of paranoia are not useful in identifying people who should be denied firearms. Those characteristics are all too common.

While it might be possible to develop an algorithm to assess an individual's risk of becoming violent, such a tool is unlikely to be useful for regulatory purposes. Many studies have found that alcohol abuse is a major risk factor for all types of gun violence.[48] We know other factors such as gender, age, impulsivity, and lack of family support are stronger predictors of violent behavior than mental illness. John Monahan, a psychologist at the University of Virginia, developed a software program that uses 106 risk factors to predict the potential for violence for patients being discharged from psychiatric hospital units.[49] The model shows promise: only 10 percent of those who were deemed low-risk committed a violent act over the next six months while 49 percent of those deemed high-risk did so. Nevertheless, such a model will have little utility for regulatory policy. It might be helpful in determining whom to release from a mental-health facility, but it will never stop people without criminal or mental-health records from purchasing guns. There is, first, the practical problem of getting the data. Monahan acquired his information in extensive interviews of patients prior to discharge, but how would the government learn that someone in the general population sometimes has five drinks in a row or does not have good relationships with family members? Second, there are legal barriers. The Supreme Court has held that individuals possess a constitutional right to own handguns for self-defense. The courts will likely continue to allow a regulatory system that denies firearms to felons and people who have been adjudicated a danger to themselves or others, but they are not going to sanction algorithms of the kind Monahan has developed.

The good guy/bad guy model is widely accepted though generally unexamined.[50] There is a strong incentive not to reach this conclusion—not even to consider it, in fact—because it leads to pessimism, even despair. Occasionally, however, people who examine the data and think hard about the options realize the futility of the good guy/bad guy model. In October 2016, the *New York Times* published an extensive examination of the issue that began on the front page and took up two full interior pages. Titled "In 130 of Worst Shootings, Vision of Porous Gun Laws," the story contained this observation:

> An examination of high-casualty shootings emphasizes not only how porous existing firearm regulations are, but also how difficult tightening them in a meaningful way can be. . . . The findings are dispiriting to anyone hoping for simple legislative fixes to gun violence. In more than half the 130 cases, at

least one assailant was already barred by federal law from having a weapon, usually because of a felony conviction, but nonetheless acquired a gun. . . . Of the remaining assailants, 40 percent had never had a serious run-in with the law and probably could have bought a gun even in states with the strictest firearm control.[51]

The hard truth is that the possibility of reducing mass shootings by improving the mental health system or the records used for background checks run into four implacable problems. First, most perpetrators of gun violence do not suffer from serious mental illness. Second, among the perpetrators of gun violence that do suffer from mental illness, few seek treatment. Third, among people who do seek help for mental illness, psychiatrists and other mental health professionals cannot distinguish between those who are dangerous and those who are not. Fourth, people identified as dangerous and barred from purchasing a gun may prevail on someone else to serve as a "straw purchaser," that is, to purchase the gun for him. Police sting operations have shown that some licensed gun dealers readily sell a gun to A even when they know all of the following three things: A is serving as a straw purchaser for B, B is legally prohibited from purchasing a gun, and B intends to use the gun to commit a crime.[52] There are grossly irresponsible private, unlicensed sellers too. The two teenagers who committed the Columbine High School massacre were too young to legally purchase long guns, so they recruited an eighteen-year-old to purchase two shotguns and a semiautomatic rifle from a private seller at a gun show for them.[53]

We shall now more broadly examine gun violence in America.

There were, according to the FBI Uniform Crime Reports, 13,455 murders in the United States in 2015.[54] Firearms accounted for 9,616—71.5 percent—of those murders. And handguns were the most commonly used firearm. In fact, handguns were used to commit at least 6,447 murders—67 percent of all firearm homicides and 48 percent of all homicides. I say "at least" because we do not know what type of firearm was used for 2,648 murders. We do know that long guns—shotguns and rifles—were used to commit 521 murders, which represent less than 4 percent of all homicides. If we assume the division between handguns and long guns for the category "other guns or type not stated" in the FBI's Uniform Crime Reports is in the same proportion as when the type of firearm used was known and reported, then handguns accounted for about 61 percent of all murders in the United States. The next most commonly used weapons are knives or cutting instruments, which account for approximately 11 percent of all murders in the United States. Personal weapons (hands and feet) and blunt objects are used to commit roughly 4 percent and 3 percent, respectively, of all murders. All other weapons combined—including poison, explosives, and fire—plus other methods of murder, such as pushing someone off a cliff, account for well under 1 percent of all murders. This has long been the U.S. pattern.[55] Handguns are therefore, by far, the most common murder method in the United States.

In what types of situations do handgun-related murders occur? According to the FBI, about 17 percent of all handgun murders in 2015 occurred in connection with a felony or suspected felony—such as robbery, rape, and narcotics violations—while about 23 percent occurred during arguments or brawls.[56] These were followed by juvenile gang killings and gangland killings, which constituted about 9 percent and 2 percent, respectively, of handgun-related homicides. Law enforcement did not know the circumstances in which about 38 percent of all handgun-related murders were committed. For these purposes, however, we cannot reasonably assume that the circumstances in the unknown category mirror those in the known categories. Perhaps a higher proportion of murders that occurred in unknown circumstances arose from robberies and other felonies than from arguments, brawls, and romantic triangles than was the case when police were able to discern the circumstances of the killing. It is a reasonable guess, therefore, that about half of all handgun murders occur during other crimes and about half arise from arguments, brawls, romantic triangles, and the like.

The FBI also reports that, among all the 13,455 murders in 2015, 1,721 victims (12.8 percent) were family members of the perpetrator, 1,013 (7.5 percent) were a friend, boyfriend, or—most commonly—a girlfriend of the perpetrator, and 2,801 (20.8 percent) were an acquaintance of the perpetrator.[57] These three categories—relative, friend, and acquaintance—are all somewhat larger than the numbers suggest because in many instances the police are unable to identify the perpetrator. The rough rule of thumb used by criminologists and sociologists familiar with these data is that in about half of homicides the perpetrator and victim knew each other, about a quarter of all female victims are killed by husbands and boyfriends, and about one-third of all homicides arise from arguments.[58]

The largest category of gun violence is suicide. According to the Centers for Disease Control and Prevention (CDC), there were 21,334 suicides by firearms in the United States in 2014 (the latest year for which the CDC has supplied data).[59] While the CDC does not report the type of firearm, handguns are almost always the type of firearm used, both because they are more prevalent and because of the physical difficulty of using a long gun to shoot oneself.

The smallest category of gun fatalities is accidents. About six hundred people die annually from unintentional shootings.[60] While there are relatively few accidents in terms of the total number of fatalities, they are often poignant and include, on average, 62 children age 14 or younger per year.[61] Many of these are quite young—toddlers who find a parent's handgun in a nightstand drawer or under socks in a bedroom dresser and accidently kill themselves, siblings, or playmates.

Of course, many shootings are not fatal. In 2010, hospital emergency rooms treated 73,505 nonfatal gunshot injuries.[62] These include gunshots resulting from murder attempts, robberies, assaults, accidents, and suicide attempts. Firearms, therefore, impose a heavy financial cost on the U.S. health care system. Firearms were also used to commit 123,358 robberies and 170,941 aggravated assaults in the United States during 2015.[63] That accounts for about 41 percent of all robberies and nearly a quarter of all aggravated assaults.[64] Guns, therefore, have an impact on American life that extends well beyond the numbers of people killed and injured.

So far we have been examining the cost side of the ledger. Let's now turn to the benefit side: how often handguns and other firearms are used in self-defense. This is a subject of hot debate. The NRA and its allies claim that guns are frequently used for self-defense and prevent many crimes, most often by merely brandishing a gun and frightening a robber or attacker away. That is a convenient claim because it largely relies on unverified stories by gun owners. For example, a gun owner says that he heard someone attempting to break into his home at night. He got his gun and shouted, "Come in at your own risk. I am armed!" He then heard footsteps running away. Or a gun owner claims he was walking alone at night when a menacing-looking individual crossed the street in his direction, apparently bent upon robbery. The gun owner drew his previously concealed handgun from its holster and displayed it to the approaching individual, who promptly turned tail and ran away. Such stories are legion. Even assuming good faith by a storyteller, how do we know whether he was mistaken about the intent of the person he frightened away? To take a famous situation, George Zimmerman may have been convinced in his mind that he was a law-abiding citizen and Trayvon Martin was a dangerous criminal, yet things surely appeared quite different to Trayvon Martin.[65] In a study conducted by a researcher at the Harvard School of Public Health, a panel of judges reviewed incidents in which gun owners said they fired a single shot in self-defense. The judges concluded that in a majority of those incidents the action was not, in fact, a legitimate act of self-defense.[66]

We do, however, have hard data that can give us a better idea about how often guns are used in self-defense, namely, the number of justifiable homicides in which handguns were used. Unlike unverified stories about brandishing a gun, when someone is shot and killed there is a dead body and a police investigation. According to the FBI, private handguns were used in 215 justifiable homicides in 2015.[67] (Long guns were used in just 21 justifiable homicides.) Justifiable homicides occur when someone reasonably believes it is necessary to use deadly force in defense of himself or someone else. Of course, not every use of handgun for self-defense results in a fatality. It is reasonable to assume the rule of thumb that there are five to seven nonfatal injuries for every fatal gun injury applies.[68] And there are surely occasions when merely brandishing a weapon is, by itself, an effective mode of self-defense. Nevertheless, comparing the number of justifiable handgun homicides to handgun murders is extremely useful in making a cost-benefit analysis of handguns in America. To repeat the figures, there were 215 justifiable homicides and 6,447 murders committed with handguns in 2015. Thus, 96.8 percent of all nonsuicidal killings committed with handguns were murders. This is, of course, not the whole story, but it gives us a solid apple-to-apple comparison.

Also on the benefit side of the ledger are the feelings of security that handguns give their owners. It must be noted, however, that as comforting as those feelings may be, they provide gun owners with a false sense of security. Most Americans who own handguns do so for self-defense. Undoubtedly, they believe they are making a prudent decision to protect themselves and their families, but data suggest otherwise. Another study has shown that for each incident in which a gun in the home is used to shoot an intruder, there are four accidental shootings of members of their households or their guests, seven criminal assaults or homicides, and eleven attempted or completed suicides.[69] Having a gun at home increases the chance of successful suicide in that home by a factor of five.[70] Teenagers are especially at risk. Many teens go through periods of angst and depression, and a gun is all too easy to grab and use in a moment of even brief despair. Moreover, once the trigger is pulled, there is no turning back as sometimes happens when someone swallows pills or sits in a running automobile in a closed garage.

The gun lobby has long argued that guns in the home deter home invasions or "hot burglaries," that is, burglaries occurring when homeowners are present. The theory is that burglars do not want to be confronted by armed homeowners. Thus, burglars seek to avoid neighborhoods where they believe there are a higher proportion of armed homeowners, work harder to ensure the home is unoccupied before burglarizing it, or are more likely to take up other lines of work in states and regions with high rates of gun ownership. The theory may be superficially appealing, but data do not support it. First, guns in the home are rarely used against intruders. In one study, researchers working with the police found that in only 3 out of 198 instances (1.5 percent) of unwanted home entries that occurred in Atlanta over a three-month period were handguns used in self-defense.[71] Second, according to one study, hot burglary rates increase rather than decrease along with the prevalence of gun ownership.[72] A 10 percent increase in gun ownership appeared to increase burglary rates by 3 to 7 percent.

I suspect that even if gun owners knew all these data, many would nonetheless feel confident that owning a handgun is a prudent decision for them and their families. Tragedies happen to less careful people. Just as 90 percent of all drivers believe they are better than average, most gun owners likely believe that they are more trustworthy than the average gun owner.[73] Jamie Gilt, a thirty-one-year-old gun activist in Jacksonville, Florida, may have been just such a person. Gilt maintained a Facebook page titled "Jamie Gilt for Gun Sense," on which she ridiculed the idea of relying on the police for protection instead of owning a gun.[74] Her whole family knew how to shoot, Gilt noted, adding, "Even my 4-year-old gets jacked up to target shoot the .22." On Monday, March 7, 2016, while Gilt was driving a pickup truck, her four-year-old son, who was sitting in the backseat, accidentally shot Gilt with a handgun. The bullet entered Gilt's back and exited the front of her torso. A police officer quickly came to the rescue when he observed Gilt behaving frantically inside the truck. Fortunately, she survived.

We shall now examine the existing system of firearm regulation in the United States.

Federal law requires that people wishing to purchase a firearm— handgun, rifle, or shotgun—from licensed gun dealers fill out a Firearms Transaction Form and have their names run through the National Instant Criminal Background Check System (NICS), which is operated by the FBI.

In the main, the system is designed to prevent sales to people who have been convicted of a felony; people who have been convicted of a domestic violence misdemeanor or are under a restraining order; people adjudicated to be "a mental defective" or involuntarily committed to a mental institution; drug addicts; aliens unlawfully in the United States; fugitives from justice; and people dishonorably discharged from the armed forces.[75] In the good guy/bad guy model, these are the bad guys. Everyone else over eighteen years of age may purchase a long gun, and those twenty-one or older may purchase a handgun. Under federal law, background checks must be completed within three days, although nearly all checks are completed within just seconds. There are some additional state restrictions—most notably, about a dozen states require a license or permit to own a handgun.[76]

For political reasons, the system has enormous loopholes. Most significantly, only sales by licensed gun dealers are covered. Private sales are exempt under federal law. These include, notoriously, sales made by private sellers at the 4,000 gun shows that are held annually across the country. Private sellers constitute between a quarter and a half of all gun sellers at gun shows.[77] No one really knows what portion of all firearm sales are private and therefore take place without background checks. According to a rather old survey, 40 percent of all gun sales are private. In a more recent survey of prison inmates who used a gun in their most recent crime, only one in nine (11 percent) said they bought the gun from a store or a pawnshop, which are generally the venues of licensed gun dealers. Only sixteen states require background checks for private handgun sales, and only six states require background checks for private sales of all firearms, including long guns.[78]

Another strange aspect of federal law is that federal agencies must destroy their records relating to approved background checks within twenty-four hours of completed gun sales.[79] Congress routinely includes this requirement in appropriation bills for the Department of Justice (which includes both the FBI and ATF). The reason for the requirement is that the NRA is adamantly opposed to the government possessing records of gun ownership so that, should it fall into tyrannical hands, the government would not have records to aid it in gun confiscation.[80] However, the requirement handicaps investigations relating to gun sales where background checks failed to find disqualifying information.[81]

Moreover, Congress has deliberately included other provisions in the federal firearm laws to make research about gun regulation in the United States by criminologists, public health experts, and others more difficult. In 1995, Congress directed that the $2.6 million that had been budgeted for gun-related research by the Centers for Disease Control and Prevention be used for other purposes instead, and it has since repeatedly instructed that no CDC research money be "used to advocate or promote gun control."[82] Note that Congress' direction was not evenhanded; it did *not* say, for example, that CDC funds were not to be used to advocate for or against gun control. Not only the CDC but researchers based at universities that obtain federal grants to study crime or public health issues got the message: stop researching gun violence. That effectively ended federally funded gun research for more than a decade.

In 2009, the National Institutes of Health (NIH) began to make small but regular research grants related to guns. At the behest of the NRA, Congress also passed legislation designed to foreclose another promising area of research related to ATF traces of guns used in crimes. When police recover a gun at a crime scene, ATF initiates a trace, using the weapon's serial number, to follow the gun from manufacturer, to distributor, to dealer, to the person who purchased the gun from the dealer. Using trace data, researchers discovered that a disproportionate number of crime guns were being sold by a relatively few gun shops. In fact, the data were astonishing: 1 percent of licensed gun dealers were selling nearly 60 percent of the guns ultimately used in crimes.[83] This presented a new area of inquiry: could gun crimes be reduced by eliminating "bad apple" dealers or otherwise improving the distribution chain? Continuing its three-monkey approach—see no evil, hear no evil, speak no evil—Congress, in 2003, enacted legislation that effectively prohibits ATF from disclosing trace data, even non-individual aggregated data, to the public.[84]

The NRA, and thus Congress, wants as weak and ineffective an ATF as possible. Congress expressly prohibits ATF from conducting more than one unannounced visit of a gun dealer per year—no matter how questionable the history of the dealer—and the funding that Congress provides is barely sufficient to allow ATF to visit a gun dealer, on average, every five years.[85] Congress forbids ATF from computerizing trace data; all traces have to be conducted by hand. And Congress prohibits ATF from requiring that dealers maintain an inventory, which, of course, makes it difficult or impossible for ATF to tell whether a dealer's guns are being stolen, lost, or deliberately diverted to the black market.

Let's assume for the sake of argument that the loopholes could be closed and the political obstacles removed. Suppose the law required that all gun sales in all states—whether made by licensed dealers or private sellers—were subject to NICS background checks.[86] Suppose the ATF were adequately funded and permitted to inspect dealers as reasonably necessary to ensure compliance with law. Suppose record reporting were improved to ensure that criminal and mental health records were timely entered into the system. If the basic regulatory model was improved as much as possible, would it reasonably protect America from gun violence?

The answer is no. Even with a perfect record system covering all gun sales, the good guy/bad guy model will not do the job. Let's start with the criminal side. Only 40 percent of people convicted of murder had prior felony records.[87] Moreover, even if we require that all private sales be subject to background checks, people with felony records will still borrow guns from friends and family members, steal guns, and purchase them on the black market. When surveyed, only 20 percent of prisoners say they purchased the gun they used for the last crime from a store.[88] Things are even bleaker on the mental health side. As previously mentioned, only a small fraction of people who commit murder are mentally ill. There are serious mental illnesses such as schizophrenia, bipolar disorder, and severe depression that are associated with increased risks of violent behavior, but one study found that only 7 percent of people who were hospitalized for these conditions were hospitalized involuntarily, and federal law prohibits only that subgroup from owning a firearm.[89] Even if the NICS records and federal law were to be expanded to prohibit everyone suffering from a severe mental illness from owning a gun—regardless of whether they were hospitalized involuntarily, or even hospitalized at all—the records will still be woefully over-inclusive and under-inclusive. On the one hand, only a fraction of people with serious mental illness will ever wind up in the NICS; on the other hand, the vast majority of people with serious mental illnesses are not violent. Moreover, it is estimated that only 5 percent of violent crimes are committed by people with serious mental illness.[90] (At present, we are making it easier for mentally ill people to buy guns. At the NRA's behest, Congress passed and President Donald J. Trump signed legislation abolishing a federal regulation that required the Social Security Administration to report to the NICS people who receive disability checks because they are mentally disabled or unable to handle their own financial affairs.[91])

Currently, most states require psychotherapists to report patients who present a serious danger of violence to an identifiable individual.[92] This generally means that a psychotherapist must report a patient who expressly says he intends to harm a specific person. A few states also require psychotherapists to report individuals who they believe present a serious danger to society at-large, regardless of whether they have said they want to harm a particular individual. Either way, this is very different from reporting all patients with serious mental illness. Requiring psychotherapists to report to the government everyone with a serious mental illness who comes to them for help, regardless of whether the psychotherapist has reason to believe the particular patient is dangerous, would likely do far more harm than good. It would discourage people from seeking treatment, and it would weaken the patients' trust in their relationships with their psychotherapists, which is essential to successful treatment. Discouraging people with serious mental illnesses from getting treatment is hardly a recipe for improving public health and safety.

Scientists have begun to identify genes that are associated with violent behavior.[93] Suppose, for the sake of argument, they get much better at this—so much better that a DNA test can identify people who are likely to commit violent acts in the future. Should such individuals be prohibited from buying or possessing a firearm, even if they have not yet committed a violent act? In view of the fact that the Supreme Court has held that people have a constitutional right to own handguns, it would, as a matter of law, be extremely difficult to deny that right to people who have, to date, been law-abiding citizens. If we can deny them that constitutional right, is not the next logical step preventive detention?[94]

Thus, for a host of reasons—involving law, public policy, fundamental American values, medical ethics, sociology, and much more—the good guy/bad guy model is never going to be adequate to the task, even if it is improved as much as practicably possible. It should be no surprise, therefore, that the best evidence is that gun control measures based on that system have been ineffective.

The statutory genesis of our current federal system was the Brady Handgun Violence Prevention Act of 1994. That law imposed a five-day waiting period for handgun purchases. The purpose was twofold: (1) to provide a cooling-off period for people who may be purchasing handguns because they were angry at someone and intending harm, and (2) to have local police conduct a background check of putative handgun purchasers during the waiting period.[95] When the law went into effect, eighteen states already had similar laws in place. This set up something of a natural experiment to measure the efficacy of the Brady Act. Crime rises and falls for many reasons, so just seeing whether homicide rates increased or declined after the law went into effect would not tell us much. A crime decrease may have happened anyway. However, researchers were able to compare the thirty-two states with new waiting periods and background checks with the eighteen states that already had such requirements to see whether there were greater changes in one group of states than in the other. They discovered that the average homicide rates in both groups followed nearly exactly the same trajectories.[96] There was no discernable impact of the Brady Act on crime rates.

Further research has confirmed that the Brady Act has no discernable effect on reducing criminal violence by purchasers who were blocked from purchasing a gun because of their previous criminal histories. Researchers found evidence that the Act might have had "some positive effect" among purchasers who were disqualified exclusively by their mental health histories, that is, people with serious mental illness and without criminal records.[97] But that is a pretty small subgroup. In the study, it comprised only 5 percent of the people blocked from purchasing a gun.

The fact that the Brady Act is not associated with a decline in homicides often surprises gun control advocates. On its website, the Brady Campaign to Prevent Handgun Violence, which was the principal advocate for the Brady Act, makes the following claim: "Since the Brady law took effect in 1994, over 2.4 million prohibited purchases have been blocked and countless lives have been saved."[98] It is true that 2.4 million sales by licensed gun dealers were blocked because purchasers were determined to be ineligible to purchase a gun, but it is, I believe, nothing more than an assumption that the blocked sales saved lives—at least as a result of homicides, robberies, and criminal assault. That is why, I suspect, the Brady Campaign says that "countless" lives were saved, without any supporting citation. The most obvious explanation as to why blocked sales do not appear to translate into saved lives is that buyers turned away by licensed dealers get guns elsewhere. While we do not know how often such buyers are redirected to private sellers or the black market, there is plenty of anecdotal evidence of people shopping at guns shows being turned away by licensed dealers and immediately going to unlicensed dealers at adjacent tables.[99]

This does not mean, however, that effective gun control is impossible. Other nations have it. They have reduced firearm homicides to a tiny fraction of what we experience in the United States, and as a result their total homicide rates are also much lower than ours. I do not say "as a result" blithely, but before speaking of cause and effect let's look at some data.

The first bar for the United Kingdom is not missing; you cannot see it because the firearm homicide rate was zero. The firearm death rate for the United States towers above the other three countries: the U.S. rate is more than seven times the next highest rate. By contrast, the non-firearm homicide rate in the United States is not even twice the Canadian rate. As

Total Death Rates per 100,000 Population, 2010

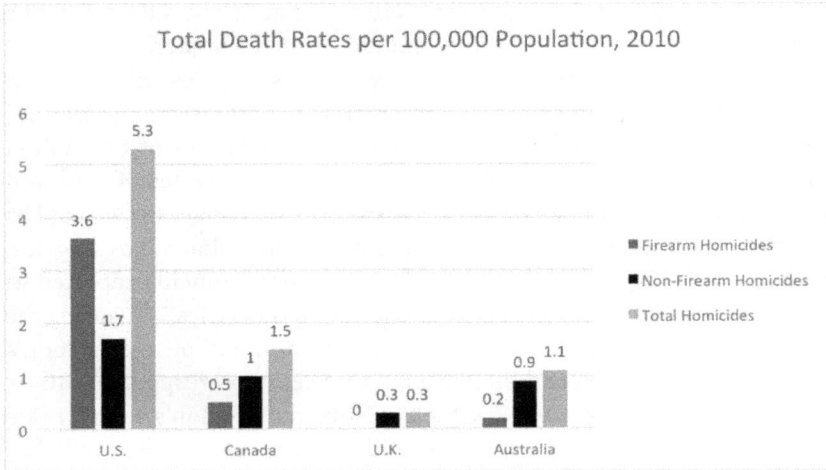

Data from: Erin Grinshteyn and David Hemenway, "Violent Death Rates: The US Compared with Other High-income OECD Countries, 2010," American Journal of Medicine 129 (2016): 266.

one can clearly see, that towering third bar of total homicides in the United States comprises, in the main, the first bar—homicides with guns.

Franklin E. Zimring and Gordon Hawkins convincingly demonstrated that the United States is not exceptional because Americans are more violent than citizens in other affluent countries. Rates of robberies and assaults in America are not far different from those in other affluent nations. For example, during their study period, the assault rates for Canada and England were within 30 percent of the U.S. rate, while the assault rate in Australia was a bit more than 30 percent above the U.S. rate. What makes America so different is its extraordinarily high rate of *lethal* violence, and what makes violence in America lethal much more often is the far greater prevalence of guns. Guns are, quite simply, far more lethal than other weapons. The robbery rates in Canada, England, and Australia were, for the year studied, within 30 percent of the U.S. rate.[101] Robberies, however, are more likely to turn deadly when they are at gunpoint. It is so much easier to shoot a victim who resists, or flees, or whom the robber just does not like than it is to stab or bludgeon him, and someone who is shot is more likely to die than someone who is stabbed or bludgeoned. Guns are used in about 40 percent of New York robberies yet accounted for 85 percent of robbery killings.[102] The same dynamic plays out in assaults.[103] Guns are used in 26 percent of assaults in New York but only 1 percent of assaults in London.[104]

Consider that last statistic, and then look again at the bars depicting the homicide rates in the United States and the United Kingdom.

Zimring and Hawkins compared crime in Los Angeles with crime in Sydney, Australia, and crime in New York City with crime in London, England.[105] Los Angeles and Sydney both had populations of 3.6 million during the study period, and they had roughly similar rates of theft and burglary. And yet, Sydney's robbery rate was only 12.5 percent of that of Los Angeles, and its homicide rate was only 4.8 percent of that of Los Angeles. Thus, as Zimring and Hawkins put it, "For every homicide reported in Sydney, twenty bodies are added to the count in Los Angeles."[106] During the study period, New York City's population was seven million and London's was 6.6 million. London's theft and burglary rates were, respectively, 166.5 percent and 157 percent of New York's. However, London's robbery rate was 19.4 percent of New York's rate, and its homicide rate was only 8.9 percent of New York's rate. Thus, even though London's burglary and theft rates were higher than New York's rates, New York's robbery rate was five times that of London, and New York's murder rate was *more than eleven times* London's rate.

One famous study by other researchers examined crime over a seven-year period in both Seattle, Washington, and Vancouver, British Columbia.[107] During the study period, these two cities—located 140 miles apart—were nearly identical in population size, unemployment rate, and median household income. They had strong cultural similarities as well; for example, a majority of the top-ten rated television shows were the same in both cities. As one might expect of twin cities, the burglary rates in Seattle and Vancouver were nearly identical. The aggravated assault rate was slightly higher in Seattle, but when researchers examined that more closely they found something quite interesting. The aggravated assault rates with knives were almost identical. So were the aggravated assault rates with all other weapons besides firearms. However, Seattle's rate of aggravated assaults with firearms was nearly eight times Vancouver's rate. The murder rates between the cities were very different. In fact, there were nearly twice as many murders in Seattle than in Vancouver over the study period. The pattern here was much the same: the murder rates with knives, and with all other weapons other than firearms, were quite close, but Seattle's homicide firearm rate was nearly five times Vancouver's rate. The most salient difference between the two cities was the prevalence of handguns: 41 percent of Seattle households had handguns compared to 12 percent of Vancouver households.

It is, more than anything else, the prevalence of guns that accounts for why the United States is similar to other affluent nations in nonlethal crime rates and yet so vastly dissimilar in lethal crime rates. Other international comparisons have found that major gun laws reduce homicides while modest regulations do not.[108] And researchers have discovered that, within the United States, residents of states with higher gun prevalence are more likely to be murdered than residents of states with lower gun prevalence.[109] Indeed, residents of states with the very highest gun prevalence (Louisiana, Alabama, Mississippi, Wyoming, West Virginia, and Arkansas) are 2.5 times more likely to be homicide victims than are residents of states with the very lowest gun prevalence (Hawaii, Massachusetts, Rhode Island, and New Jersey).[110]

"No program for the prevention of lethal violence can possess even superficial credibility without paying sustained attention to guns," wrote Zimring and Hawkins.[111] "The basic choice," they continued, "is between trying to deny handguns to only high-risk groups and attempting to curtail the availability of handguns generally."[112] That is, the United States follows the good guy/bad guy model, which allows everyone except those in prohibited categories to own firearms while other high-income nations allow only people in certain special categories to own firearms. Zimring and Hawkins recognized that the choice is either to bring "U.S. handgun policy to the standard of the rest of the developed world" or be content with making "minor adjustments to current regulations that will all but guarantee persisting high rates of death."[113] It was, they observed, an "unpalatable" choice—unpalatable for reasons of public opinion and politics.

Since they made that observation, the option of joining the rest of the world seems even more unrealistic. Constitutional law has become a second obstacle. It is entirely understandable that gun control advocacy groups today try to content themselves with fighting off ever more radical proposals by the gun lobby—such as requiring states to honor concealed weapon permits issued by other states, or making gun silencers legal[114]—or seeking modifications in the existing good guy/bad guy model. Yet, as I shall explain shortly, that strategy is counterproductive because it accepts and entrenches the good guy/bad guy model. I am not arguing that we can overthrow the good guy/bad guy model and join the rest of the developed world soon. Rather, I shall argue that we must take a long-term view. Neither public opinion nor constitutional law is unalterable. Both can be changed through concerted and sustained effort.

It was, not that long ago, settled constitutional law that the Second Amendment grants the people a right to keep and bear arms within the government-regulated militia. The higher federal courts, including the U.S. Supreme Court, had consistently so held throughout American jurisprudential history, and all legal commentators agreed. Yet, beginning in the 1970s, the NRA and its allies launched a campaign to change that basic understanding. They knew this was not an easy task; they knew it would take sustained effort over considerable time. I have told some of the story elsewhere.[115] Suffice it to say here that they proceeded incrementally, gained momentum slowly but continuously, and succeeded with a dramatic reversal of Supreme Court precedent. It took almost thirty years. Had they contented themselves with easier but less consequential short-term projects, Second Amendment jurisprudence would never have changed.

Can Second Amendment jurisprudence be changed again? If America is someday to have a rational public policy and reasonable public safety, it must be changed. Moreover, it can be changed without constitutional amendment because the historical background to the Second Amendment demonstrates that the Supreme Court's decisions in *Heller*—the 5–4 decision that reversed two centuries of precedent—was wrong. I shall next try to give you just a flavor of that history.

Almost exactly 100 years before James Madison and the First Congress drafted the Second Amendment, the English Parliament included a right-to-possess-arms provision in its Bill of Rights of 1689. Although the English and American provisions are not identical, they were written to deal with parallel problems, namely, competing governmental authorities. Both were fundamentally separation of powers provisions. In England, the question was whether Parliament had the sole right to regulate guns, or whether the king could dispense with those laws; in America, it was whether the states had some minimum right to armed militia even though the newly adopted Constitution gave Congress the sole authority to organize and arm the militia.

The English provision arose out of the Glorious Revolution of 1688. The genesis of the revolution was the ascension to the throne of King James II.[116] That set England's teeth on edge. Some years earlier, Parliament had enacted the Test Acts, which required that all political and military officials take an oath renouncing any belief in Catholicism.[117] James, who was the brother of then-ruling King Charles II, shocked the nation by refusing to take the oath and instead resigning his position as Lord High Admiral. When Charles died unexpectedly in 1685 without an heir, James succeeded him.

Although historians estimate that England's Catholic population was only between 2 and 10 percent at the time, Protestant England nonetheless feared an attempt to restore the nation to Catholicism, whether by invasion or subversion. That is why Parliament enacted the Test Acts in the first place. James began ignoring the Test Acts by appointing Catholic army officers. While the king could "dispense" with the law under certain circumstances, many considered this an abuse of that authority. There was fear that James intended to disarm Protestants and arm Catholics by replacing Protestant military officers with Catholics, as James's friend, the Earl of Tyrconnell, was doing in Ireland. James, however, was 55, then an advanced age, and neither hale nor hearty. His second wife was also Catholic, but she was believed to be infertile. Next in line to the throne was James's daughter Mary. There was no problem there. Mary's deceased mother, James's first wife, had been a Protestant, and Mary's husband—William of Orange, the Stadtholder of Holland—was the principal defender of Protestantism on the Continent. The hope, therefore, was that the danger posed by James II would be a fleeting one.

That hope was dashed in June of 1688 when the Queen gave birth to a baby boy, who by virtue of his gender became first in line to the throne. The prospect of a line of Catholic kings was intolerable. Leaders of Parliament invited William of Orange to invade England, precipitating the Glorious Revolution. Finding himself with no political or military support in the face of William's advancing army, James fled to France.

Parliament then negotiated the terms under which it would offer William the throne.[118] It presented him with a Declaration of Rights, and asked him to accept it as a condition of being made king of England. Parliament wanted assurances that its lawmaking authority would be recognized and not curtailed. For example, the Declaration accused James II of "assuming and exercising a power of dispensing with and suspending of laws and the execution of laws without consent of Parliament," and provided that "the pretended power of dispensing with laws or the execution of laws by regal authority, as it hath been assumed and exercised of late, is illegal."[119] Most relevant for our purposes, the Declaration accused James II of "causing several good subjects being Protestants to be disarmed at the same time when papists were both armed and employed contrary to law." Article VII of the Declaration provided that "the subjects which are Protestants may have arms for their defence suitable to their conditions and as allowed by law."[120] William accepted the Declaration but insisted that he rule as king and not merely as Mary's consort. Parliament agreed that William and Mary would be joint sovereigns but that William would administer the kingdom. When, ten months later, Parliament formally enacted the Declaration by statute, it became the English Bill of Rights of 1689.

The right-to-have-arms provision of the Bill of Rights was not designed to grant the people a right to have weapons regardless of what Parliament might decide. It was precisely the opposite: it reaffirmed that firearm ownership was regulated by law, and that Parliament made the laws. Moreover, Parliament had long and vigorously regulated gun ownership and use in England. It had, for example, always restricted ownership of guns to the wealthy. In 1523, Parliament made it unlawful for anyone with an annual income of less than £100—a considerable income at the time—to own a gun, a restriction that remained in place in 1689 and well beyond.[121] Crossbows were similarly regulated. One of the reasons for allowing the wealthy to own handguns was that military officers were drawn from the aristocracy. (Proposals that officers should instead be appointed on the basis of competency or merit were repeatedly rejected. This lasted through World War I and even to some extent into World War II, when the aristocracy still provided a majority of military officers. The view was that a "British military officer should be a gentleman first and an officer second.")[122] It was sensible that military officers be familiar with the handguns, which were their principal weapon, and the view, no doubt, was that gentlemen could be trusted with handguns. The gun laws were supplemented with game laws that made it unlawful for anyone except those meeting real property qualifications to either possess or use a gun for hunting. Parliament enacted game laws to restrict hunting to the landed gentry—or, as one modern historian cleverly put it, the game laws "protected pheasants from peasants."[123] The laws regulating arms—guns and crossbows—were, of course, public safety measures.

It is quite interesting that even as early as the sixteenth century Parliament distinguished between what we today think of as handguns—that is, a gun small enough to conceal on one's person—and longer guns, and between urban and rural areas. In 1541, Parliament noted that "little shorte hand-guns and little hagbuttes" were responsible for "destestable and shameful murders, robberies, felonies, riot and route," and prohibited the possession of guns shorter than one yard in length. Residents living outside urban areas were allowed to own guns of the prescribed length to protect their households, and residents living near the seacoast or the Scottish border were also permitted to own guns as a defense against invasion.[124] Residents in urban areas with annual incomes of more than £10 were required to own weapons to help provide for the national defense and public order, but they were required to keep those weapons in public storage facilities.[125]

Both the gun laws and the hunting laws were, of course, modified from time to time. The central point is this: Parliament vigorously regulated arms.

There was no tradition of granting all subjects a right to own guns. Historian Lois Schwoerer writes: "A striking feature of England's early modern gun culture was its restrictive nature: English subjects whose socioeconomic standing was below a certain level (usually an annual income of £100) were legally disallowed to possess or use a firearm. This limit affected about 98 percent of the population."[126]

And Parliament wanted the king to acknowledge that it—that is, Parliament, as the law-making body of the nation—had the sole authority to decide how arms were to be regulated. Prior to James II, there had been at least one previous episode of a king exercising his claimed dispensing power regarding Parliament's gun laws. In 1544, while England was at war with both Scotland and France, King Henry VII proclaimed that all native-born subjects could possess guns, notwithstanding any statute to the contrary.[127] But that was during war, and it was brief; two years later the king rescinded that proclamation. James II's program of disarming Protestants and arming Catholics was another matter entirely. Article VII was not intended to curtail gun regulation but to specify which branch of government had the authority to regulate guns. Its most salient phrase was *as allowed by law*, which meant that possession and use of arms was entirely contingent upon parliamentary regulation. The main point was to have the king accept that phrase.[128]

The American founders were well aware of the English Bill of Rights, and it should not be a surprise that the Second Amendment of the U.S. Constitution was also a separation of powers provision. The new Constitution adopted by the founders in Philadelphia on September 17, 1787, radically changed governmental authority over the militia. Previously, the militia had been creatures of the states. The Constitution changed that. It placed the militia under the joint control of the federal and state governments, but it gave the lion's share of power to the federal government. Article I, Section 8, Clause 16 of the Constitution gave Congress the power "to provide for organizing, arming, and disciplining, the Militia, and for governing such Part of them as may be employed in the Service of the United States, reserving to the States respectively, the Appointment of the Officers, and the Authority of training the Militia according to the discipline prescribed by Congress." That meant that Congress could organize and govern the militia as it saw fit. Congress was also empowered to call forth the militia to execute the laws of the Union and to suppress insurrections and repel invasions. The states were left with only the power to appoint officers and to train the militia, although they had to train the militia as Congress would prescribe. Congress, moreover, was not required to rely principally on the militia for national defense. Although it had been a topic of some controversy in Philadelphia, the Constitution ultimately gave Congress the power to maintain standing armies and a navy. Congress was therefore free to decide to what extent it wanted to maintain a citizen militia.

I have told the remarkable story of what happened next at length elsewhere,[129] and will give only a snapshot description here. When James Madison sought to have his home state of Virginia ratify the new Constitution at a convention in Richmond, Virginia, in June 1788, his Antifederalist opponents—led by Patrick Henry and George Mason—accused him of creating a militia clause that presented grave dangers for Virginia and the South. The Antifederalists accepted the representation that the Constitution did not give Congress the power to eliminate slavery—not directly, that is. But, they argued, the Constitution gave Congress the power to undermine the slave system by disarming the state militia, on which the South relied for slave control. Under the Constitution, only Congress was empowered to arm the militia, they argued, and thus Congress could effectively disarm the militia. As everyone in Richmond well understood at the time, that would leave the South defenseless against slave revolts. (George Mason also argued that Congress might stimulate slave uprisings by, for example, sending Georgia's militia to New Hampshire.)

Even with an armed and ever-present militia, the South then lived in constant terror of slave revolts.[130] Henry and Mason's suggestion that Congress might deprive Virginia of an armed militia had to be profoundly disturbing. They went as far as to suggest that Congress might deliberately disarm the militia to undermine the slave system. "Slavery is detested," Patrick Henry reminded his audience.[131] "The majority of Congress is to the north," he added, "and the slaves are to the South."[132] When Madison tried to rebut these arguments by suggesting that if Congress did not arm the militia, the states could do so themselves, he was ridiculed. What did it mean to provide that Congress had specific powers over the militia and the states had other specific powers? Certainly that did not mean that all those powers were concurrent between the national and state governments.

Madison and the Federalists ultimately prevailed, albeit only by a vote of 88–80, and Virginia ratified the Constitution and joined the Union. But, I believe, when Madison went off to the First Congress the following year representing Virginia in the House of Representatives and politically committed to writing a Bill of Rights, he sought to fix the problem identified by Henry and Mason and to ensure that the states could have an armed militia regardless of Congress's desire.

With all this in mind, consider the words of the Second Amendment anew: "A well regulated Militia, being necessary to the security of a free State, the right of the people to keep and bear Arms, shall not be infringed."

I shall conclude with two short, personal stories.

In 1987, I was elected to the board of directors of the organization that is known today as the Brady Campaign. It was then Handgun Control, Inc. (HCI). At about the time I joined the board, HCI decided to make the Brady Bill its flagship objective. In its original form, the Brady Bill would have created a nationwide, seven-day waiting period for handgun purchases. I questioned the wisdom of that effort. Nearly half the states already had waiting periods, some longer than seven days. California, I believe, had a fifteen-day waiting period. I knew of no data suggesting that waiting periods were effective in reducing handgun deaths. Why, therefore, should we put all our effort behind this proposal? The top officers believed that HCI needed a legislative victory to show its members it was making progress, and they wanted that victory in the next congressional session. The Brady Bill was so reasonable, so moderate, and so commonsensical that even the NRA could not oppose it without humiliating itself. The bill would breeze through the next session of Congress, they argued.

The NRA, however, did not seem embarrassed about opposing the bill. It did so with the same passion and fury it would have mustered if HCI had sought to confiscate all guns. In fact, that was pretty much the NRA argument: the Brady Bill was a ploy to get America to take a first step on a slippery slope that would eventually lead to banning guns. Not so, countered HCI. We favor only common-sense gun control measures. We do not support banning handguns.

Public opinion was overwhelmingly on HCI's side. According to the Gallup Poll, 91 percent of Americans supported the Brady Bill in 1988. By 1991 public support had risen to 95 percent.[133] That level of support was practically unheard of, then or now, for any issue. Nevertheless, year after year the NRA successfully held off the legislation. The reason for its success was simple: while the overwhelming majority of people favored the bill, for them the issue was not do-or-die. It was not a decisive factor in the voting booth. Meanwhile, although voters opposing a waiting period represented a relatively tiny percentage of voters, many of them considered gun control the most important issue of all. They told their congressional representatives that they would never again for vote for them if they voted for the Brady Bill, and they clearly meant it. I remember discussing the bill at the time with a Democratic congressman representing a mostly suburban Philadelphia district that stretched into rural areas. I told him that supporting the measure would cost him no more than 1 percent of the electorate. "Do you know what my margin was in the last election?" he asked. It had been less than 1 percent. "This is not an issue over which I am prepared to lose my seat," he said. And why should it have been? There was no evidence—then or now—that the Brady Bill would actually save lives.

The Brady Act was enacted in 1993. In fact, its passage did provide some political momentum; the following year a federal assault weapons ban was included in the Violent Crime Control and Law Enforcement Act. The argument for banning assault weapons was that there is no legitimate reason for private citizens to own military-style weapons. The weapons were defined by certain features, including whether they had a pistol grip, flash suppressor, barrel shroud, folding stock, or bayonet mount. A gun containing at least two of nineteen specified features was deemed to be an assault weapon. The NRA argued that the objection to these weapons was merely cosmetic; they might look more dangerous than standard hunting rifles, but they were functionally the same. All semiautomatic weapons, including those not designated as assault weapons, are capable of firing rounds as rapidly as the shooter can pull the trigger, allowing for rates of fire approaching or even exceeding a round per second.[34] The NRA had a legitimate point. Nevertheless, the assault weapons looked especially fearsome, and this measure too enjoyed broad public support. When it passed the House on August 21, 1994, forty-six Republicans voted for it.[35]

There was, however, one aspect of the assault weapon ban that was of potential consequence: large-capacity magazines. The legislation essentially defined gun magazines capable of holding more than ten rounds to be assault weapons. Thirty-round magazines had been common. Large-capacity magazines provide little benefit for hunters and target shooters—but they are enormously useful to mass murderers. The legislation purported to ban magazines holding more than ten rounds. Someone equipped with ten-round magazines must replace empty magazines with full magazines three times more often than someone equipped with thirty-round magazines. While it only takes a few seconds to reload this way, those few seconds give victims a chance to escape or to attack the shooter. For example, the man who shot Congresswoman Gabrielle Giffords and eighteen other people in Tucson, Arizona, in 2011 was successfully tackled by bystanders while he was attempting to replace the empty magazine in his Glock 19 handgun, and the following year nine children successfully fled from a classroom at the Sandy Hook Elementary School in Newtown, Connecticut, while the shooter was reloading.[136]

The ban on large-capacity magazines was, however, a mirage. Not only did the legislation exempt assault weapons that were manufactured before the legislation passed, it also grandfathered large-capacity magazines manufactured before that date. An estimated 25 million large-capacity magazines were in private hands when the legislation was passed—they were, in fact, heavily promoted while the legislation was pending in Congress, and sold like hotcakes—and another 4.7 million exempted large-capacity magazines were imported to the United States during the first five years the legislation was in effect.[137] Large-capacity magazines remained readily available throughout the ten-year life of the ban. Researchers at the University of Pennsylvania found that while the number of assault weapons in private hands declined while the law was in effect, that decline was offset by a rise in weapons equipped with large-capacity magazines.[138]

The Brady Campaign expended its political capital on legislation that did not, in fact, make America safer. While Brady and other gun control advocates may have thought they would improve these pieces of legislation down the road, the public believed that the best available gun control measures had been enacted and lost interest in the issue. Meanwhile, the NRA and its allies worked assiduously to persuade the political class that the Brady Act and the assault weapons ban had politically injured their supporters.[139] This was, at best, a dubious proposition, but the NRA's effort was successful nonetheless. It succeeded in persuading the political class that gun control cost a number of prominent Democratic members of Congress their seats. The NRA reprised this approach in the aftermath of the 2000 presidential election; it argued that gun control cost Al Gore three states—Arkansas, West Virginia, and Tennessee—and took credit for George W. Bush winning the presidency. This too was a dubious proposition. In fact, Gore was so silent about gun control during the general election that one national poll found that most Americans thought Bush was the more pro-gun control candidate.[140] Yet politicians came to accept the NRA claim.

The gun control movement has never recovered from its pyrrhic victories in 1993 and 1994. Congress allowed the assault weapon ban to expire in 2004, and there has been no serious effort in Congress to enact any new gun control legislation in the last twenty-four years. In every national election cycle, Republicans proclaim their devotion to the Second Amendment and their opposition to any form of gun control while Democrats largely remain silent. President Obama decried massacres that occurred during his presidency—especially those at the Sandy Hook Elementary School in Newtown, Connecticut, and the Pulse Nightclub in Orlando, Florida—and called for Congress to act. Specifically, he pleaded for Congress to close the loophole exempting private sales from the national instant background check system. Congress, of course, did not act. Although there has been some activity within the states in response to mass shootings, only eight states and the District of Columbia require universal background checks for all firearms, including those purchased from unlicensed sellers,[141] and only three states and the District of Columbia ban all large-capacity magazines.[142]

Nevertheless, the NRA and other gun-rights organizations constantly sound the tocsins, warning that any form of gun control will lead to gun confiscation and tyranny.[143] One might think hysterical claims would only make the NRA look ridiculous; but, in fact, the strategy has been effective. Even a character in a mystery novel I happened to be reading last night remarked: "What happens after every mass shooting? The gun control nuts come crawling out of the woodwork talking about banning this and banning that and the next thing you know everybody and his cousin wants a gun."[144] That neatly sums up what nearly everyone thinks. Gun sales do surge after mass shootings because buyers fear new gun control measures will make their purchases unlawful.[145] Yet at the federal level gun control organizations have largely confined themselves to trying to stop NRA initiatives to loosen gun laws and have refrained from launching campaigns for new legislation.[146] The more extreme the NRA gets, the more moderate gun control organizations try to become. Even the term "gun control" is too extreme for gun control organizations today. They now characterize themselves as "gun safety" groups.[147]

What has the gun control movement achieved by its strategy of meeting NRA absolutism with moderation and "common sense"? Its only achievement has been to shift the Overton Window in a pro-NRA direction. The Overton Window is a simple concept that holds that for any issue there is a spectrum of possible public policy proposals, and at any given time along this spectrum there are proposals that fall within a "window of political possibility."[148] Politicians feel comfortable advocating proposals within the window, but they are loath to advocate policies falling outside it because voters consider them too extreme. The important point is that the size and location of the window is determined by, and changes with, the zeitgeist. As one of the originators of the concept puts it, "If you shift the position or size of the window, you change what is politically possible."[149] Social and political movements shift Overton Windows. So can public discourse. If advocacy groups or prominent individuals advocate proposals that fall outside the window, the window is likely to expand or shift in the direction of those proposals even if it does not move far enough to embrace those particular proposals. Conversely, if prominent groups and individuals stop advocating certain policies, the window may shrink or shift to exclude those proposals.

In 1959, the Gallup Poll reported that 60 percent of Americans favored banning handguns.[150] Clearly, banning handguns was not then considered extreme or unthinkable. It was within the Overton Window, notwithstanding that it may have been politically extremely difficult or impossible. By 1975, the fraction of Americans favoring a handgun ban had fallen to 41 percent. A handgun ban was still within the Overton Window. Someone who supported a handgun ban would not have been considered crazy or irresponsible. Two gun control organizations were established at about that time. One called itself the National Council to Control Handguns, the other the National Coalition to Ban Handguns.[151] The first organization soon changed its name to Handgun Control, Inc. A complete handgun ban did not seem politically feasible, so HCI adopted a strategy of advocating a ban on a certain class of handguns—Saturday Night Specials, cheap handguns with short barrels, which made them readily concealable.[152] When it did not achieve that objective, it moved back a step to what seemed like an even more moderate position—a seven-day waiting period for handgun purchases, which was the original version of the Brady Bill—and changed its name again to the Brady Organization. In 1990, the National Coalition to Ban Handguns changed its name to the Coalition to Stop Gun Violence.[153] Very few people continued to advocate for a handgun ban.[154] By 2008, only 29 percent of Americans thought that handguns should be banned while 69 percent thought they should not be banned. A handgun ban now fell outside the Overton Window.

It was in 2008 that Supreme Court decided for the first time that people have a constitutional right to have handguns in their homes. In making that decision, the Court attached great importance to handguns being widely accepted by American society.[155] It is entirely possible that the justices did not think their decision greatly endangered public safety because, along with the rest of the public, they had become accustomed to thinking about gun control exclusively in terms of the good guy/bad guy model. "Nothing in our opinion should be taken to cast doubt on the longstanding prohibitions on the possession of firearms by felons and the mentally ill," they wrote.[156]

Here is the second story. In 1996, Common Cause of Rhode Island
launched a campaign to get Rhode Island to recognize the principle of
separation of powers in its state government.[157] The state legislature took
the position that Rhode Island government was unique and did not accept
that principle. As a result, the legislature could—in addition to creating
and funding administrative agencies—also operate them. The legislature accomplished this by creating agencies controlled by a commission
or a board, and gave itself—i.e., the legislature—the ability to appoint a
majority of the controlling body. In the federal system, that would violate
the principle of separation of powers and be flatly unconstitutional. The
Rhode Island legislature even appointed sitting legislators to agency boards
and commissions. This was a system vulnerable to—some might even say
designed for—corruption.[158]

The state Common Cause chapter took on the issue. First, Common
Cause took the matter to the Rhode Island Supreme Court. But the court,
whose members had also been effectively selected by the legislature, upheld
the legislature's position.[159] Common Cause then launched a campaign for
a constitutional amendment. Most people, including the state's savviest
political strategists, considered that a fool's errand. The state constitution
could not be amended without the consent of the legislature. The legislature
would not willingly yield an enormous source of its power absent a firestorm
of voter displeasure. Voters cared about issues such as schools, taxes, and
potholes, and were not going to understand, let alone become outraged
over, an abstract principle of political philosophy. And yet, Common Cause
persisted. It educated journalists and community leaders; it sent speakers to
community groups of all kinds; it organized forums, lectures, and debates;
its members wrote op-eds and letters-to-the-editor for newspapers. It was
a vigorous and sustained effort of public education. During the seven-
year campaign, the *Providence Journal* published nearly 800 news articles,
editorials, commentary articles, and letters-to-the-editor about separation
of powers.

Other good government groups initially joined the effort but fell by the
wayside as the campaign stretched on. Their familiar calculation was that
they had to show their members they had achieved something recently. Yet,
year after year, separation of powers remained Common Cause's flagship
proposal. Voters began peppering state legislators with questions—and
increasingly passionate demands—about separation of powers. Legislators
started offering cosmetic concessions that would have allowed Common
Cause to claim victory while actually accomplishing little. Common Cause

rejected those offers. Eventually, a government scandal provided the spark that ignited a firestorm. For days on end, local talk radio was all about separation of powers. Voters sent the General Assembly so many emails that its system crashed. In the end, the legislature and voters approved a truly meaningful constitutional amendment.

The lesson of these two stories—as well as the NRA's successful campaign to change how the Supreme Court interpreted the Second Amendment—is that it is sometimes necessary and possible to take the long view. Despite conventional wisdom, neither the NRA nor Common Cause of Rhode Island were institutionally weakened by doing so.

What would a decades-long campaign look like? Both the Common Cause campaign to amend the Rhode Island Constitution and the NRA campaign to change the meaning of the Second Amendment had strong similarities. Both campaigns began with academic writings, which were used to give the nonconsensus view legitimacy and persuade opinion makers such as leaders of advocacy groups, potential financial supporters, politicians, other academics and teachers, and—perhaps most importantly—journalists. The writings were expanded to popular venues such as the op-ed pages of newspapers. In the case of gun control, op-eds could be produced by authors with recognized expertise, such as criminologists, sociologists, epidemiologists, and public health experts, or, more often, by newspaper columnists and journalists describing the work of researchers. The message must be the simple, hard truth about gun control: effective gun control is available, but it requires reducing handguns in general circulation. It is a message that the American public has not heard because gun control advocates, for political and institutional reasons, have led Americans to believe the myth that less draconian, "common sense" measures are available. At first the message will seem jarring, but that may help it get attention. Because this is a long campaign, it is not necessary—indeed, it may even be counterproductive—to combine it with a plea of quick political action. The first, essential task is to tell the simple, hard truth and let it sink in. Both the message and its importance should be repeated wherever it is relevant. In debates over health care costs, for example, it should be noted that reducing gun violence would reduce public health care costs because gunshot wounds result in extremely expensive emergency room and trauma center visits. Both the NRA and Common Cause also effectively sent speakers to every venue that would have them—community groups, college clubs, social action committees of churches and other religious organizations, and radio talk shows.

What I have described so far is necessary but by itself insufficient. Arguments based on facts and logic may persuade a necessary cohort of opinion leaders, but they will not, by themselves, create a sea change in public opinion. Consider this statement by the eighteenth-century Scottish politician Andrew Fletcher: "I knew a very wise man [who] believed if a man were permitted to make all the ballads he need not care who should make the laws of a nation, and we find that most of the ancient legislators thought that they could not well reform the manners of any city without the help of a lyric, and sometimes of a dramatic poet."[160]

Everyone today is familiar with the term "designated driver." Many of us have been one or had someone else be one when going out on the town with a group of friends. It was not always so. When I was a college student, neither the term nor the concept was known. In 1986, experts at the Harvard School of Public Health who wanted to do something about drunk driving met with hundreds of Hollywood screenwriters and producers, introduced them to the term, and asked them to include it in television scripts.[161] Over a four-year period, the term "designated driver" was used in 160 prime-time television shows. In some shows, it was mentioned only in passing; in other shows, it was integral to the main plot line. This campaign had a profound effect on public attitudes and behavior. My point is not that the gun control movement must replicate the designated driver campaign; every campaign is different. My point is that, just as Andrew Fletcher suggested three hundred years ago, sea changes in public attitudes require help from artists and storytellers.

Storytellers are evocative. I can create a bar chart, but storytellers know how to paint indelible images in their audience's mind. For example, a moment ago I made a point about the costs of treating gunshot wounds in hospital emergency rooms. In his novel *Balance of Power,* Richard North Patterson has a fictional president of the United States also speak about gunshot wounds and emergency rooms while advocating stricter gun control in a speech to Congress. Here is the line Patterson wrote for his fictitious president: "Only in America, in *this* city, do surgeons prepare for combat duty by training at an urban hospital."[162]

We should also listen to the storytellers for their instincts about how public opinion on the issue might be shaped. Patterson's *Balance of Power* is about an effort to persuade the nation to accept more rigorous gun control, and so is John Madden's 2016 film *Miss Sloane.*[163] In both stories, gun control advocates successfully employ strategies based upon making gun control a more salient issue for women and exposing the commercial interests of the gun lobby, as well as the self-interest of politicians who do its bidding. Moreover, in both stories the winning strategies are built on a combination of public education and carefully crafted evocative approaches.

The NRA has been a master of the evocative stratagem. It had, for example, the foresight to make Charlton Heston its president for a five-year period beginning in 1998. The famous actor's value to the NRA was extremely simple—it was nothing more than the image of Heston holding a musket over his head and declaring, "From my cold, dead hands!" This became ritual at the NRA's annual convention and was inevitably included in that evening's television newscasts. It was a double-barreled subliminal image. It semi-consciously evoked Moses, whom Heston famously played in Cecil B. DeMille's 1956 movie *The Ten Commandments*,[164] holding up his staff against Pharaoh and leading his people to freedom under divine guidance. Probably more significantly, it simultaneously evoked the Minutemen at Lexington and Concord. The power of such images should not be underestimated, and when deployed must be decoded and rebutted. That second image can be turned completely around by communicating that the Second Amendment was not written to protect the musket in the hands of the minuteman in Lexington; it was written to protect the musket in the hands of the militia slave patrols in the South.[165] I have written a law review article laying out that case, but to be effective it needs to be turned into a movie.

In October 2017, I heard a talk by John Feinblatt, who is president of Everytown for Gun Safety.[166] He talked about the moderate strategy his organization pursues, and explained why he believes that approach is essential for success. As I listened, I could not help but be struck by how much Feinblatt's thinking echoed recommendations that political consultants gave Pete Shields forty years earlier. Pete had been an executive at Du Pont when in 1974 his son was shot to death during the so-called Zebra killings in San Francisco. The following year, Pete left Du Pont to work with the National Coalition to Control Handguns (now the Brady Campaign), and he led the group from 1976 to 1989.[167] Pete had no prior experience in politics or political advocacy, and he engaged consultants to advise him on what strategy to pursue. Their advice was: Take a moderate approach. Whatever you do, don't advocate banning handguns because that sounds extreme.[168] That has been the gun control movement's approach ever since. Where has it led? During his talk, Feinblatt said he expected to stop the Concealed Carry Reciprocity Act from becoming law by holding the number of senators voting for it to no more than fifty-eight, short of the sixty votes necessary to invoke cloture and bring a filibustered bill to the floor for a vote. In the not too distant past, this legislation would have been considered too extreme to have any feasible chance of becoming law—a proposal well outside the Overton Window. The proposal is, among other things, deeply offensive to the traditional conservative principle of respecting states' rights. Yet the bill comfortably passed the House, and the president has said he will sign it when it reaches his desk. The gun control movement hopes to stop the legislation because *only* fifty-seven or fifty-eight senators support it. This is where a forty-year strategy of appearing moderate at all costs and focusing exclusively on short-term goals has led.

We need to be clear-eyed about the choice before us. The choice is not whether America will have truly effective gun control today. It cannot. That does not mean that nothing can be done under the present system. We could, for example, improve the existing background check system, repeal right-to-carry laws, prohibit large-capacity magazines, and impose longer prison sentences on people convicted of committing robberies with a gun as opposed to a less lethal weapon.[169] Nevertheless, our present system is so fundamentally flawed that it can never be truly effective. The choice before us is whether America will have truly effective gun control in the future. While public opinion, politics, and constitutional law currently bar the way, all three are malleable. The public, politicians, and judges can all be educated. That must begin, however, with telling the hard, simple truth about gun control.

Notes

The author thanks Hannah Pfeiffer for her superb research assistance, and Sandra G. Mayson and participants in a seminar for the Department of Law, Jurisprudence, and Social Thought at Amherst College for insightful comments on earlier drafts of this chapter.

1. A search in the Westlaw news database for articles that contain the phrase "common sense" within ten words of the phrase "gun control," conducted on January 13, 2017, found more than 3,000 such articles. Typically, those advocating for "common sense gun control" are gun control advocates, but occasionally gun control opponents also use the phrase.

2. https://www.hillaryclinton.com/issues/gun-violence-prevention/.

3. https://assets.donaldjtrump.com/Second_Amendment_Rights.pdf. (This document accessed by hyper-jump from https://www.donaldjtrump.com/policies/constitution -and-second-amendment.)

4. See Salman Rushdie, "The Disappeared: How the Fatwa Changed a Writer's Life," *New Yorker*, September 17, 2012, http://www.newyorker.com/magazine/2012/09/17 /the-disappeared.

5. I say "might" because there are different kinds of stalkers, some more dangerous than others, and there would have to be a determination that an applicant for a gun permit reasonably fears physical attack. It is indisputable, however, that stalking threats are serious and widespread. Each year in the United States about 3.4 million people are victims of stalking. Nearly a third of stalking victims fear bodily harm, a quarter fear that their child

or some other family member will be hurt or kidnapped, and about 9 percent fear being killed. All too often, these fears are not groundless: 39,000 people in the United States are raped or sexually assaulted each year and 52,000 are seriously injured by stalkers. About 3 percent of stalking victims get a gun for self-protection. See Katrina Baum et al., "Stalking Victimization in the United States," Bureau of Justice Statistics, January 2009, 1, 7, 8, 6, https://victimsofcrime.org/docs/src/baum-k-catalano-s-rand-m-rose-k-2009.pdf?sfvrsn=0.

6. *District of Columbia v. Heller*, 554 U.S. 570, 628–30 (2008).

7. The five states are California, Florida, Illinois, New York, and South Carolina. See "Open Carrying: Summary of State Laws," Law Center to Prevent Gun Violence, http://smartgunlaws.org/gun-laws/policy-areas/firearms-in-public-places/open-carrying/#state.

8. A few states have mixed regulations. Pennsylvania, for example, requires a license to openly carry a firearm in the city of Philadelphia, but does not require a license to do so elsewhere in the state. In North Dakota, someone without a concealed weapons permit may openly carry an unloaded handgun during daylight hours, while someone with such a permit may openly carry a handgun during the day or night. Ibid.

9. Stephen Clark, "After Altercation, Philadelphia Police Say They Won't Look the Other Way on Open-Carry Gun Owners," Fox News, May 21, 2011, http://www.foxnews.com/politics/2011/05/21/altercation-philadelphia-police-say-wont-look-way-open-carry-gun-owners.html. An open-carry gun activist who was inconvenienced in this manner sued Philadelphia and won a $25,000 judgment. http://www.newsworks.org/index.php/local/philadelphia/35164-25000-judgment-in-suit-against-philly-over-permitted-gun.

10. http://www.opencarry.org/.

11. http://www.opencarry.org/is-open-carry-disorderly-conduct/.

12. https://www.nraila.org/articles/20170113/national-concealed-carry-reciprocity-lies-an8.d-the-lying-liars-who-tell-them.

13. Dennis A. Henigan, *"Guns Don't Kill People, People Kill People": And Other Myths about Gun Control* (Boston: Beacon Press, 2016), 122.

14. John R. Lott and David B. Mustard, "Crime, Deterrence, and the Right-to-Carry Concealed Handguns," *Journal of Legal Studies* 26, no. 1 (1997).

15. John R. Lott, *More Guns, Less Crime* (Chicago: University of Chicago Press, 1998).

16. Ibid., 19.

17. Ibid., 19 and 54.

18. For example, on August 2, 1996, *USA Today* ran a prominent story about the paper titled "Fewer Rapes, Killings Found Where Concealed Guns Legal." A. Henigan, *"Guns Don't Kill People,"* 130.

19. Robert J. Spitzer, *The Politics of Gun Control*, 6th ed. (Boulder, CO: Paradigm Publishers, 2015), 68.

20. Justine E. Johnson-Makuch, Comment, "Statutory Restrictions on Concealed Carry: A Five-Circuit Shoot-Out," *Fordham Law Review* 83 (2015): 2757, 2758.

21. John J. Donohue, "The Impact of Concealed-Carry Law," in *Evaluating Gun Policy: Effects on Crime and Violence*, ed. Jens Ludwig and Philip Cook (New York: Oxford University Press, 2003), 289. The price of powdered cocaine was falling sharply during the late 1980s, and by 1991 crack cocaine was found on more than 60 percent of people arrested in Manhattan. Franklin E. Zimring, *The City That Became Safe: New York's Lessons for Urban Crime and its Control* (New York: Oxford University Press, 2012), 96–99.

22. Donohue, "The Impact of Concealed-Carry Law" (original emphasis). See also Ian Ayres and John J. Donohue, "Shooting Down the 'More Guns, Less Crime' Hypothesis," *Stanford Law Review* 55 (2003): 1193.

23. Ian Ayres and John J. Donohue, "More Guns, Less Crime Fails Again: The Latest Evidence from 1977–2006," *Econ Journal Watch* 6 (2009): 218.

24. Donohue, "The Impact of Concealed-Carry Law," 293.

25. Dan A. Black and Daniel A. Nagin, "Do Right-to-Carry Laws Deter Crime?," *Journal of Legal Studies* 27 (1998): 209.

26. See generally David Hemenway, *Private Guns, Public Health* (Ann Arbor: University of Michigan Press, 2004), 101–4; Henigan, *"Guns Don't Kill People,"* 130–31; Spitzer, *The Politics of Gun Control*, 70–74. The pro-gun criminologist is Gary Kleck of Florida State University.

27. Philip J. Cook and John J. Donohue, "Saving Lives by Regulating Guns: Evidence for Policy," *Science* 358 (2017): 1259, 1260.

28. Ibid., 1260.

29. Johnson-Makuch, Comment, "Statutory Restrictions on Concealed Carry," 2758.

30. This was the count as of January 3, 2018. Violence Policy Center, "Concealed Carry Killers," http://concealedcarrykillers.org.

31. According to the NRA, only eight states—California, Delaware, Hawaii, Maryland, Massachusetts, Rhode Island, New Jersey, New York—deny concealed carry to most citizens. See https://www.nraila.org/gun-laws.aspx.

32. H.R. 38, 115th Congress (2017–18). See https://www.congress.gov/bill/115th -congress/house-bill/38?q=%7B%22search%22%3A%5B%22Concealed+Carry+Reciprocity +Act+of+2017%22%5D%7D&r=1.

33. http://clerk.house.gov/evs/2017/roll663.xml.

34. I include Whitman's wife and mother, whom he killed earlier that morning, and three individuals he killed in The Tower. The total does not include Whitman himself.

35. See History News Network, "The Deadliest Mass Killings in American History by a Single Shooter," June 17, 2016, http://historynewsnetwork.org/article/153325.

36. The impression that mass shootings were rare before 1966 is confirmed by criminologist Grant Duwe, who has studied more than 1,300 mass shootings occurring from 1900 to 2013. See N.R. Kleinfeld et al., "Killers Fit a Profile, but So Do Many Others," *New York Times*, October 14, 2015, 1.

37. Data for all entries except the last three were taken from Violence Policy Center, "Large-capacity Ammunition Magazines Are Common Thread Running through Most Mass Shootings in the United States," http://www.vpc.org/fact_sht/VPCshootinglist.pdf. Data for the last three entries (Las Vegas, Sutherland Springs, Parkland) were taken from http://www.gunviolencearchive.org/mass-shooting?page=1.

38. See generally Christopher Ingraham, "What Makes a 'Mass Shooting' in America?," *Washington Post*, December 3, 2015, https://www.washingtonpost.com/news/wonk /wp/2015/12/03/what-makes-a-mass-shooting-in-america/?utm_term=.3f98ff6118fd.

39. See http://www.gunviolencearchive.org/. For definitions used by the organization, see the Methodology section of its website.

40. For purposes of its survey, the *Washington Post* defined a mass shooting as an event in which four or more people are killed by a lone shooter or, in three instances, by two shooters. Bonnier Berkowitz et al., "50 Years of Mass Shootings in the U.S.," *Washington Post*, December 13, 2015, A10.

41. During one four-year period, 57 percent of mass shooters killed a current or former intimate partner, together with others. Philip J. Cook and Kristin A. Goss, *The Gun Debate: What Everyone Needs to Know* (New York: Oxford University Press, 2014), 50.

42. Sixty-three percent of Americans blame mass shootings on failings in the mental health system. See Michael S. Rosenwald, "Most Mass Shooters Aren't Mentally Ill," *Washington Post*, May 19, 2016, A1.

43. Ibid.

44. See Kleinfeld et al., "Killers Fit a Profile" (quoting Fox).

45. Jeffrey W. Swanson et al., "Preventing Gun Violence Involving People with Serious Mental Illness," in *Reducing Gun Violence in America: Informing Policy with Evidence and*

Analysis, ed. Daniel W. Webster and Jon S. Vernick (Baltimore: Johns Hopkins University Press, 2013), 33, 36.

46. See Kleinfeld et al., "Killers Fit a Profile" (quoting Fox).

47. Ibid.

48. David Brown, "No Easy Task to Identify a Mass Killer," *Washington Post,* January 4, 2003, A1.

49. Ibid.

50. For example, Philip Cook and Kristin Goss use the terms "good guys" and "bad guys" to describe the U.S. model and recognize that other nations employ the other, more effective model, but nevertheless restrict themselves to making proposals to improve the fatally flawed model. Cook and Goss, *The Gun Debate*, 55, 118, and 214–20, respectively.

51. Sharon LaFraniere and Emily Palmer, "In 130 of Worst Shootings, Vision of Porous Gun Laws," *New York Times,* October 22, 2016, A1.

52. Hemenway, *Private Guns, Public Health*, 142–43.

53. Henigan, *"Guns Don't Kill People,"* 36–39.

54. FBI, "Crime in the U.S. 2015," Expanded Homicide Data, Table 9. The full report is available at https://ucr.fbi.gov/crime-in-the-u.s/2015/crime-in-the-u.s.-2015.

55. See Carl T. Bogus, "Gun Control and America's Cities: Public Policy and Politics," *Albany Government Law Review* 1 (2008): 440, 447 and sources cited therein.

56. FBI, Crime in the U.S., 2015, Expanded Homicide Data, Table 11.

57. Ibid., Table 10.

58. See, e.g., Anthony A. Braga and Philip J. Cook, "The Criminal Records of Gun Offenders," *Georgetown Journal of Law and Public Policy* 14 (2016): 1, 7.

59. https://www.cdc.gov/nchs/fastats/suicide.htm.

60. See Cook and Goss, *The Gun Debate*, 34 (reporting 606 unintentional firearm-related killings in 2010), and Henigan, *"Guns Don't Kill People,"* 71–72 (reporting "almost 3,800" accidental gun fatalities in 2005–2010).

61. Henigan, *"Guns Don't Kill People,"* 72 (reporting data from a six-year CDC study).

62. Cook and Goss, *The Gun Debate*, 34.

63. FBI, Crime in the U.S. 2015, Table 15.

64. FBI, Crime in the U.S. 2015, Robbery, Table 3, and Aggravated Assault Table.

65. Trayvon Martin, a seventeen-year-old black youth, was shot and killed by George Zimmerman, a twenty-six-year-old white neighborhood watch captain. On the evening of February 26, 2012, Martin had been walking through a predominately white, gated community in Sanford, Florida, returning to a home where he was a guest after buying snacks at a convenience store. Martin was unarmed. Martin called his girlfriend on his cell phone to say he was going to walk fast because someone was following him. At roughly the same time, Zimmerman, who was carrying a handgun, called 911 and said he was observing someone behaving suspiciously. Zimmerman told the police the person was starting to run and that he was following him. "We don't need you to do that," the police dispatcher told Zimmerman. Witnesses saw the two individuals engaged in a fight and heard one of them cry for help, but they didn't know whose voice they heard. There was then a gun shot. Zimmerman said he shot Martin in self-defense after Martin attacked him. Zimmerman was charged with second-degree murder but found not guilty. Dan Barry et al., "Race, Tragedy and Outrage Collide after a Shot in Florida," *New York Times,* April 1, 2002, https://www.nytimes.com/2012/04/02/us/trayvon-martin-shooting-prompts-a-review-of-ideals.

66. See Cook and Goss, *The Gun Debate*, 19–20 (describing a study conducted by David Hemenway).

67. FBI, Crime in the U.S. 2015, Expanded Homicide Data, Table 15.

68. Spitzer, *The Politics of Gun Control*, 54.

69. Henigan, *"Guns Don't Kill People,"* 116–17.

70. Ibid. See also Matthew Miller et al., "Firearm and Suicide in the United States: Is Risk Independent of Underlying Suicidal Behavior?" *American Journal of Epidemiology* 178 (2013): 946, 951 (finding that "higher rates of firearm ownership are associated with higher rates of overall suicide, but not with nonfirearm suicide").

71. Henigan, *"Guns Don't Kill People,"* 116–17.

72. Ibid., 105–6 (describing study by Cook and Ludwig).

73. Daniel Kahneman, *Thinking, Fast and Slow* (New York: Farrar, Straus and Giroux, 2011), 259–60.

74. Joe Daraskevich, "Woman Tells Putnam County Deputy That Son, 4, Shot Her in Back while She Was Driving," *Florida Times Union*, March 8, 2016, http://jacksonville.com/2016–05–02/stub-3.

75. 18 U.S.C. § 922(g). For good descriptions of the system, see Cook and Goss, *The Gun Debate*, 101–18; Henigan, *"Guns Don't Kill People,"* 143–46 and 205–6; Spitzer, *The Politics of Gun Control*, 158–64.

76. Cook and Goss, *The Gun Debate*, 107.

77. Ibid., 81.

78. Ibid., 144.

79. Henigan, *"Guns Don't Kill People,"* 144–46. However, the gun shop is required to retain the Firearm Transaction Record, signed by both the seller and the purchaser, for a period of twenty years. See Notices, Instructions, and Definitions, ATF Form 4473 (revised October 2016).

80. For more about the view that the Second Amendment exists as a check on government tyranny, see Carl T. Bogus, "Heller and Insurrectionism," *Syracuse Law Review* 59 (2008): 255.

81. Henigan, *"Guns Don't Kill People,"* 145. See also note 17 at http://lawcenter.giffords.org/gun-laws/policy-areas/gun-sales/maintaining-records-of-gun-sales.

82. Henigan, *"Guns Don't Kill People,"* 119; Spitzer, *The Politics of Gun Control*, 49–50.

83. Henigan, *"Guns Don't Kill People,"* 169.

84. Ibid., 175–87.

85. Cook and Goss, *The Gun Debate*, 117; Spitzer, *The Politics of Gun Control*, 170–82.

86. About one-third of the states require that private sales also go through the background check system. To accomplish this, private sellers and buyers visit Walmart or another local gun dealer, fill out the Firearms Transaction Form, and pay the dealer a modest fee to run the background check through the system.

87. Cook and Goss, *The Gun Debate*, 56. This does not mean, however, that 60 percent of murderers would have been eligible under federal law to purchase a gun. About 37 percent of persons arrested for murder, robbery, assault, or illegal gun possession would have been eligible to purchase a gun under federal law. Braga and Cook, "The Criminal Records of Gun Offenders," 2.

88. Cook and Goss, *The Gun Debate*, 57.

89. Ibid., 149.

90. Ibid., 72.

91. The regulation was promulgated in the waning days of the Obama administration. It is estimated that about 75,000 people are categorized as mentally disabled or unable to handle their own financial affairs. President Trump signed the legislation abolishing the regulation on February 28, 2017. https://www.washingtonpost.com/news/powerpost/paloma/daily-202/2017/03/03/daily-202-what-trump-didn-t-want-you-to-see-him-signing/58b923fae9b69b1406c75d33/?utm_term=.43032ede9038.

92. Most of these statutes were stimulated by and follow the reasoning of *Tarasoff v. Regents of University of California*, 17 Cal.3d 425 (1976), involving a patient who told his

psychotherapist that he intended to kill someone whom he did, in fact, later murder. A duty to report only arises when the psychotherapist believes a particular patient presents a serious danger of violence to a readily identifiable victim. Some have advocated broadening that rule. E.g., Sally Satel, "Loosen Restrictions for Therapists to Report Danger," *New York Times,* August 20, 2013, http://www.nytimes.com/roomfordebate/2014/05/29 /can-therapists-prevent-violence/loosen-restrictions-for-therapists-to-report-danger.

93. Melissa Hogenboom, "Two Genes Linked with Violent Crime," BBC News, October 28, 2014, http://www.bbc.com/news/science-environment-29760212.

94. Not everyone is horrified by preventive detention. See, e.g., Adam Klein and Benjamin Wittes, "Preventive Detention in American Theory and Practice," *Harvard National Security Journal* 2 (2011): 85, http://harvardnsj.org/wp-content/uploads/2015/01 /Preventative-Detention-in-American-Theory-and-Practice.pdf.

95. By its original terms, the five-day waiting period was to be replaced by the NICS within ten years. In 1997, the Supreme Court held that the federal government could not require state and local police to conduct background checks of putative handgun purchasers. *Printz v. U.S.,* 521 U.S. 898 (1997).

96. Philip J. Cook and Jens Ludwig, "The Limited Impact of the Brady Bill: Evaluation and Implication," in *Reducing Gun Violence in America,* 2. See also Cook and Goss, *The Gun Debate,* 142–43. But see Michael Luca et al., "Handgun Waiting Periods Reduce Gun Deaths," *PNAS Early Edition,* September 21, 2017, http://www.pnas.org/content /early/2017/10/11/1619896114.full (finding that waiting periods reduce gun homicides by 17 percent and gun suicides by 7–11 percent). Luca looked at the same data as Cook and Ludwig, but he coded some key data differently. At the time of this writing, other researchers have not yet commented on the differences between the Cook-Ludwig and Luca studies.

97. Swanson et al., "Preventing Gun Violence Involving People with Serious Mental Illness," 45.

98. http://www.bradycampaign.org/bradys-solutions-0.

99. Garen J. Wintemute, "Broadening Denial Criteria for the Purchase and Possession of Firearms: Need, Feasibility, and Effectiveness," in *Reducing Gun Violence in America,* 77, 84.

100. The data is derived from Erin Grinshteyn and David Hemenway, "Violent Death Rates: The US Compared with Other High-income OECD Countries, 2010," *American Journal of Medicine* 129 (2016): 266.

101. Franklin E. Zimring and Gordon Hawkins, *Crime Is Not the Problem: Lethal Violence in America* (New York: Oxford University Press, 1997), 38. The year studied was 1991.

102. Ibid., 45.

103. The researchers note that in Los Angeles, for example, a far greater proportion of homicides "grow out of arguments and other social encounters between acquaintances" than out of robbery. Ibid., 16.

104. Ibid., 47.

105. Ibid., 4–7.

106. Ibid., 16.

107. John Henry Sloan et al., "Handgun Regulations, Crime, Assaults, and Homicide," *New England Journal of Medicine,* November 10, 1988, 1256–62. See also discussion in Carl T. Bogus, "The Strong Case for Gun Control," *American Prospect* (Summer 1992): 19.

108. Hemenway, *Private Guns, Public Health,* 169–70.

109. Henigan, *"Guns Don't Kill People,"* 103.

110. Ibid., 104.

111. Ibid., 200.

112. Ibid.

113. Ibid., 201.

114. See Robert Spitzer, "Silencing Lifesaving Noise," *Washington Post*, January 25, 2017, A17 (regarding an NRA push to eliminate registration requirements for owning gun silencers).

115. See Carl T. Bogus, "The History and Politics of Second Amendment Scholarship," *Chicago-Kent Law Review* 76 (2000): 3.

116. For an abbreviated history, see Carl T. Bogus, "The Hidden History of the Second Amendment," *UC Davis Law Review* 31 (1998): 309, 375–86. See also Lois G. Schwoerer, *Gun Culture in Early Modern England* (Charlottesville: University of Virginia Press, 2016), 156–70.

117. The Test Act of 1673 required civil and military officers to "declare that I do believe that there is not any transubstantiation in the sacrament of the Lord's Supper, or in the elements of the bread and wine, at or after the consecration thereof by any person whatsoever."

118. Parliament sat as a Convention because Parliament could not be formally convened.

119. English Bill of Rights of 1689, http://avalon.law.yale.edu/17th_century/england.asp.

120. Parliament had no objection if the mayor of London decided that public safety required disarming all Catholics in his city, which, in fact, he was doing at the very moment that Parliament was presenting its Declaration of Rights to William of Orange.

121. See Schwoerer, *Gun Culture in Early Modern England,* 48 and 162. The statute referred to handguns, but in early modern England the words "handgun" or "hand gonnes" referred to almost all firearms and included pistols and muskets. See generally Schwoerer, *Gun Culture*, Appendix A, "What Is a Gun?" A handgun was defined as "a firearm that one person could discharge with or without a rest." Schwoerer, *Gun Culture*, 181.

122. Ibid., 79.

123. Ibid., 50 (quoting Edmund S. Morgan).

124. Ibid.

125. Ibid., 81.

126. Ibid., 171.

127. Ibid., 60. Sixteenth-century gun laws authorized the king to grant gun licenses to people who were otherwise ineligible to own guns. In significant part, this appears to have been used as a means of enabling landholding aristocrats—who were willing to pay a considerable licensing fee—to arm a small number of designated servants in order to help protect their estates from intruders, poachers, or pests, such as buzzards. Some aristocrats also purchased licenses for friends they wanted to take hunting with them but were otherwise not authorized to possess guns. The practice ended in 1604, however. See generally ibid., 65–73.

128. The Bill of Rights did not cause Parliament to relax firearm regulation, either then or now. In England today, people may only possess shotguns or "section 1 firearms," which are mainly limited to manually loaded cartridge pistols and manually loaded rifles. Possession requires either a Shotgun Certificate or a Firearm Certificate. Handguns, revolvers, and automatic and semiautomatic guns of any kind are banned to the general public. See Walter Hickey, "How Australia and Other Developed Nations Have Put a Stop to Gun Violence," *Business Insider,* January 15, 2013, http://www.businessinsider.com/canada-australia-japan-britain-gun-control-2013-1. See also http://www.cps.gov.uk/legal/d_to_g/firearms/#a12.

129. Bogus, "The Hidden History of the Second Amendment."

130. Ibid. For a brief supplement about the South's fear of slave uprisings, see http://www.carltbogus.com/edmund-a-blog/72-the-hidden-history-of-the-second-amendment-redux.

131. See Bogus, "The Hidden History of the Second Amendment," 352, and sources cited therein.

132. See ibid., 353, and sources cited therein.

133. See Bogus, "Gun Control and America's Cities," 268, and sources cited therein.

134. In a recent opinion, the majority and dissent argued over the possible rate of fire of semiautomatic assault rifles. The majority cited studies showing that rates of fire can exceed two rounds per second, while the dissent cited authorities placing the rate of fire at 45 to 60 rounds per minute. *Kolbe v. Hogan*, No. 14–1945, slip. op. at 19 and 103, 2017 WL 679687 *7 and *33 (4th Cir. Feb. 21, 2017) (en banc). It is possible that the difference results from some studies calculating rate of fire on a single magazine while other studies calculate how many rounds can be fired per minute using standard 30-round magazines and thus including the time it takes to change magazines.

135. Spitzer, *The Politics of Gun Control*, 152.

136. See http://www.cnn.com/2013/06/10/us/arizona-safeway-shootings-fast-facts (regarding Tucson, Arizona) and *Kolbe v. Hogan*, 6, 2017 WL 679687 *1 (regarding Newtown, Connecticut).

137. Christopher S. Koper, "Updated Assessment of the Federal Assault Weapons Ban: Impacts on Gun Markets and Gun Violence, 1994–2003," Report to the National Institute of Justice, June 2004, https://www.ncjrs.gov/pdffiles1/nij/grants/204431.pdf.

138. Ibid., 2.

139. Bogus, "Gun Control and America's Cities," 269–76.

140. Ibid., 274.

141. This excludes Nevada, which has a universal background check law but is currently not enforcing it, as well as two states that mandate universal background checks for only certain types of firearms. See http://lawcenter.giffords.org/gun-laws/policy-areas /background-checks/universal-background-checks/#state.

142. The three states are California, New Jersey, and New York. Five other states ban large-capacity magazines but exempt those manufactured before their laws went into effect. See http://lawcenter.giffords.org/gun-laws/policy-areas/hardware-ammunition /large-capacity-magazines/#state.

143. Henigan, *"Guns Don't Kill People,"* 81–97; Spitzer, *The Politics of Gun Control*, 111–15.

144. Jode Ide, *IQ* (New York: Mulholland Books), 163.

145. http://time.com/money/4965030/gun-stocks-rise-las-vegas-shooting/.

146. See, e.g., Cook and Goss, *The Gun Debate*, 77.

147. The best-funded gun control organization today is Everytown for Gun Safety. See, e.g., Spitzer, *The Politics of Gun Control*, 118–20.

148. Joseph Lehman, "A Brief Explanation of the Overton Window," https://www .mackinac.org/OvertonWindow#Explanation.

149. Ibid.

150. http://news.gallup.com/poll/1645/guns.aspx.

151. Spitzer, *The Politics of Gun Control*, 115.

152. Ibid., 115–16. See also Pete Shields, *Guns Don't Die—People Do* (New York: Arbor House, 1981), 46.

153. Spitzer, *The Politics of Gun Control*, 115–16.

154. The only national organization still advocating a ban was the Violence Policy Center, which was formed in 1988. Its executive director has cogently advocated for a handgun ban in Josh Sugarmann, *Every Handgun Is Aimed at You: The Case for Banning Handguns* (New York: New Press, 2001).

155. *Heller*, 628–34.

156. Ibid., 626. They also declared that the government could forbid carrying firearms into sensitive places such as schools and government building, and they suggested that the government could prohibit the carrying of concealed weapons.

157. For a more complete recounting of this story, see Carl T. Bogus, "The Battle for Separation of Powers in Rhode Island," *Administrative Law Review* 56 (2004): 77.

158. The battle for separation of powers in Rhode Island began when U.S. Attorney (now U.S. Senator) Sheldon Whitehouse published an article explaining why not recognizing

separation of powers exacerbated corruption. Sheldon Whitehouse, "Appointments by the Legislature under the Rhode Island Separations of Powers Doctrine: The Hazards of the Road Less Traveled," *Roger Williams University Law Review* 1, no. 1 (1996).

159. Bogus, "The Battle for Separation of Powers in Rhode Island," 124–26.

160. https://en.wikiquote.org/wiki/Andrew_Fletcher.

161. Bogus, *Why Lawsuits Are Good for America*, 143–44.

162. Richard North Patterson, *Balance of Power* (New York: Ballantine Books, 2003), 188.

163. *Miss Sloane* (EuropaCorp, 2016).

164. *The Ten Commandments* (Paramount Films, 1956).

165. See Bogus, "The Hidden History of the Second Amendment."

166. Talk by John Feinblatt, titled "From Third Rail to Silver Lining: The Politics of Gun Safety," delivered at the Shasha Seminar at Wesleyan University, Middletown, Connecticut, October 27, 2017.

167. Shields, *Guns Don't Die—People Do*, 11–24. See also http://www.nytimes.com /1993/01/27/obituaries/nelson-shields-3d-69-gun-control-advocate.html.

168. This is based on my recall of private conversations with Pete Shields that took place when I was a member of the HCI board of directors.

169. One of the most effective improvements to the background check system took place in 1996, when Congress added people convicted of domestic violence misdemeanors to the list of persons prohibited from possessing firearms. This reduced gun homicides of females by intimate partners by 17 percent without increasing homicides by other weapons. Cook and Donohue, "Saving Lives by Regulating Guns," 1261. There is also evidence that states have been able to reduce their firearm-robbery rates by about 5 percent by imposing longer prison sentences on persons who commit aggravated assaults or robberies with a gun instead of a less-lethal weapon. Ibid.

CHAPTER 5

Merely Regulation?
How Gun Law Matters for Public Law Enforcement

JENNIFER CARLSON

Under the so-called "War on Crime," the American society and the American state have become emboldened with force. On the one hand, the War on Crime has been deployed as a rallying cry to enlarge the prerogative of everyday (law-abiding) Americans and embrace gun rights as a "sensible" response to crime.[1] By the 2010s, millions of gun carriers began to see themselves as crime-stoppers and even symbolically embraced an identity as citizen-protectors.[2] On the other hand, the politics of crime has been used to legitimize and expand state prerogatives to aggressively combat crime.[3] The consequences, especially for African Americans, have been profound: black boys and men are disproportionately likely to be arrested and incarcerated as well as killed in gun homicides, whether state agents deem those homicides to be felonious or justifiable.

Police are central to these dynamics. Police, after all, are the state agents tasked with addressing gun law enforcement at its frontline. It is the police who define themselves by the gun and the badge,[4] often declining to relinquish their guns at the end of the work day and instead arming themselves as 24/7 peace officers.[5] And it is the police who are attached to their own guns as practically and morally powerful crime-fighting tools[6] as they (alongside other criminal justice actors)[7] discursively champion the rights of crime victims.

At a time in the not-so-distant past, many police appeared to favor a restrictive approach to firearms in the hands of private citizens.[8] Consider the police embrace of President Clinton's Violent Crime Control and Law Enforcement Act of 1994. Promising a surge of funding to law enforcement that would deepen divisions between public law enforcement and those they police through expanded police militarization, the law also put into effect an assault weapons ban, outlawing certain firearms, firearms features, and firearms accessories. Clinton signed the bill in a ceremony on the South Lawn of the White House, surrounded by law enforcement. Yet today, while some police organizations continue to endorse tightened gun restrictions[9], it appears that many police—even police chiefs—endorse gun rights over gun control. A recent survey from Pew[10] confirms the limited literature on contemporary police attitudes on guns[11] to show that at the national level, police outpace the public in support of gun rights. The vast majority of police—74 percent—say it is more important to "protect the right of Americans to own guns," compared to 53 percent of the public.[12]

Meanwhile, police seem increasingly apt to make high-profile statements in favor of armed civilians. Sheriffs, perhaps under their political pressures as elected office-holders, have led the way: in 2011, former Arizona sheriff and police officer Richard Mack founded the Constitutional Sheriffs and Peace Officers Association, a law enforcement organization aimed at promoting gun rights. Other sheriffs have made headlines for their pro-gun stances, such as Wisconsin's Milwaukee County sheriff David Clark Jr. and Oregon's Douglas County sheriff John Hanlin. Police chiefs—known for staying out of the spotlight by virtue of often being appointed rather than elected—have also made unexpected waves. In 2014, the Detroit police chief appeared in the NRA magazine *America's First Freedom,* endorsing law-abiding civilians who choose to carry guns with concealed pistol licenses in Detroit as he admitted police shortcomings, especially slow response times. Such police are no longer simply gun law enforcers; these high-profile officials are taking political stands on gun laws in favor of expanded private civilian access.

How do police reconcile an embrace of a "tough on crime" mandate with an endorsement of gun rights for private civilians? What precisely do police, as state agents, stand to gain from embracing a pro-gun stance? How might this embrace, for example, buttress state power and entrench social, especially racial, division? This chapter explores these questions by examining in-depth interviews with thirty-six members of public law enforcement who, because of where they police and at what level, might be expected to most heavily endorse restrictions on civilian access to firearms: California's police chiefs.

U.S. gun laws have often been interrogated by scholars in terms of their impact on *society,* for example, in the robust political movement for expanded gun access (dominated, though not exclusively, by white conservative men)[13] and in the heightened levels of gun death and gun injury (disproportionately impacting urban African American boys and men with respect to felonious and justifiable homicides and rural white men with respect to suicides).[14] In this chapter, my goal is to shift attention toward the *state*. Specifically, I show how state agents deploy particular stances on California's relatively restrictive gun laws to assert particular state prerogatives and practices that, in turn, buttress the broader dynamics of the War on Crime.

This chapter situates the political struggle over American gun laws within the so-called myth of the "weak" American state[15] to suggest that contemporary gun politics can be understood as part of a "weak state" effect whereby American state power is exerted, and with consequences for racial disparities and divisions.[16] It explores the specific context of the War on Crime, examining how the myth of "weak" statehood makes the American state particularly pervious to populist mobilizations such as the War on Crime, on the one hand, and increases the attractiveness of state-society sharing of legitimate violence, on the other hand. The chapter then turns to interviews with California police chiefs, showing that for police, gun laws are not simply a mechanism of enforcement. Rather, gun laws are symbolically mobilized as a means to assert particular relationships between themselves and the communities they police (and, in doing so, substantiate the social, particularly racial, divisions therein); affirm the legitimacy of their own police guns; and distance themselves from arms of the state, particularly the legislature, that they see as ineffective, inept, and even illegitimate.

From Gun Laws to State Effects

Debates surrounding American gun laws, culture, and politics are often embedded in an implicit understanding of the United States as a "weak" state. This perspective is rehearsed by both sides of the gun debate. Take the National Rifle Association (NRA), which asserts the colorblind value of gun rights as residing in the inherent weakness of the American state apparatus to protect civilians from crime, chaos, and disaster. As Wayne LaPierre remarked in a U.S. Senate hearing:

> What people all over the country fear today is being abandoned by their government if a tornado hits, if a hurricane hits, if a riot occurs, that they're going to be out there alone, and the only way they're going to protect themselves in the cold, in the dark, when they're vulnerable, is with a firearm.[17]

In this commentary, LaPierre juxtaposes tornados, hurricanes, and riots as intractable sources of insecurity for "people all over the country"; this juxtaposition draws a link between human-aggravated natural disasters (for example, Hurricane Katrina in New Orleans) and responses to conditions of acute inequality and vulnerability (for example, protests in response to police brutality), but it glosses over the structural conditions of insecurity that undergirds them. Through this doomsday depiction of natural disasters and social upheaval, the NRA paints the weakness of the American state with a broad brush with regard to gun law enforcement. Over the years, the NRA has highlighted a variety of threats—including the racialized specter of the armed criminal—as aided and abetted by underenforced gun laws. Indeed, the NRA countered the Obama administration's pursuit of further gun regulations by highlighting inadequate enforcement of gun laws "already on the books," especially laws that target "violent felons" who use guns in the commission of crime. On the other side of the gun debate, Everytown for Gun Safety, an organization that emerged in the aftermath of the Sandy Hook School Shooting in Newtown, Connecticut, likewise explains loose gun laws in the United States by referencing a weak state alongside weak politicians presumably unwilling to take on the NRA. One series of memes developed by Everytown's Moms Demand Action illustrates the rhetorical power of the "weak" American state for proponents of tightened gun restrictions: two children are juxtaposed, one of whom holds an AR-15-style rifle, the other of whom holds a seemingly innocuous object (a basketball, a book, a candy). The reader is instructed: "One child is holding something that's been banned in America to protect them. Guess which one." Spoiler alert: it is never the gun. This juxtaposition glosses over the trend that, when laws regulating possession—for example, in the case of drugs—*are* on the books and enforced, they are disproportionately and most punitively enforced against poor boys and men of color. Thus, on both sides of the gun debate, the state is imagined in broadly similar, colorblind terms[18]—as a weak enforcer—and this imaginary of the weak state, in turn, is the basis upon which to advance certain perspectives on gun laws.

That gun politics is grounded in what William Novak calls the "myth of the 'weak' American state" is not surprising. This notion has been lionized into an overarching narrative of American history. As Novak[19] summarizes, "It is the absence of a sense of a state that has been the great hallmark of American political culture":

> The phrase "the American state" is seen as something of an oxymoron in a land of alleged "anti-statism" and "statelessness." When acknowledged at all, the American version of a state is viewed as something not quite fully

formed—something less, something laggard, something underdeveloped compared to the mature governmental regimes that dominate modern European history. An enduring and exceptional tendency to view the American state throughout its history as distinctively "weak" continues to frustrate a reckoning with American power in the twenty-first century.[20]

This presumption of a "weak" American state can be contrasted with what Michael Mann[21] defines as "despotic" power: "The range of actions which the [state] elite is empowered to undertake without routine, institutionalized negotiation with civil society groups . . . despotic power is also usually what is meant in the literature by 'autonomy of power.'" When viewed through the lens of despotism,[22] the American state may indeed appear weak. But, as Novak and others suggest, another reading of the American state is possible. Consider the notion of infrastructural power, or "the positive capacity of the state to 'penetrate civil society' and implement policies throughout a given territory."[23] Such penetration is usually conceptualized in terms of communications and economy: "The state can assess and tax our income and wealth at source, without our consent or that of our neighbours or kin . . . ; it stores and can recall immediately a massive amount of information about all of us; it can enforce its will within the day almost anywhere in its domains; its influence on the overall economy is enormous; it even directly provides the subsistence of most of us (in state employment, in pensions, in family allowances, etc.)"[24] Under this formulation of state power, law is never autonomous from state power but constitutive of it: "The choice between law and power is a false dichotomy."[25]

How does this distinction between two "analytically autonomous dimensions of power"[26] help us understand the persistence of the "myth of the 'weak' American state"? As Novak[27] notes, "While the despotic power of the American state (until recent times) might have been limited, the scale and scope of its infrastructural power is and always has been extensive." This leads to an "intriguing interpretive possibility": that part of the power of the American state is its capacity to penetrate civil society in ways that do not pass muster as state power, or, as Novak[28] suggests, "that the very anti-despotic organization of the American state might actually increase its infrastructural capacity."

This demarcation of the line between civil society and the state in ways that enhance state prerogative is what Mitchell[29] defines as the "state effect": "the state should be addressed as an effect of detailed processes of spatial organization, temporal arrangement, functional specification, and supervision and surveillance, which create the appearance of a world fundamentally divided into state and society." States, whether weak or strong, may produce "strong state" or "weak state" effects[30]; indeed, the "myth of the 'weak' American state" persists despite a historically elaborate American regulatory state[31] as well as a vast contemporary carceral apparatus spanning from the criminal justice system "proper" (e.g., police, courts, prisons, probation, and parole) to the "shadow carceral state,"[32] including schools, immigration enforcement, welfare sanctions, and beyond.[33] Indeed, across a wide variety of settings and historical time periods, scholars have shown that U.S. state apparatuses, including police, are outgrowths of an array of organized attempts among white Americans (particularly white American elites) to constitutively control, contain, and/or exclude racially subordinate groups.[34]

This line of reasoning raises two questions. First, to whom is this "weak state effect" directed? Second, how might the most quintessentially "despotic" elements of state power—e.g., the state's historic harnessing of violence—be imagined, enacted, and effective under a state apparatus in which power is largely infrastructural?[35] After all, the framing of the American state as "weak" resonates with regard to the exceptional violence of American society, as evidenced by the circulation of more than 300 million guns in the hands of civilians,[36] high rates of violent crime,[37] and vigilante violence, historically ranging from slave patrols to mob lynching to posses to militias to (at times armed) neighborhood watch groups.[38] Across historical time and geographical space, civilian-comprised, arms-wielding groups have emerged to enforce social, oftentimes racial, orders in the absence of, at the behest of, and at times in collaboration with state agents. Infrastructural power, when viewed against the backdrop of American racial politics, is not just a mechanism of state power; it is also a means of reinforcing racial boundaries both by devolving enforcement capacities onto white American men (who, with notable exceptions, have generally composed civilian-organized policing units) and by generating consent among those engaged in collaborative activities (whether formal or informal) with the state.

Thus, rather than debating the "weakness" of the American state, might we instead extend the notion of infrastructural power to understand the mobilization and deployment of legitimate violence? This reframes the question of gun laws away from mere regulation and toward a more productive tactic[39] of state-society relations. After all, state inaction in the face of civilian violence oftentimes *is* interested state action: for example, the willingness of southern sheriffs from the late nineteenth century through the mid-twentieth century to allow detained African Americans to be kidnapped, tortured, and killed in lynching mob spectacles[40] should not be read as direct evidence of a "weak" state. Rather, it can be viewed as evidence of a "weak state" effect, whereby state objectives (white supremacy) are achieved via overt social channels that state actors—in a show of "weakness"—facilitate. Thus, in terms of "state effects,"[41] these phenomena might be interpreted *not* as an example of state weakness but rather indicators of a unique kind of state power, one in which the dirty work of violence is shared between state and society (rather than monopolized by police; contra Bittner)[42] and thus resembles a more capillary, diffuse power[43] more impervious to resistance than a centralized despot.

Many—including five U.S. Supreme Court justices in the landmark case *District of Columbia v. Heller* (2008)—have argued that it is precisely such sharing of violence across state and society that the Second Amendment sanctioned by stipulating an individual right to keep arms alongside the militia as a vehicle of citizen-sanctioned social order.[44] Thus, taking seriously the myth of the "weak" state opens the door for a different kind of relationship to violence than the despotic framework of a state monopoly on legitimate force, one that situates gun laws, gun cultures, and gun politics not as a reflection of a "weak state" but rather as constitutive of a "weak state" effect. And just as lynching became acceptable in specific contexts of moral panic over perceived social breakdown (in that case, regarding white supremacy under Jim Crow),[45] so too might the contemporary appeal of lenient gun laws to both everyday civilians and (certain) state agents be grounded in the more contemporary machinery for the enforcement of social order,[46] one that has called for "lethal violence as a legitimate response to lethal violence":[47] the War on Crime.

A "Weak" State at War

Consider that under the "myth of the 'weak' American state," the state's execution of violent coercion is presumed to be weak, vulnerable, clipped—even neutered. What kinds of social and state responses appear appropriate in such contexts of apparent broad-based breakdown in social order? If state-craft "as usual" is presumed to be weak, then "emergency" responses may well seem not just urgent—but urgently acceptable. This helps explain why the American state's "ambiguous" approach to policing oscillates between weakness and war: "The state has an ambiguous role . . . it sets and administers the rules of civilized conduct—but it is, in its judicial form, always a three days' ride away. Or it turns up in its military form as the 11th-hour cavalry rescue."[48] In this way, the presumed weakness of the American state can open the door for histrionic displays of coercion in the context of crime, terrorism, immigration, and other social issues deemed indicative of the threat that the "weak" American state poses to Americans. The so-called War on Crime is one such instance. The War on Crime is understood by scholars to reference a set of moral frameworks, justificatory discourses, political strategies, and forms of statecraft to aggressively address the problem of crime.[49] At the heart of the War on Crime is fear: not only fear of racialized criminals,[50] but also fear that the social apparatus in place to protect would-be victims from crime—namely, the state—is ill equipped to do so.[51] While crime did spike from the 1960s until the early 1990s,[52] the fearsome politics that this crime wave was mobilized to justify far exceeded proportions.[53] Likewise, the perception of the state as a failed Leviathan was part truth, part effect: while the likelihood of an individual crime-doer facing arrest, much less incarceration, was relatively low in the 1960s,[54] powerful criminal justice interests—most notably, the California Correctional Peace Officer Association (CCPOA), as documented by Page[55]—transformed this statistical observation into a formidable political project that emotionally galvanized voters by asking them to see themselves as potential victims. As Beckett[56] shows, fear of crime did not drive politics; a state-driven politics of racial resentment (such as Nixon's "Southern Strategy") drove fear of crime in ways that sanctified crime victimhood and provided state agencies with a blank check—both politically and financially—to wage war on crime.

Since the early 1990s, California has carved out the frontlines of the War on Crime: the state made headlines for its zero-tolerance crime policies, including the infamous 1994 "Three Strikes" ballot measure.[57] An interesting set of allies championed the measure, most notably the CCPOA and the NRA, which Zimring, Hawkins, and Kamin[58] described as "a gun owners' group that welcomes punitive sentencing programs as a method of addressing violent crimes without inconveniencing gun owners." But guns would be next on the agenda. A follow-up proposal, the 1996 "Use a Gun and You're Done" legislation, was billed at its passing as one of the harshest gun laws in the United States: it added enhancements of ten years, twenty years, and up to life for first, second, and third offenses of crimes involving firearms. At the time, the NRA was uninterested in funding a bill that zeroed in on guns, but the measure was later revived as a compromise measure between California Republicans, who presented it as an alternative to more direct gun control, and California Democrats, who used it to maintain their own "tough on crime" credentials.[59] This broad shift toward mandatory minimums and enhanced sentencing led to California's prison overcrowding crisis, disproportionately impacting boys and men of color, which the U.S. Supreme Court declared unconstitutional in 2011 in *Brown v. Plata*.[60]

As state policies and practices politicized social breakdown, many Americans[61] became more proactive themselves; the swelling of prisons coincided with the swelling of registers selling home security systems, car alarms, and other security gadgets.[62] It was in this particular moment that Simon[63] argues that the Second Amendment became rehabilitated as living law rather than a "dead letter": guns became increasingly appealing ways of securing the middle-class, white suburban home, and they provided a means of everyday people to practice a "tough on crime" sensibility in their everyday lives. The payoff was twofold: by the 2010s, not only did Americans feel more secure from crime with guns than without them,[64] but armed Americans used guns to make a moral assertion, distinguishing themselves against criminals by their willingness to use lethal force to defend innocent life.[65]

This embrace of crime-fighting reminds us that, alongside the calls for expansion of the punitive state, the War on Crime also enjoyed popular appeal. As Steinert[66] argues, "The war metaphor is strong and socially valid because it is connected to very basic social values and their everyday practices: community, patriarchy, masculinity":

> The proud father of a family who plants the American flag on his front lawn and arms himself against burglar attacks acts out a social validation of war. So does the woman who asks for male protection at night (even if she probably knows that it may not be worth much if the unfortunate occasion should arise). So do youth gangs that form to defend 'the hood' against invaders.

Indeed, Steinert[67] argues that when marshalled under a war metaphor, populism works in two ways: first, it emboldens society's embrace of state prerogatives as everyday practices of crime-fighting (i.e., the armed civilian), and second, it legitimates the state by reference to American myths of populist—that is, non-state—wielding of violence. One illustration of this is the close tracking between police and civilian-perpetrated justifiable homicides according to the FBI's yearly counts. Thus, police may be celebrated as vigilantes (e.g., *Dirty Harry*; see Lenz)[68] that model the heroic masculinity made salient through the very "statelessness" of American society that police aim to address.[69]

While the War on Crime has transformed state and social sensibilities regarding the control of crime, both as an end in itself and as a metaphor for other social issues,[70] some of the more "despotic" state actions under the War on Crime, such as mandatory minimums, have begun to outlive their original luster. By the 2010s, the tides began to shift as crime persistently declined and budgets increasingly tightened: politicians in states as diverse as Texas and California began morally questioning and fiscally defunding the project of mass incarceration, releasing prisoners and decriminalizing offenses.[71] In the aftermath of *Brown v. Plata*, California embarked on a project of decarceration by "realigning" the onus of incarceration onto the counties that convict, releasing early inmates with so-called "non-non-non" (non-violent, non-sexual, non-serious) convictions, and de-felonizing drug use and other "victimless" and nonviolent crimes.[72]

Against Sacramento's strategies to reduce the prison population, police attitudes on guns take on an interesting significance. Rather than reflecting the letter of the law, police attitudes on guns reveal a brand of legal consciousness[73] that depends on, and reproduces, particular state effects surrounding the role of police in this unsettled[74] context of the aftermath of the War on Crime. My analysis thus approaches gun law as a socio-legal phenomenon in two related ways: first, as a set of normative values that are codified by the state but that circulate through social channels, and second, as a set of tools that allow for the drawing of moral boundaries *both* between state and society *and* within the state. While California chiefs show meaningful variation in how they talk about gun law to understand and assert their prerogatives as police, they often coalesced around expanded civilian gun access in ways that allowed them to draw on popular sensibilities and thereby reinforce their prerogatives as police. As I will show, *both* critique of California's restrictive gun laws *as well as* support for lawful access to guns provide police with an occasion to assert themselves as crime fighters, to justify their own use of violence, to align themselves with victims, and to counterpose themselves to policymakers looking to roll back the War on Crime. Police support for civilian access to lawful guns makes little sense if the state is understood in terms of its monopoly on violence (and indeed, the relatively small portion of chiefs who *did* understand the state in this way tended to oppose expanded gun access); in contrast, if state power is understood in terms of its capacity to penetrate civil society, then loosening gun law to facilitate civilian access to firearms can be a symbolically potent moment of infrastructural power for police.

Gun Law Enforcement in California

This essay is part of a larger study that examines how state agents make sense of and enforce gun law. While the gun debate often takes place at the national level, the laws and enforcement mechanisms in place to regulate gun ownership, gun carrying, and gun use are fragmented across local, state, and national levels.[75] California gun laws are highly unique within a country that has largely loosened gun laws and embraced nondiscretionary concealed carry licensing; praised by gun control organizations and condemned by gun rights organizations, the state of California both regulates and restricts which guns residents can own, which residents can own them, and whether and how they can carry them.

At the time of this writing, California is one of seven states (plus the District of Columbia) that has banned "assault weapons," legally defined in California by make and model as well as generic features. California became the first state to ban such weapons when it passed the Roberti-Roos Assault Weapons Control Act of 1989. Because of the law's grandfather clause, nearly 150,000 assault weapons remain in the legal possession of Californians, although they cannot be transferred or sold. Around this ban, California has built up a regulatory apparatus that not only seeks to track registered firearms but also ensure "prohibited persons" are not in possession of firearms—known as the Armed & Prohibited Persons System, which went into effect in the early 2000s. In terms of gun carry licensing, California state law outlines a "may issue" licensing system whereby, in addition to fulfilling statutory requirements, applicants must prove "good cause" to local licensing officials (either municipal police chiefs or county sheriffs) in order to obtain a license to carry a firearm concealed. This is a more restrictive system than the majority of U.S. states; most states issue licenses on a nondiscretionary basis, and roughly a quarter of states require no license at all to carry a firearm concealed.

With these unique aspects of California gun law in mind, I analyze in-depth interviews with thirty-six police chiefs in California. To solicit interviews, I first compiled a list of municipalities in California, identified police chiefs based on public information available online, and contacted prospective interviewees accordingly. Among interviewees, the modal police chief was an older white man who had decades of police experience, with interviewees split across the Greater Los Angeles region, the Bay Area, the Inland Empire, and the Central Valley (see Table 1 and Table 2).

Table 1. Demographic Profile of California Police Chiefs	
Average age (years)	53
% Male	86%
% White	97%
Table 2. Geographic Breakdown of Jurisdictions	
Bay Area	19%
Greater LA region	33%
Inland Empire	14%
Central Valley	33%

Data from: author's interviews.

Interviews covered policing background and experiences and attitudes on gun violence and gun policy, including experiences with violence (as victims and perpetrators), thoughts on the use of guns for self-defense, attitudes on and experiences with gun regulations on the ground (such as concealed carry licensing), and opinions on gun control measures such as background checks and assault weapons bans. Interviews lasted between 30 minutes and two hours, and as per my Human Subjects Review Board protocol, I took detailed written notes (no audio recording), which I turned into narratives the day of or day after the interview, removing all identifying information. To further ensure anonymity, I use generic markers (e.g., "Chief A") for each new quote introduced, and, following Moskos,[76] to further ensure confidentiality I refer only to the pertinent characteristics of an officer when introducing an excerpt.

"There Is Zero Difference": How Police Understand Gun-Carrying Civilians

The firearm is at the core of the quintessential police task of crime-fighting under the War on Crime. Action-oriented, "hard-charger" policing, which centers on heroic acts of self-endangerment, naturalizes firearms as a common sense, everyday tool for police.[77] As one chief remarked, "Really, [the firearm] is just part of my being." But if police define themselves by a gun and a badge, gun laws expanding civilian access to firearms—especially concealed carry laws—work to blur the boundaries of police identity, shaking the police monopoly on lawful force. Is this a problem for police, and if not, why not?

Indeed, the majority of California chiefs I interviewed supported the notion of at least some law-abiding civilians being licensed by the state to carry firearms concealed. Only 17 percent of the chiefs I interviewed outright opposed it (see Table 3).

Table 3. Attitudes on Concealed Firearm Carry	
Supported	53%
Opposed	17%
Indifferent/Mixed	31%

Data from: author's interviews.

How do we make sense of this finding? Consider a pair of police chiefs who exhibit a stark contrast in attitudes on civilian gun carry. Chief A and Chief B are both chiefs in Bay Area suburbs, but Chief A's attitudes on civilian gun carry resonates with the majority of police chiefs interviewed, while Chief B represents the minority:

Yes, I am comfortable with concealed carry. You know, the only concealed carry that is a problem are parolees with firearms in their belts—not someone who studied for carrying. I don't know who is armed around me, but my feeling is—if there's an off-duty cop next to me in the store when I need back up, I'm going to want that back up. And I don't see what's the difference between that off-duty cop and the responsible citizen. There is zero difference. (Chief A)

I think [concealed carry for civilians] is crazy. I think it is a bad idea for civilians to arm themselves. You know, sometimes people will occasionally tell me they want to get a gun—and I try to talk them out of it. Here's what I say . . . If you have a gun for defense, you better be shooting to kill if someone is doing something that calls for a gun. And the average citizen has just not thought that through. So I tell them they need to have a serious sit-down and think of the consequences—not just legal. The moral, psychological consequences. And if they are still absolutely convinced, I tell them—buy a dog. Get a bullhorn. Get an alarm system. Stay away from guns! (Chief B)

The contrast is striking in at least three ways. First, consider the framing of civilians for each chief. Chief A describes the "responsible citizen," someone who is explicitly contrasted to the criminal other[78] ("parolees," suggestive of racial difference[79] given the stark racial disparities in incarceration in California).[80] Other chiefs likewise used responsibility as the key criteria (disclaimer?) for supporting gun carrying (e.g., one chief remarked, "I have no problem with people legally carrying. They have some training, even if it is minimal, and they understand how to be responsible"; still another said, "I'm good with civilians who own and carry legally—as long as they are proficient, trained, and responsible"). Focusing on moralistic and statutory attributes—training, proficiency, responsibility—these chiefs shroud their endorsement of armed civilians in colorblind language[81] wherein lawfulness and moral standing are co-constitutive: the lawfully armed citizen is both legally and morally prepared for the use of force.[82] In contrast, Chief B emphasizes state-society distinctions by referencing an amorphous and indistinct "average citizen": for Chief B, and other chiefs who opposed civilian gun carry, the key distinction is not between "good" and "bad" civilians but rather between the state and society—another colorblind distinction, but one that rests not so much on the moral standing of particular citizens (as per Chief A) but rather on the institutional standing of the state as presumed guarantor of order. In other words, both chiefs chisel out colorblind renditions for justifying the distribution of legitimate violence; they differ on the socio-legal cues—responsible citizen versus state agent—that would qualify someone to wield legitimate violence.[83]

Next, these chiefs present different explanations for why these two brands of citizen (i.e., the "responsible" versus the "average") desire firearms: the "responsible citizen" has made some kind of deliberate, and even protracted, choice to carry a firearm (i.e., "studied for carrying") that brings into being the purposefully armed citizen, whereas the "average citizen," impulsive and blindsided, "has just not thought that through."

Third and finally, the cost-benefit analysis that each chief entertains implicates a different "worst case" scenario that places the armed citizen at the center. For Chief A, this is an imagined scenario in which police need "back up" and the citizen acts as a needed stop-gap. Here, we might even imagine the police—acting on behalf of an unnamed victim—as *standing in* for the victim and thus requiring any and all help. For Chief B, the implication is that it is the citizen who—by virtue of being armed—creates a problem, largely for herself but also ultimately for police. This is a problem that otherwise would have been averted had it not been for the presence of an impulsively acquired firearm. Here, the citizen is the potential victim; the police can at best work to prevent the civilian from hurting himself, on the one hand, and clean up the damage once it has been done, on the other. These divergences ultimately entail very different conclusions about guns in the hands of civilians: against the forces of criminality, an armed citizen is a "comfortable" (comforting?) prospect for Chief A, but given the weakness and even turpitude of everyday civilians, an armed citizen is "crazy" to Chief B.

These contrasts resonate with Herbert's[84] examination of police-community relations as *generative of* versus *separate from* society,[85] a distinction that lines up with both the literature on racialized policing throughout American history,[86] which shows that public law enforcement at turns constitutes and reinforces structures of racial difference and racial inequality within society, as well as the distinctions that Novak[87] and Mann[88] draw regarding state power more broadly. Echoing infrastructural power, Herbert found that police *generate* community by normatively channeling how civilians interact with police and by creating community (sometimes through exclusionary means) rather than merely responding to or separating from it: "Here our attention is drawn to how state agencies apprehend community. State actors employ grids of legibility upon the input they receive from the citizenry; they recognize some and not other forms of input as legitimate, they sort that input into categories, they react to it via certain prescribed routines."[89] In contrast to *generative* police-community relations, the framing of police as *separate* grows out of the mid-twentieth-century rise of police professionalism[90] and the elaboration of police expertise that encouraged a top-down relationship between civilians and police and the notion that police are separate from, and above, society.

In line with Herbert's analysis, Chief A speaks of a *generative* relationship as he collapses the forces of order into a narrative of "responsibility" that is counterposed to "criminality." This ode to responsibility is an incantation to infrastructural power: a sense that similarities between state agents and "responsible" civilians outweigh state-society distinctions. Police may be uniquely sworn to protect, but the distinction that the badge offers evaporates in the demanding messiness of "real" police work. Whether we label this rhetorical move "shared policing," an "anti-state effect," or even "community policing with a vengeance," the point is that this chief levels the distance between the state and some civilians (i.e., the trained, proficient, and responsible civilian, who is juxtaposed against the "parolee"). This inclusionary moment is thus also exclusionary: it creates continuity between police and law-abiding civilians only in contrast to "criminals," a term saturated with racial, class, and gender connotations given the disproportionate number of poor men and boys of color entangled in the criminal justice system.[91] In contrast, Chief B broadens this divide by ascribing impulsiveness and lack of serious forethought to civilians looking to carry guns: this is a state-society relation of *separation*. Accordingly, police are fundamentally separate from the "average civilian." The effect is an imaginary of a state independent from, and above, society, an imaginary captured by the iconic SWAT units developed by California police[92] and deployed by law enforcement across the United States to wage the War on Drugs against civilians.[93]

From this perspective, how police understand laws regulating civilian gun access far exceeds the question of how guns should be regulated. Police attitudes on guns reveal how police imagine the relationship between the state and society, a relationship that in turn reflects their own under-standings of themselves as policing agents. In doing so, police reflect the contradictory socio-legal sensibilities of the War on Crime.[94] The majority of police chiefs, like Chief A, opt to side with an abstract law-abiding civil-ian; a minority double-down on police expertise, like Chief B, and oppose ruptures to police monopoly on force.

"I'm Not Going to Be a Walking Victim": How Police Understand Their Own Guns

If gun laws codify presumptions about the capacity of everyday civilians, the boundaries of community, and the relationship between state agents and society (all against the backdrop of the cultural politics of a waning War on Crime), such presumptions in turn shape how police understand their own guns. Police have long been socially expected if not legally required to carry off-duty (this legal requirement has loosened since the 1980s), but police off-duty guns have historically been treated as a separate phenomenon from civilian guns. As Fyfe writes:

> Police, unlike most handgun owners, are psychologically screened and tested, trained, and sworn to protect life and property. Police possess weapons to protect public interests, whereas citizens possess weapons to protect their own private interests. Thus it is likely that even handgun control advocates, if they have thought about the issue at all, regard police off-duty guns as a category of weapons separate and distinct from those in the hands of private citizens.[95]

Yet, California chiefs' attitudes on off-duty gun carry suggest that the cul-tural politics of crime has not only reinvented the Second Amendment for everyday civilians[96] but also reshaped police understandings of their own firearms.

Consider how these two chiefs, both of whom hail from the Greater Los Angeles region, answered the question of whether they carry while off-duty:

> *Yes I do! First, because I legally can. Second, because a lot of people know what I do. And third, because I don't want to be caught in the middle of some movie the-ater where someone is shooting—I'm going to be that person that does something. I'm not going to be a walking victim. Because you never know—whether it's road rage or whatever. There are a bunch of examples . . . where people are unarmed, and here you have someone shooting for the hell of it. So I'm not going to be one of those guys. I am going to protect my family and stop—or at least try to stop it.*
> (Chief C)

Yes [now I carry off-duty]—there have been times when I didn't. But I'm not going to intervene in something—I have my cell phone, and I will call. But my goal is to never get involved unless I absolutely have to—unless someone is going to get killed. I tell my officers in training, don't get involved . . . There was an [off-duty] officer whose son was shot because he intervened. So I say, if you are with your family—don't get involved. Be the best witness! Help with the investigation. Because you don't have a radio, you don't have a vest—and I carry a 6-shot .380 pistol. So, it's about protecting myself, and you never know, but it's better to be a good witness. (Chief D)

These two excerpts reveal that the language of gun rights shapes police understandings of their own guns, especially for Chief C (who represents the majority of interviewed police with regard to off-duty carry) but also for Chief D (who represents the minority). In contrast to Fyfe's analysis, which emphasized police prerogative, for both Chief C and Chief D we hear the clarion call not just of *public* interest but also of *private* protection: "I am going to protect my family and stop—or at least try to stop it [a crime]" (Chief C) and "So, it's about protecting myself, and you never know" (Chief D).[97] As both chiefs frame their decisions regarding off-duty in an imagined scenario in which a crime suddenly unfolds before their eyes, it is worth noting that these chiefs turn to the same kinds of examples that circulate as justifications for why civilians carry:[98] the "snap" violence associated with active shootings that can occur in places like "schools, theaters, Best Buy," as one chief explained.

For Chief C, such scenarios subsume his obligations as a state agent into commitments that exceed the state proper: acknowledging that he carries off-duty "because I legally can," he asserts that "I'm going to be that person that does something. I'm not going to be a walking victim . . . I'm not going to be one of those guys." This resonates with a logic uncovered by Fyfe at the height of the War on Crime: "the prevailing definition [among police] of the appropriate off-duty police role is that of active intervener."[99] For Chief C, his occupational identity as a state agent makes possible, but does not circumscribe, his relationship to his firearm: his gun is a symbolic refusal to be a victim, a refusal that he is particularly committed to as a police officer. However, in contrast to Fyfe's[100] analysis of the off-duty police gun, this refusal transcends his police identity as such: Chief C frames himself (armed with his off-duty gun) as a civilian who happens to be a police officer rather than a police officer who happens (by virtue of being off-duty) to be a civilian. If "tough-on-crime" politics, championed by police, prison guards, and politicians, had encouraged civilians to take security measures into their own hands under the War on Crime, the populist prowess of the armed citizen also affirms this chief's off-duty gun.

Chief C was not the only time I heard pro-gun discourse seeping in to make sense of *police* use of force. Consider the following statement from another chief on why he supports concealed carry among civilians: "If they think that will make them safer—I mean, it's the same reasons that I would carry! And I'm no better than they are. I just have a job where I carry a gun, but that doesn't change why I should be able to carry a gun. They are no less qualified." This chief could be read as transferring police prerogative to civilians in a show of solidarity with "responsible citizens" (as per Chief A), blurring the lines between state and (some factions within) society. At the same time, though, this blurring goes both ways: "They are no less qualified" nods to the blurring of state into society, but it also blurs society (or a social justification of lethal force) into the state by highlighting the similarity between police and certain civilians (i.e., the civilians carrying guns for "the same reasons I would carry"). Thus, these chiefs are not just comfortable with civilian guns; support for civilian guns allows them to make moral sense of—and even legitimize—their own guns. One is reminded of Mann's[101] observation that, although capitalist societies show "few signs of . . . despotic" power, early state-civil society relations were embroiled in a dialectical process: "a range of infrastructural techniques are pioneered by despotic states, then appropriated by civil societies (or vice versa); then further opportunities for centralized coordination present themselves, and the process begins anew." Thus, perhaps the story of the state's monopoly on policing does not stop with the eclipse of the twentieth-century professional policing paradigm by the boom in private policing, concealed carry, and a variety of private-public partnerships;[102] this boom, in turn, may breathe new life into police prerogatives—or, at least, this is what the articulation of pro-gun discourse by police might suggest.[103] If armed private citizens can model themselves after police, police can likewise model themselves after private citizens.

Returning to Chief C and Chief D, it is thus perhaps not surprising that they have different attitudes on the issue of civilian gun carry. While Chief C describes himself as "a strong believer in the Second Amendment. I think law-abiding citizens should be able to own and carry guns," Chief D asserts his refusal to even issue licenses: "I don't have to do it [issue concealed pistol licenses], and I just don't believe people should be having weapons." For Chief D, the felt obligation to protect is, as with Chief B above, circumscribed by the state: police are fundamentally separated from society by way of police know-how, police equipment, and police coordination that even an off-duty cop must accept this chasm. Without a vest and a radio, a police officer may well be disempowered by his firearm, rather than empowered by it, as his reference to "an officer whose son was shot because he intervened" suggests.[104] Chief D thus recognizes that even as a sworn officer, he too must (as his life may rely on it) cede to the police once he loses his own status as an *on-duty* cop. Thus, with a brief nod to self-protection (which this chief acknowledges as a concern), his understanding of his off-duty gun asserts that the state inheres not in individuals but in institutions, reinforcing a chasm between state and society. Rather than appeal to a populist, pro-gun sentiment, Chief D has an entirely different lexicon of justifications related to the use of force: here, state protocol, rather than social practice, operates as a form of police expertise that enhances police as separate and above society.

While a minority of police assertively separated themselves from those they police with regard to access to firearms, many did not draw thick lines between themselves and private citizens (a pattern that echoes the moral improvisation and identity work observed to shape frontline work more generally).[105] This finding is reflective of the "tough on crime" politics under the War on Crime, which provided fertile ground for gun-involved understandings of citizenship (centered on gun carry as an individual right and civic duty) to flourish even as citizens demanded greater and greater action from the state. Rather than a threat to public law enforcement's purview, police appear to have absorbed this rendition of social citizenship by transforming it into a mechanism for buttressing, rather than undermining, public law enforcement.

"The California Legislature Has Completely Lost Its Mind!": How Police Understand Gun-Regulating Legislators

In discussing gun laws, police not only asserted particular relationships across state and society (i.e., between public law enforcement and the private citizens they police); they also asserted distinctions *within* the state, that is, between themselves and other arms of the state, especially legislators viewed as "soft on crime." When viewed from the perspective of infrastructural power, these assertions provide a source of power and legitimacy to those state agents able to harness it to their advantage.[106] If police repeatedly voiced support for "Three Strikes" and other laws that expanded and intensified punishment in California, they chided the newfound push for reduced sentencing and decriminalization. In this shifting context, gun laws allowed police to distance themselves from policymakers and assert their own moral worth as state agents who understand, they assert, the fine line between crime and criminalization, and between impactful laws versus laws that merely make legislators feels impactful.

From chiefs who had little direct contact with legislators to chiefs who had worked with legislators intimately, nearly all the interviewed chiefs were dismayed, for one reason or another, at California's attempts to regulate firearms. The police chiefs I interviewed often blamed the sheer incompetence of lawmakers; a few highlighted good but misguided intentions; and a couple explicitly blamed George Soros for allegedly commandeering control of the state's political process. Perhaps the most memorable diagnosis of legislative ineptitude came from a chief who explained, "I have a strong sense that the California legislature has completely lost its mind!" This reflects a broad finding in the literature on policy innovation in crime control that "many officers see . . . innovative policies as a reflection of political whims, the politicization of law enforcement, and a distraction from basic 'good police work.' "[107]

In critiquing California gun laws, several chiefs fell back on the stylized binary between the "good guys" with guns and the "bad guys" with guns, breathing into gun law a moralistic stance that resonates not only with the colorblind narratives popularized by pro-gun interests such as the NRA[108] but also with broader "criminology of the other"[109] under the War on Crime that sublimated racial politics into the politics of crime.[110] For example, one chief evoked the bucolic imagery of a rancher[111] in contrast to the "gangster who was just in LA with a stolen gun," implicitly drawing racial and class boundaries by erecting a line between allegedly harmless rural gun use and presumably dangerous urban gun crime:

> Look, I'm not worried about the guy who has a ranch and who has his guns responsibly locked up in a safe . . . . I'm really worried about the gangster who just was in LA with a stolen gun. Creating all these laws just doesn't help with that! I'm not worried about the rancher with a gun, or the school teacher with a gun. Most people—most citizens—it's Law, Shlaw! They don't actually care about the laws. They care that their problems are being solved by police. And so, do I sleep good at night knowing that there are [high-capacity] magazines out there? It just doesn't matter. (Chief R)

This chief articulated the view that restrictive gun laws put pressure on the police's relationship with those they police. In his view, because everyday civilians cannot be expected to keep track of California's myriad of gun laws, California laws risk creating a population of otherwise law-abiding "criminals" according to many of the chiefs interviewed. This, of course, further suggests that the boundaries many chiefs drew around the "proficient, trained, and responsible" armed civilian were less about the law and more about moralistic, colorblind sensibilities that are informed by, but exceed, the law proper.

Other chiefs shared this apprehension regarding the impact of gun laws, concerned that California gun laws are so misguidedly expansive that they hamper meaningful police work:

> *Look at this thick penal code. If the court system would just enforce it, and put people away so that if they have a gun or use a gun they never see the light of day— well, that's what I'd prefer . . . [Banning guns] is not effective at all. Once again, we have laws on the books already, but they are not being enforced. And no, those guns [assault weapons] don't bother me. It would not bother me that they are out. We have regulation, and yes, people have to be accountable to the laws, but as far as banning—we are in the position where we have to do the work that others just write about. Lawmakers think they are helping the situation, but really, they are making feel-good laws that appeal to their constituents.* (Chief T)

This chief and others questioned the ability of lawmakers to adequately regulate guns by emphasizing the sheer impracticalities of enforcing what they see as elaborate law. Slipped into their critiques is an appeal to "tough on crime" sensibilities: rather than broadly ban guns, lawmakers should be looking for ways to aggressively enforce gun laws against criminals.

This subtle appeal to "tough on crime" politics is key to understanding how gun laws can become a wedge between police and legislators while welding police to the general public (or, at least, the "law-abiding" portions of it): California's gun laws, in the view of many police, provide yet another example of how legislators have lost their way as fellow crime fighters. Echoing the NRA's support of strict enforcement against "violent crimi-nals," chiefs wanted harsher penalties and stricter enforcement, generally believing that the crime drop of the last two decades was the result not of gun control but of "tough on crime" policies. When asked about the impact of enhanced sentencing on crime rates, Chief P responded,

> *I am a believer that crime went down because of the harsh penalties we had in the early 1990s to put people away. Well, now we say about Prop 47—"everything's a misdemeanor"—date rape drugs, guns. So, 70–80% of crime—people are going to continue to commit it, but most crime is recidivist—it's not the first crime that someone commits.*

Whether they saw themselves as in favor of expanded gun rights or restrictive gun controls, police chiefs across California voiced antipathy toward the political process that shaped crime policies—including gun policies—and the resulting laws that they believed failed to harshly sanction "real" criminals while criminalizing "innocent" people. Police often railed against the top-down attempts of lawmakers to pass blanket gun laws by asserting their own moral obligations to good, law-abiding people.[112] Their grievances over California's current matrix of crime policy suggests that gun laws are not simply about guns: they are also about effecting a particular, populist imaginary of the state that maintains the authority of police, in defense of and sometimes in collaboration with "good" civilians.

Conclusion

Scholars have largely looked at the *social* dimensions of American gun culture, and its codification into American gun laws, as a reflection of the punitive politics of race, class, and gender throughout the American experience.[113] Less attention, however, has been paid to the *state* effects of American gun laws. The endorsement of gun rights by many police suggests that gun laws provide a symbolic mechanism by which police are able to forge moralistic, colorblind distinctions between "good guys" and "bad guys" and situate themselves as radically supportive of victims, critically positioning themselves vis-à-vis other arms of the state as they do. Drawing on the distinction between state power as despotic versus infrastructural[114] and extending this distinction to how contemporary American gun politics, gun culture, and gun laws may be mobilized by police to enact particular state effects,[115] this essay suggests that gun laws provide a discourse for police to assert a relationship between themselves and certain civilians and for emboldening their own prerogatives while questioning those of other state actors. As such, gun laws contain and communicate implicit norms surrounding citizenship and state-society relations not just for civilians but also for state agents, especially where police implicitly rely on and reproduce particular racial imaginaries regarding criminality and responsibility. This is certainly not the only instance in which criminal justice agents have circulated "myths" related to crime and its control, but this instance does clarify that these myths are directed both outward, to private citizens, but also inward, to police themselves, and upward, to other arms of the state.

To that end, this chapter has examined California police chiefs' attitudes on gun laws. By virtue of their occupational status as well as their state politics, California chiefs might be expected to be particularly anathema to the notion of private citizens owning and carrying firearms. In contrast to these expectations, California chiefs find in gun rights a symbolic assertion of an idealized sharing of legitimate violence with the "good guys," against both the criminal intent of the presumed "bad guys" and the legislative incompetence of policymakers. This essay thus reveals how gun law becomes "useful" to state agents insofar as it allows them to make sense of their relationships with private citizens, with their own guns, and with other state actors—all against the backdrop of particular visions of state and social order.

Notes

1. Jonathan Simon, "Gun Rights and the Constitutional Significance of Violent Crime," *William & Mary Bill of Rights Journal* 12 (2003): 335.

2. Jennifer Carlson, *Citizen-Protectors: The Everyday Politics of Guns in an Age of Decline* (New York: Oxford University Press, 2015).

3. Radley Balko, *Rise of the Warrior Cop: The Militarization of America's Police Forces* (London: Hachette, 2013); Peter B. Kraska, "Enjoying Militarism: Political/Personal Dilemmas in Studying US Police Paramilitary Units," *Justice Quarterly* 13, no. 3 (1996): 405–29; Peter B. Kraska and Victor E. Kappeler, "Militarizing American Police: The Rise and Normalization of Paramilitary Units," *Social Problems* 44, no. 1 (1997): 1–18; Jonathan Simon, *Governing through Crime* (New York: Oxford University Press, 2007).

4. David H. Bayley, *Forces of Order: Police Behavior in Japan and the United States* (Berkeley: University of California Press, 1978); Egon Bittner, *The Functions of the Police in Modern Society* (Chevy Chase, MD: National Institute of Mental Health, Center for Studies of Crime and Delinquency, 1973); Steven Herbert, "'Hard Charger' or 'Station Queen'? Policing and the Masculinist State," *Gender, Place and Culture: A Journal of Feminist Geography* 8, no. 1 (2001): 55–71.

5. James J. Fyfe, "Always Prepared: Police Off-duty Guns," *The ANNALS of the American Academy of Political and Social Science* 452, no. 1 (1980): 72–81.

6. Herbert, "'Hard Charger' or 'Station Queen'?," 4.

7. Joshua Page, *The Toughest Beat: Politics, Punishment, and the Prison Officers Union in California* (New York: Oxford University Press, 2011).

8. Note that in this essay, I use the terms "civilian," "citizen," and "private citizen" somewhat interchangeably to draw attention to armed individuals acting out of private, rather than state, interests; rather than reifying a binary between police and those they police, my goal is to explore this very boundary between police and those they police with as succinct language as possible.

9. A 2013 proposed assault weapons ban enjoyed support from the International Association of Chiefs of Police, the Police Foundation, Major Cities Chiefs Association, the National Association of Women Law Enforcement Executives, and the National Organization of Black Law Enforcement Executives, among others. See http://www.feinstein.senate.gov/public/index.cfm/assault-weapons-ban-endorsements.

10. R. Morin, K. Parker, R. Stepler, and A. Mercer, "Behind the Badge," *Pew,* http://www.pewsocialtrends.org/2017/01/11/behind-the-badge/ (accessed January 20, 2017).

11. Amy Thompson, James H. Price, Joseph A. Dake, and Thomas Tatchell, "Police Chiefs' Perceptions of the Regulation of Firearms," *American Journal of Preventive*

Medicine 30, no. 4 (2006): 305–12; Amy Thompson, James H. Price, Jagdish Khubchandani, and Jamie Dowling, "Sheriffs Perceptions of Firearm Control Polices," *Journal of Community Health* 36, no. 5 (2011): 715–20; Rachael A. Woldoff, Robert C. Litchfield, and Angela Sycafoose Matthews, "Unpacking Heat: Dueling Identities and Complex Views on Gun Control among Rural Police," *Rural Sociology* 82, no. 3 (2017): 444–72.

12. Morin et al., "Behind the Badge," 10. As compared to the general public, police were slightly less in favor of a "federal database tracking gun sales" (61 percent versus 71 percent) and only slightly favored "laws to prevent mentally ill from purchasing guns" (95 percent versus 87 percent) and "making private gun sales and sales at gun shows subject to background checks" (88 percent versus 86 percent). While these figures should certainly be interpreted as displaying broad police and public consensus regarding universal background checks and mental health precautions, they throw in stark relief presumptions that police monolithically favor gun restrictions.

13. Carlson, *Citizen-Protectors*, 2. See also Jeffrey Jones, "Men, Married, Southerners Most Likely to be Gun Owners," http://news.gallup.com/poll/160223/men-married-southerners-likely-gun-owners.aspx (accessed January 10, 2018).

14. John Roman, "Race, Justifiable Homicide, and Stand Your Ground Laws: Analysis of FBI Supplementary Homicide Report Data," *Urban Institute,* https://www.urban.org/sites/default/files/publication/23856/412873-Race-Justifiable-Homicide-and-Stand-Your-Ground-Laws.pdf (accessed January 8, 2018); Roberto Ferdman, "The Racial Divide in America's Gun Deaths," *Washington Post,* https://www.washingtonpost.com/news/wonk/wp/2014/09/19/the-racial-divide-in-americas-gun-deaths/?utm_term=.8c4a6d0ec2dd. (accessed January 18, 2018).

15. William J. Novak, "The Myth of the 'Weak' American State," *American Historical Review* 113, no. 3 (2008): 752–72.

16. Emine Fidan Elcioglu, "The State Effect: Theorizing Immigration Politics in Arizona," *Social Problems* 64, no. 2 (2017): 239–55; Timothy Mitchell, "The Limits of the State: Beyond Statist Approaches and Their Critics," *American Political Science Review* 85, no. 1 (1991): 77–96.

17. Melanie Mason, "NRA's Wayne LaPierre Blasts Obama's State of the Union Speech," *Los Angeles Times,* http://articles.latimes.com/2013/feb/14/nation/la-na-nra-response-20130215 (accessed January 31, 2017).

18. Needless to say, the normative value of a weak state is different on the two sides (the NRA, despite its lambasting of government abandonment, embraces an individualist ethic that runs counter to a strong state). But the work that the state does vis-à-vis gun laws is strikingly similar: these divergent stances on American gun laws both depend on—and in a sense are *used* to prop up—a myth of a "weak" state.

19. Stephen Skowronek, *Building a New American State: The Expansion of National Administrative Capacities, 1877–1920* (Cambridge: Cambridge University Press, 1982), 3.

20. Novak, "The Myth of the 'Weak' American State," 15, 754.

21. Michael Mann, "The Autonomous Power of the State," in *States in History,* ed. John A. Hall (New York: Oxford University Press, 1986).

22. Weber, Max, *The Vocation Lectures* (Indianapolis: Hackett Publishing, 2004); Carl Schmitt, *Political Theology: Four Chapters on the Concept of Sovereignty* (Chicago: University of Chicago Press, 1985); Charles Tilly, "War-making and State-making as Organized Crime," in *Violence: A Reader,* ed. C. Besteman (New York: New York University Press, 1985).

23. Novak, "The Myth of the 'Weak' American State," 15, 763; see also Mann, "The Autonomous Power of the State," 21.

24. Ibid., 114.

25. J. F. Witt, "Law and War in American History," *American Historical Review* 115, no. 3 (June 2010): 770.

26. Mann, "The Autonomous Power of the State," 21, 115.

27. Novak, "The Myth of the 'Weak' American State," 15, 763.

28. Ibid., 763; Mann, "The Autonomous Power of the State," 21, 114.

29. Elcioglu, "The State Effect: Theorizing Immigration Politics in Arizona," 239.

30. Mitchell, "The Limits of the State," 16, 95.

31. Suzanne Mettler, *The Submerged State: How Invisible Government Policies Undermine American Democracy* (Chicago: University of Chicago Press, 2011); William J. Novak, *The People's Welfare: Law and Regulation in Nineteenth-Century America* (Chapel Hill: University of North Carolina Press, 1996); Skowronek, *Building a New American State*, 19; Joe Soss, Richard C. Fording, and Sanford Schram, *Disciplining the Poor: Neoliberal Paternalism and the Persistent Power of Race* (Chicago: University of Chicago Press, 2011).

32. Katherine Beckett and Naomi Murakawa, "Mapping the Shadow Carceral State: Toward an Institutionally Capacious Approach to Punishment," *Theoretical Criminology* 16, no. 2 (2012): 221–44.

33. E.g., Amada Armenta, *Protect, Serve, and Deport: The Rise of Policing as Immigration Enforcement* (Berkeley: University of California Press, 2017); Jennifer Carlson, "The Hidden Arm of the Law: Examining Administrative Justice in Gun Carry Licensing," *Law and Society Review* 51, no. 2 (2017): 346–78; Kaaryn S. Gustafson, *Cheating Welfare: Public Assistance and the Criminalization of Poverty* (New York: New York University Press, 2011); Doris Marie Provine, Monica W. Varsanyi, Paul G. Lewis, and Scott H. Decker, *Policing Immigrants: Local Law Enforcement on the Front Lines* (Chicago: University of Chicago Press, 2016); Victor M. Rios, *Punished: Policing the Lives of Black and Latino Boys* (New York: New York University Press, 2011); Soss, Fording, and Schram, *Disciplining the Poor*, 30.

34. See, e.g., Patricia Hill Collins, *Black Feminist Thought: Knowledge, Consciousness, and the Politics of Empowerment* (New York: Routledge, 2002); Joe R. Feagin, *The White Racial Frame: Centuries of Racial Framing and Counter-Framing* (New York: Routledge, 2013); Ibram X. Kendi, *Stamped from the Beginning: The Definitive History of Racist Ideas in America* (New York: Nation Books, 2016); Michael Omi and Howard Winant, *Racial Formation in the United States* (New York: Routledge, 2014). On the contemporary relationship between police and constitution of racialized communities, see Laurence Ralph, *Renegade Dreams: Living through Injury in Gangland Chicago* (Chicago: University of Chicago Press, 2014); Robert Vargas, *Wounded City: Violent Turf Wars in a Chicago Barrio* (New York: Oxford University Press, 2016). Scholars further note the variegated forms of resistance—including, at times, turning to firearms—as a means of political, social, and physical survival for African Americans; see Joshua Bloom and Waldo E. Martin, *Black against Empire: The History and Politics of the Black Panther Party* (Berkeley: University of California Press, 2013); Nicholas Johnson, *Negroes and the Gun* (New York: Prometheus Books, 2014); Akinyele O. Umoja, "The Ballot and the Bullet: A Comparative Analysis of Armed Resistance in the Civil Rights Movement," *Journal of Black Studies* 29, no. 4 (1999): 558–78. Finally, on private and public legitimate violence as a dynamic historical process, see Jonathan Obert, *The Six-Shooter State: Public and Private Violence in American Politics* (Cambridge: Cambridge University Press, 2018).

35. Note that this is not the focus in either Novak's or Mann's analyses.

36. C. Ingraham, "There Are Now More Guns than People in the United States," *Washington Post*, https://www.washingtonpost.com/news/wonk/wp/2015/10/05/guns-in-the-united-statesone-for-every-man-woman-and-child-and-then-some/ (accessed July 25, 2016).

37. Philip J. Cook and Jens Ludwig, *Gun Violence: The Real Costs* (New York: Oxford University Press, 2000).

38. Carlson, *Citizen-Protectors*, 2; David Mark Chalmers, *Hooded Americanism: The History of the Ku Klux Klan* (Durham, NC: Duke University Press, 1981); Amy B. Cooter,

"Americanness, Masculinity, and Whiteness: How Michigan Militia Men Navigate Evolving Social Norms," PhD dissertation, University of Michigan, 2013; Carl Bogus, "The Hidden History of the Second Amendment," *UC Davis Law Review* 31 (1997): 309; Crystal Nicole Feimster, *Southern Horrors: Women and the Politics of Rape and Lynching* (Cambridge, MA: Harvard University Press, 2009); Carolyn Gallaher, *On the Fault Line: Race, Class, and the American Patriot Movement* (New York: Rowman and Littlefield, 2003); Martin Alan Greenberg, *Citizens Defending America: From Colonial Times to the Age of Terrorism* (Pittsburgh: University of Pittsburgh Press, 2005); Sally E. Hadden, *Slave Patrols: Law and Violence in Virginia and the Carolinas* (Cambridge, MA: Harvard University Press, 2001); Johnson, *Negroes and the Gun*, 33; Amy Louise Wood, *Lynching and Spectacle: Witnessing Racial Violence in America, 1890–1940* (Chapel Hill, NC: University of North Carolina Press, 2011).

39. Michel Foucault, *Discipline and Punish* (New York: Vintage, 2012).

40. Feimster, *Southern Horrors*, 37; Wood, *Lynching and Spectacle*, 37.

41. Elcioglu, "The State Effect," 16; Mitchell, "The Limits of the State," 16.

42. Bittner, *The Functions of the Police in Modern Society*, 4.

43. Foucault, *Discipline and Punish*, 38.

44. Saul Cornell, "Don't Know Much about History: The Current Crisis in Second Amendment Scholarship," *Northern Kentucky Law Review* 29 (2002): 657; Saul Cornell, "Originalism on Trial: The Use and Abuse of History in District of Columbia v. Heller," *Ohio State Law Journal* 69 (2008): 625; Nicholas J. Johnson, "A Second Amendment Moment: The Constitutional Politics of Gun Control," *Brooklyn Law Review* 71 (2005): 715; Adam Winkler, *Gunfight: The Battle over the Right to Bear Arms in America* (New York: W. W. Norton & Company, 2011).

45. Feimster, *Southern Horrors*, 37; Wood, *Lynching and Spectacle*, 37.

46. Michelle Alexander, *The New Jim Crow: Mass Incarceration in the Age of Colorblindness* (New York: New Press, 2012); Paul Butler, *Chokehold: Policing Black Men* (New York: New Press, 2017); Alex S. Vitale, *The End of Policing* (New York: Verso Books, 2017).

47. Simon, "Gun Rights and the Constitutional Significance of Violent Crime," 1, 356.

48. Heinz Steinert, "The Indispensable Metaphor of War: On Populist Politics and the Contradictions of the State's Monopoly of Force," *Theoretical Criminology* 7, no. 3 (2003): 269. See also David Garland, "Limits of the Sovereign State: Strategies of Crime Control in Contemporary Society," *British Journal of Criminology* 36, no. 4 (1996): 445–71; David Garland, *The Culture of Control* (New York: Oxford University Press, 2001).

49. Katherine Beckett, *Making Crime Pay: Law and Order in Contemporary American Politics* (New York: Oxford University Press, 1999); Page, *The Toughest Beat*, 7; Simon, *Governing through Crime*, 3.

50. Beckett, *Making Crime Pay*; Ted Chiricos, Ranee McEntire, and Marc Gertz, "Perceived Racial and Ethnic Composition of Neighborhood and Perceived Risk of Crime," *Social Problems* 48, no. 3 (2001): 322–40.

51. Garland, "Limits of the Sovereign State," 47. Note that these fears about state inefficacy were not confined to white Americans; as scholars are beginning to reveal, communities hit hardest by increasing social disorder and crime (often comprised of racial minorities) made demands for increased police support alongside other forms of social support. See Butler, *Chokehold*, 45; James Forman Jr., *Locking Up Our Own: Crime and Punishment in Black America* (New York: Farrar, Straus and Giroux, 2017); Michael Javen Fortner, *Black Silent Majority: The Rockefeller Drug Laws and the Politics of Punishment* (Cambridge, MA: Harvard University Press, 2015).

52. Steven Pinker, *The Better Angels of Our Nature: Why Violence Has Declined* (New York: Penguin Books, 2012).

53. Beckett, *Making Crime Pay*, 48.

54. Pinker, *The Better Angels of Our Nature*, 51.

55. Page, *The Toughest Beat*, 7.

56. Beckett, *Making Crime Pay*, 48.

57. Page, *The Toughest Beat*, 7; Franklin E. Zimring, Gordon Hawkins, and Sam Kamin, *Punishment and Democracy: Three Strikes and You're Out in California* (New York: Oxford University Press, 2001).

58. Zimring, Hawkins, and Kamin, *Punishment and Democracy*, 5.

59. Ibid., 142–43.

60. Jonathan Simon, *Mass Incarceration on Trial: A Remarkable Court Decision and the Future of Prisons in America* (New York: New Press, 2014).

61. Married white southern men are disproportionately represented among gun owners; see Jones, "Men, Married, Southerners Most Likely to be Gun Owners," 12. Nevertheless, the appeal of proactive security, even with respect to guns, crosses racial, class, gender, age, and regional boundaries; see Justin McCarthy, "More than Six in 10 Americans Say Guns Make Homes Safer," *Gallup* http://news.gallup.com/poll/179213/six-americans-say-guns-homes-safer.aspx (accessed January 8, 2018).

62. Simon, *Governing through Crime*, 3.

63. Simon, "Gun Rights and the Constitutional Significance of Violent Crime," 1.

64. John Burnett, "Does Carrying a Pistol Make You Safer?," National Public Radio, http://www.npr.org/2016/04/12/473391286/does-carrying-a-pistol-make-you-safer (accessed July 18, 2016); Frank Newport, "Majority Say More Concealed Weapons Would Make US Safer," http://www.gallup.com/poll/186263/majority-say-concealed-weapons-safer.aspx (accessed July 25, 2016).

65. Carlson, *Citizen-Protectors*, 2.

66. Steinert, "The Indispensable Metaphor of War," 47, 281.

67. Ibid.

68. Timothy O. Lenz, "Conservatism in American Crime Films," *Journal of Criminal Justice and Popular Culture* 12, no. 2 (2005): 116–34.

69. Richard Slotkin, *Gunfighter Nation: The Myth of the Frontier in Twentieth-Century America* (Norman: University of Oklahoma Press, 1992); Pieter Spierenburg, ed., *Men and Violence: Gender, Honor, and Rituals in Modern Europe and America* (Columbus: Ohio State University Press, 1998).

70. Simon, *Governing through Crime*, 3.

71. Hadar Aviram, *Cheap on Crime: Recession-Era Politics and the Transformation of American Punishment* (Berkeley: University of California Press, 2015); Philip Goodman, Joshua Page, and Michelle Phelps, "The Long Struggle: An Agonistic Perspective on Penal Development," *Theoretical Criminology* 19, no. 3 (2015): 315–35.

72. Aviram, *Cheap on Crime*, 70; Barbara Owen and Alan Mobley, "Realignment in California," *Western Criminology Review* 13, no. 2 (2012): 46–52; Anjuli Verma, "The Law Before: Legacies and Gaps in Penal Reform," *Law and Society Review* 49, no. 4 (2015): 847–82; Anjuli Verma, "A Turning Point in Mass Incarceration? Local Imprisonment Trajectories and Decarceration under California's Realignment," *Annals of the American Academy of Political and Social Science* 664, no. 1 (2016): 108–35.

73. Patricia Ewick and Susan S. Silbey, *The Common Place of Law: Stories from Everyday Life* (Chicago: University of Chicago Press, 1998); Susan S. Silbey, "After Legal Consciousness," *Annual Review Law Society Science* 1 (2005): 323–68.

74. Ann Swidler, "Culture in Action: Symbols and Strategies." *American Sociological Review* 51, no. 2 (April 1986): 273–86.

75. Robert J. Spitzer, *The Politics of Gun Control*, 6th ed. (New York: Routledge, 2015).

76. Peter Moskos, *Cop in the Hood: My Year Policing Baltimore's Eastern District* (Princeton, NJ: Princeton University Press, 2008).

77. Herbert, "'Hard Charger' or 'Station Queen'?," 4; Kraska, "Enjoying Militarism," 3; Kraska and Kappeler, "Militarizing American Police," 3.

78. Garland, *The Culture of Control*, 47.

79. Omi and Winant, *Racial Formation in the United States*, 33, on racial code words; Van Cleve, *Crook County: Racism and Injustice in America's Largest Criminal Court* (Palo Alto, CA: Stanford University Press, 2016).

80. Simon, *Mass Incarceration on Trial*, 59.

81. Eduardo Bonilla-Silva, *Racism without Racists: Color-Blind Racism and the Persistence of Racial Inequality in America* (New York: Rowman and Littlefield, 2017).

82. Fredrick Harris, *The Price of the Ticket: Barack Obama and Rise and Decline of Black Politics* (New York: Oxford University Press, 2012).

83. Alexander, *The New Jim Crow*, 45; Bonilla-Silva, *Racism without Racists*, 80; Butler, *Chokehold*, 45; Nicole Gonzalez Van Cleve and Lauren Mayes, "Criminal Justice through 'Colorblind' Lenses: A Call to Examine the Mutual Constitution of Race and Criminal Justice," *Law & Social Inquiry* 40, no. 2 (2015): 406–32.

84. Steven Herbert, *Citizens, Cops, and Power: Recognizing the Limits of Community* (Chicago: University of Chicago Press, 2009).

85. See also David Alan Sklansky, "The Persistent Pull of Police Professionalism: New Perspectives in Policing," *UC Berkeley Public Law Research Paper No. 1788463*, https://ssrn.com/abstract=1788463 (accessed July 10, 2016); Forrest Stuart, *Down, Out, and Under Arrest: Policing and Everyday Life in Skid Row* (Chicago: University of Chicago Press, 2016).

86. Alexander, *The New Jim Crow*, 45; Balko, *Rise of the Warrior Cop*, 3; Butler, *Chokehold*, 45; Greenberg, *Citizens Defending America*, 37; Stuart, *Down, Out, and Under Arrest*, 84; Van Cleve, *Crook County*, 78; Van Cleve and Mayes, "Criminal Justice through 'Colorblind' Lenses," 82; Vitale, *The End of Policing*, 45.

87. Novak, "The Myth of the 'Weak' American State," 15.

88. Mann, "The Autonomous Power of the State," 21.

89. Herbert, *Citizens, Cops, and Power*, 74, 83.

90. Sklansky, "The Persistent Pull of Police Professionalism," 84.

91. Alexander, *The New Jim Crow*, 45; Butler, *Chokehold*, 45; Omi and Winant, *Racial Formation in the United States*, 33; Van Cleve, *Crook County*, 78; Van Cleve and Mayes, "Criminal Justice through 'Colorblind' Lenses," 82.

92. Balko, *Rise of the Warrior Cop*, 3; Vitale, *The End of Policing*, 45.

93. Although SWAT has been a vehicle for exacerbating racial disparities in law enforcement since its inception in the 1960s, it has been increasingly used to target whites, particularly poor rural whites, in the context of the so-called War on Meth. See Balko, *Rise of the Warrior Cop*, 3; Travis Linnemann, *Meth Wars: Police, Media, Power* (New York: New York University Press, 2016); Vitale, *The End of Policing*, 45.

94. Garland, "Limits of the Sovereign State," 47; Garland, *The Culture of Control*, 47; Simon, *Governing through Crime*, 3.

95. Fyfe, "Always Prepared," 5, 73.

96. Simon, "Gun Rights and the Constitutional Significance of Violent Crime," 1.

97. Although Fyfe, "Always Prepared," emphasizes the distinctions between police and civilians by reference to the importance of "public interest," and argues that maintenance of these differences requires implementing policies *against* off-duty police guns, he cites a study conducted on NYPD shootings in the mid-1970s showing that "self-defense" accounted for 55.8 percent of the shootings.

98. Carlson, *Citizen-Protectors*, 2.

99. Fyfe, "Always Prepared," 5, 75.

100. Ibid., 80.

101. Mann, "The Autonomous Power of the State," 21, 132, 130.

102. David H. Bayley and Clifford D. Shearing, "The Future of Policing," *Law and Society Review* 30, no. 3 (1996): 585–606; Lucia Zedner, "Policing before and after the Police: The Historical Antecedents of Contemporary Crime Control," *British Journal of Criminology* 46, no. 1 (2006): 78–96.

103. Mann is specifically interested in the rise and fall of states in describing this dialectic; my goal in using his insight is simply to call attention to how state power ebbs and flows "between the state and civil society . . . as continuously, temporally entwined." See Mann, "The Autonomous Power of the State," 21, 130.

104. Interestingly, this call to be a "good witness" is not unlike the encouragement that takes place in the context of self-defense manuals, pro-gun Internet boards, shooting ranges, and other gun-involved spaces. Here, armed civilians may be encouraged to walk away from fights and stand down from incitement, although this message is often simultaneously counteracted by louder moral incantations to be (to paraphrase) "judged by twelve rather than carried by six" (Carlson, *Citizen-Protectors*).

105. See Steven Maynard-Moody and Michael Musheno, *Cops, Teachers, Counselors: Stories from the Front Lines of Public Service* (Ann Arbor: University of Michigan Press, 2003).

106. Pierre Bourdieu, "The Force of Law: Toward a Sociology of the Juridical Field," *Hastings Law Journal* 38 (1986): 805; Yves Dezalay and Mikael Rask Madsen, "The Force of Law and Lawyers: Pierre Bourdieu and the Reflexive Sociology of Law," *Annual Review of Law and Social Science* 8 (2012): 433–52; Page, *The Toughest Beat*, 7.

107. Valerie Jenness and Ryken Grattet, "The Law-in-Between: The Effects of Organizational Perviousness on the Policing of Hate Crime," *Social Problems* 52, no. 3 (2005): 337.

108. Scott Melzer, *Gun Crusaders: The NRA's Culture War* (New York: New York University Press, 2012).

109. Garland, *The Culture of Control*, 47.

110. Carlson, *Citizen-Protectors*, 2; Simon, "Gun Rights and the Constitutional Significance of Violent Crime," 1.

111. Slotkin, *Gunfighter Nation*, 68.

112. Note that they often, though not always, glossed over the racial politics of the War on Crime as they did so. Indeed, some commentators have noted that much like drug law enforcement, gun law enforcement may well exhibit similarly dramatic racial disparities, even when accounting for differences across racial groups. Radley Balko, "Shaneen Allen, Race and Gun Control," https://www.washingtonpost.com/news/the-watch/wp/2014/07/22/shaneen-allen-race-and-gun-control/?utm_term=.13855f6508b5 (accessed January 2, 2018); Maya Schenwar, "Reduce Gun Penalties," *New York Times*, https://www.nytimes.com/2014/03/15/opinion/reduce-gun-penalties.html?_r=0 (accessed January 2, 2018). Scholars have paid less attention to racial disparities in gun law enforcement as compared to drug law enforcement, but see Jennifer Carlson, "Legally Armed but Presumed Dangerous: An Intersectional Analysis of Gun Carry Licensing as a Racial/Gender Degradation Ceremony," *Gender & Society* (2017): doi: 0891243217745862.

113. Carlson, *Citizen-Protectors*, 2; Johnson, *Negroes and the Gun*, 34; Cynthia Kwei Yung Lee, "Race and Self-Defense: Toward a Normative Conception of Reasonableness," *Minnesota Law Review* 81 (1996): 367; Slotkin, *Gunfighter Nation*, 68.

114. Mann, "The Autonomous Power of the State," 21; Novak, "The Myth of the 'Weak' American State," 15.

115. Elcioglu, "The State Effect," 16; Mitchell, "The Limits of the State," 16, 95.

CHAPTER 6

Good Moms with Guns

Individual and Relational Rights in the Home, Family, and Society

LAURA BETH NIELSEN

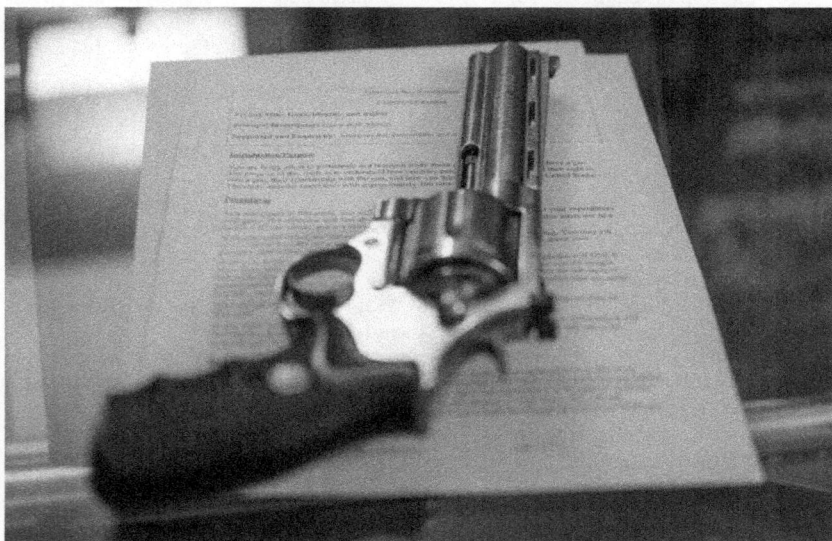

Figure 6.1. Consent form; photo courtesy Zach Sorensen-Nielsen Photography.

Introduction

The headlines seem to come daily. Toddler shoots and kills mother on a Wisconsin highway.[1] Police officer's toddler son kills himself with his father's service weapon.[2] Toddler kills older sibling despite being trained in gun use.[3] "Armed toddlers kill twice as many Americans each year as terrorists," screams another headline attempting to combat President

Trump's proposed Muslim ban.[4] Meant as a critique of the travel policy, the compilation of data does not lie. Dozens of toddlers and small children die every year in the United States from accidental self-inflicted gunshots, still others inadvertently are killed by siblings or playmates, and some are accidentally (or purposely) shot by adults.[5] Small children kill their parents or other adults due to accidental gun discharge.[6] While there is in fact a relatively small risk of injury or death[7] for Americans (hence the comparison to terrorism), the stories are heartbreaking and put into sharp relief precisely the kind of care that must be taken to secure a weapon in a home and family that includes small children. With facts like these, how could any "good" mom keep a gun in her home?

Gun advocacy groups promote the countermessage: a "good" mom *should* have a gun to protect herself and her children. Of course, these groups also advocate safety precautions, relaying conventional wisdom and distilled academic research about gun safety directed to mothers. The National Rifle Association (NRA), the Well Armed Women, the "Moms and Guns Blog,"[8] and any gun range or gun store has the answer to that question (though the answers differ from source to source). Epidemiologic and socio-medical scholars also try to answer this question, studying risk factors for gun tragedy,[9] which storage practices reduce accidental injury,[10] and how best to communicate those practices to gun-owning families.[11]

Fundamentally, the good moms with guns interviewed for this research fall into none of these camps, although they often make arguments that originate from (or are distilled in) the pro-gun ownership sources. Rather, the good moms with guns expressed what I identify as a "relational right" to their guns. Guns—whether they want them in their house or not—represent important, primarily male relationships in their lives. The decision to have guns and to use guns comes from a desire to signify the importance of relationships with husbands, fathers, and "creepy dudes." Unlike the husbands and fathers these women spoke about, the "creepy dudes" were imagined. None of the women whom I interviewed reported encountering a threatening stranger, but that narrative is pervasive.

The gun (or guns) that were the subject of these interviews are symbols of family togetherness, the physical embodiment of a compromise a wife makes for her husband, an "equalizer" to fend off potential threats, a sentimental object that illustrates happy times, and even all these things over the course of our conversations. At the same time, guns are recognized by these moms as the dangerous material objects they are and that, when not in use, must be stored extremely carefully to protect their children from accidental harm. The moms I interviewed went to great lengths to show me their safes, demonstrate trigger locks, and explain where the bullets were kept with pride. All these moms have thought about and made the decisions that will most probably keep their family safe. But fundamentally, the decision to have a gun is largely made with considerable thought about and often pressure from the men in these women's lives.

This essay uses participant observation at gun ranges and gun shows along with in-depth interviews with mothers of young children who have guns in their home for self-defense, sport, and sentimentality to examine the intersection between identity, objects, and rights. The connection between identity and rights has been a staple of socio-legal studies. Gun ownership (and the more abstract "right to self-defense") is a set of linked rights that provides important unique insights into the connection between identities and rights because guns are material objects. Sociological and socio-legal research often neglects the material,[12] which makes guns an interesting case study of rights. It is a rare situation in which the right is made material, touchable, ownable. Following and centering objects in socio-legal analysis can provide important new insight into law and society. After all, the guns we study exist in the world, impact the world through injury and death, and must be kept safely from the world.

This essay seeks to take seriously guns as material objects (indeed, all the women I interviewed showed us their weapons, handled weapons with us, and sometimes even shot with us). But the guns also are signifiers of complex rights and identity claims. In this way the mothers' relationships to their guns is "relational." Their understanding of and decision to exercise their right to own a gun is made within and in consideration of the relationships in which they are situated as women, wives, mothers, and daughters. The mothers interviewed indicate caution about safety matters. But gun ownership is an important part of the relationships these women have with the real and imaginary men in their lives.

The Second Amendment according to Courts, Scholars, and Ordinary Citizens

Like other areas of protected constitutional rights, the right to "bear arms" is the subject of much debate in this country, and restrictions on gun ownership are hotly contested. Does the Second Amendment confer an individual the right to bear arms? How do scholars understand guns: as inherently dangerous weapons, as cultural objects imbued with identity and meaning, or something else? And how do ordinary citizens think of their guns? Are they signifiers of natural rights? Objects that symbolize security and family bonding? Or just tools for practical use?

Prior to 2008, America's Second Amendment right to bear arms was not jurisprudentially understood to be an individual right. The plain language of the Second Amendment and two centuries of judicial interpretation conceived of the right to bear arms as a right of states (to form militias). In this new era of the individualized right to bear arms, how do ordinary citizens think about that right? How do they understand attempts to limit that right?

For courts, guns are less "objects" as they are signifiers of embodied rights. Until very recently, the jurisprudential history of the Second Amendment did not establish an individualized right to guns. But in *District of Columbia v. Heller*,[13] the Supreme Court shifted interpretation to declare that the right to almost any type of gun is an individual right that can be infringed under only very limited circumstances.[14] *McDonald v. Chicago* extended that interpretation of the right to gun ownership to the states.[15] Hailed by "new originalists," the NRA, and the political right, this kind of absolutism about individualized rights is not shared by all (or even most) Americans. Indeed, all the women interviewed for this research understood that right to be one that could be abridged in certain circumstances. In both cases the Supreme Court leaves largely undetermined the question of under what circumstances that right may be abridged:

> It is important to keep in mind that Heller, while striking down a law that prohibited the possession of handguns in the home, recognized that the right to keep and bear arms is not "a right to keep and carry any weapon whatsoever in any manner whatsoever and for whatever purpose." We made it clear in Heller that our holding did not cast doubt on such longstanding regulatory measures as "prohibitions on the possession of firearms by felons and the mentally ill," "laws forbidding the carrying of firearms in sensitive places such as schools and government buildings, or laws imposing conditions and qualifications on the commercial sale of arms." We repeat those assurances here. Despite municipal respondents' doomsday proclamations, incorporation does not imperil every law regulating firearms.[16]

For the federal courts, the right to own a gun is an individual right lawfully abridged in narrow circumstances. Conditions of the people (mentally ill, felons), locations (courthouses, schools, places where alcohol is served), and perhaps aspects of the weapon (fully automatic, semiautomatic) allow for lawful infringement of the right, but the materiality of guns is not typically addressed by the courts. The caliber of the bullet, the strength it takes to pull a trigger or rack a bullet into the chamber, whether it fits comfortably in the palm of a five-year-old's hand, and how it is stored are largely irrelevant factors in the face of the "right" conferred by the Second Amendment. State and local legislators understand that regulations on guns (or even storage practices like requiring child locks) are not likely to pass constitutional muster. For courts, guns are protected by a sweeping interpretation of an abstract right. That abstract right can be constrained in some ways, but on a very limited basis.

Empirical scholarship about guns treats weapons far more materially even though guns themselves also embody abstract concepts like identity. Whereas for courts, the physical weapon is an embodied right, empirical scholarship examines the ways in which the physical object is understood as relating to the identity of its owner. For example, in *Citizen-Protectors*, Jennifer Carlson documents the complex ways in which gun ownership and gun-carrying are not just signals of masculinity but also of citizenship.[17] Carrying a weapon in an area of urban decline where the police are not able to adequately monitor, deter, respond to, and solve crimes means that ordinary citizens must rise to the task. Rather than a vigilante mentality, these individuals view themselves as patriots and see their guns as wholly connected to their participation in governing crime. The gun is an object to be admired, a tool to be used, but most importantly a signal to everyone that the bearer is relationally connected to those around him. His gun is a marker of who he is.

In addition to being signifiers of civic participation for these men, women gun owners have been shown to think of their gun as something that allows them to be a "not-victim."[18] The gun itself is considered an equalizer that compensates for the innate vulnerability that comes with being female.[19] Guns also are understood by scholars as evidence of the (often distorted) views of ordinary people about their risk of being the target of violent crime.[20]

Although the NRA and Well Armed Woman aggressively promote guns to women as a way to proclaim their "independence," "security," and "equality," less researched is the identity of "mother" and guns. Protection and security traditionally have been considered masculine roles in the family, but part of being a "good mother" includes the mythology of a "mama bear." A mama bear is unable or unwilling to suppress her protective instinct and willing to engage in even violent defense of her children. In this way, mothers may be seen as the most legitimate of women gun owners, and acceptance of women with guns is on the rise in the United States.[21]

I use Wendy Griswold's framework for the study of culture elaborated in her now classic article "A Methodological Framework for the Sociology of Culture." She proposes an analysis of culture (and, by extension, cultural objects), which urges analysis of "(1) the intentions of creative agents, (2) the reception of cultural objects over time and space, (3) the comprehension of cultural objects in terms of intrinsic and heuristic genres, and (4) the explanation of the characteristics of objects with reference to the social and cultural experience of social groups and categories."[22] This framework provides for a better understanding of the weapon itself and how it comes to be imbued with social meaning.

What, if any, restrictions do moms with guns think are reasonable? Do attitudes change when they are considering restrictions that impact them more directly? How does their history with guns matter in their attitudes about the legal regulation of weapons? How do these attitudes change when we are talking about protecting her children versus how other people should be permitted to protect their children? What is the role of law and rights versus identity in how moms with guns express themselves as gun owners?

Methodology

To answer these questions, I began by reading gun websites and blogs targeted at women and mothers,[23] obtained my Firearm Owner Identification Card (FOID), and attended multiple gun shows in the Midwest. At these gun shows, my research assistant and I took detailed field notes and inquired about gun ownership with dozens of vendors at the shows. I also located and shot weapons at two firing ranges in different states. Using contacts from friends and acquaintances from the gun shows and ranges, I became most interested in gun-owning mothers with small children in the home. I became aware of a mother's group in a southern state that included many women who had weapons in the home. I characterize these mothers as "good" mothers because the ethic of the mother's group is careful consideration of mothering responsibilities, including the kinds of issues that middle-class women have the financial and temporal luxuries of considering, such as consumer reports about the safety of car seats, making (or buying) solely organic baby food, and the importance of nursing over formula. These moms refer to themselves and to one another as "granola" moms, meaning they are generally socially liberal on issues such as the environment, women's rights (including reproductive choice), public education, and the like.

I interviewed eight volunteers from the "granola moms" group in their homes in order to observe the storage practices with their guns and to photograph them with their weapons. This often meant meeting their children and partners (all but one were married). I then interviewed two other moms who fit the profile of a granola mom but who were not in that moms' group. My analysis is based on the interview transcripts and my field notes from gun shows and firing ranges.

Types of Moms

My research reveals three categories of "good moms with guns." This section of the paper elaborates that three-fold typology. Although each participant is categorized, the groups are porous, temporal, and unstable for the individual. In other words, when pushed by me (the interviewer), their friends, spouses, or even news accounts, these mothers can slide into other categories. Even when their rights consciousness changes, however, the gun in their home remains.

The three types of good moms with guns that I explore in this essay are: (1) the committed; (2) the compromising; and (3) the converted. *Committed moms with guns* had a commitment to and history of gun ownership prior to marriage and family. Their belief in guns—be it for protection (self-defense), entertainment (target shooting), or hunting—predates their current partner (if they have one) and the birth of their children. *Compromising moms with guns* are those who did not have a history with guns but married a man who had guns or wanted guns. For reasons that they explain, they decided to compromise with their husbands about gun ownership. This category is the only one presented with an active verb because these mothers remain in the process of negotiation with their husbands about all sorts of issues such as storage practices, whether the child should know how to access the gun, or even know the gun is in the home at all, and so on. *Converted moms with guns* are those who had no history of guns prior to marriage or children, who have a gun, and who now are enthusiastic about having guns in the home.

For each type of good mom with guns, I analyze the object of the gun itself, how they view it within the primary relationships around which the gun's meaning is constructed, and along four dimensions of the interview: (1) history of the first gun; (2) rationale for gun ownership as a mom; (3) storage practices; and (4) beliefs about teaching their children about guns.

Committed Moms: "I've Been Shooting with My Dad Since I Was Five"

Committed moms with guns are those who have always been around guns and have a sentimental attachment to particular guns or guns in general as signifiers of important early relationships with men in their lives (e.g., fathers or grandfathers). Committed moms never really questioned whether they would have guns in the home, so neither marriage nor becoming a mother centrally affected their gun ownership decision. Although they are comfortable with guns in the home, these moms are not complacent about gun safety. And, despite strong commitment to having guns, committed moms view their right to have a gun as one that could be infringed by the state. They are not Second Amendment absolutists.

Committed moms with guns that we interviewed and photographed did not have far to travel from their upbringing to the (mental) place where they are a mom with a gun because they grew up around guns. In some ways, these women might be the most predictable moms with guns and the easiest to understand. They grew up with guns, nothing terrible happened, they enjoyed guns, and often guns were the source of quality time with male relatives. After receiving a gun as a gift, keeping one from childhood, or buying them with their husbands, they now have both guns and young children in the home.

Tina is the prototypical committed mom with a gun. I interviewed her in a modestly sized trailer home in rural North Carolina. On a relatively large piece of wooded property, eight cars were parked near Tina's home, ranging from clearly inoperable old American cars to a shiny new Smartcar. The home was inaccessible through the front door due to a locked fence and detritus of toys Tina's children have outgrown or might use in the warmer months. Kiddie pools, plastic slides, cars, and push toys mingled with broken household items, yard tools, and planter pots that saw their last fresh blooms many years ago. Passing by the smoking area with large coffee cans full of cigarette butts, my research assistant and photographer (at six foot two inches tall) had to duck through the doorway and into the kitchen because of pots, pans, and utensils overloading shelves and hanging hooks in the ceiling. We stepped over newspapers and empty food containers, greeted Tina's six-year-old nephew who remained present throughout the interview, met Tina's parents, and settled into her living room. There we sat on a couch next to an imposing steel safe approximately seven feet tall, three feet wide, and five feet deep while Tina's toddler daughter slept in the room nearby. A safe like this retails for several thousand dollars.

I began by asking Tina to tell me how she came to have her first gun, and while she differentiated between pistols and long guns, her story of personal gun ownership began at age twelve:

TINA: I did not get my first *pistol* until I married my husband or just
    before, actually, so I was twenty-three. Long guns, I've had since I was
    12. . . . My grandfather had guns. My parents had one shotgun and
    that was it. . . . I got involved in a shooting team when I was in pre-
    teen years and that's how I got involved into owning firearms.
LBN: So would you say you primarily have them for safety or for shooting
    for sport or hunting?
TINA: All three . . . [laughter] . . . That's why I have so many different
    types. I do have certain ones that are set up for nothing but sport. . . .
    My husband has certain ones that are set up for hunting and then we
    have certain pistols that are for safety and concealed carry.

Tina does have "many different types" of guns. So many, in fact, that she is unsure how many guns she has in the home. Most (but not all) are stored in her safe. When I asked how many guns were in the house, she pondered:

TINA: I think collectively . . . [mentally calculating], well, this is a 64 gun
    safe, and it probably has 50 firearms in it . . . or very close to it. We
    have so many . . . It's the firearms that I use to shoot in competition
    with, and then it's the firearms my husband used shooting compe-
    tition with. He's inherited a few guns here and there from family
    members. We've purchased a few together. We have rifles, we have
    shotguns, which are used for different things.

Tina's relationship to at least some of her guns is one of pride and sen-timent because the guns embody personal and relational meaning. When I asked which gun is the most special to her, she said:

TINA: The one that I built when I was 17. I bought an off-the-shelf Ruger
    10/22 and stripped it down. The only part of that that I actually used
    was the action. I put a custom barrel, custom stock, custom sites on
    it. . . . I didn't actually build the pieces, I bought them all from distrib-
    utors and vendors.
LBN: So would you say that gun has a certain monetary value? Whatever
    it is in the world?

Figure 6.2. Tina's safe; photo courtesy Zach Sorensen-Nielsen Photography.

TINA: Yes.

LBN: Would you sell it for that much money?

TINA: No, I would never sell it. . . . I shot several competitions with it. I never actually won any awards with that particular one, but it has a lot more meaning to me than any of the rest of them. The rest of them are all pretty much stock, off the shelf firearms that I've not altered.

Figure 6.3. Tina's Ruger; photo courtesy Zach Sorensen-Nielsen Photography.

Tina brought out her customized Ruger (figure 3) and told us in depth exactly how she constructed the brightly colored wood grain. The sentimentality Tina has for this gun is more than simply that it is her own craftwork (though that is certainly part of it). It is not the gun she has been the most successful with, but it is the one she values the most highly because it represents a time in her life when she was accomplishing something difficult. In that sense, the value of this gun is tied up with memories of her pre-teen years, the fun of the competition, her father's approval, and her own work.

Tina's father was in the living room during our interview and when Tina described her competitive shooting as a teenager, he beamed. Later, when Tina spoke about hunting (which her father and husband do together), Tina's father chuckled when Tina confessed that she is "too talkative" to be a good hunting partner. When I asked her about the tradeoff between entertainment and safety (both for herself as a child and her own children now), Tina said:

TINA: We just enjoy them. . . . It's something that we can do with family. . . . It's a sport that even children who don't necessarily do main-
stream sports can excel at. So it's just a common point of interest for
us. And safety is just secondary to that.

It is not just the Ruger and the memories of childhood competition with
her father that shape how Tina relates to guns. As she told me at the beginning of the interview, she did not shoot pistols until she met her husband.
After we held, admired, and talked about the importance of the Ruger,
Tina told us she did have another gun that was particularly special to her:

TINA: Well, [there are] two others. I have an over/under shotgun that my
husband got me for my birthday, the second year we were together.
And I have . . . the first pistol I ever owned [which] actually was a gift
from my husband as well. So those three all hold more sentimental
value than they do actual monetary value, and regardless of [the] situation, I would never sell them.

Figure 6.4. Tina's pistol; photo courtesy Zach Sorensen-Nielsen Photography.

Tina is passionately committed to enjoying the guns she has and remains
committed to the idea of gun ownership and competition. Some of her guns
are signifiers of deeply personal periods of her life: her preteen years, her
early courtship with her husband, and wedding anniversary, and yet when

I asked her how, if at all, her life would change if she were not allowed to own guns, she told me:

TINA: We've never been in a situation where we've had to use it, in a defense situation. I would be quite sad that we couldn't own them because it is such a big part of our pastime and free-time enjoyment. But I don't know that it would necessarily *change* anything at that particular time. . . . I mean, yes, we'd be upset about it and we would be probably involved in protesting or whatever may happen, but as far as our everyday life, it wouldn't change anything.

Since Tina regularly carries a concealed weapon and her husband is part of the "prepper" movement (a movement of survivalists preparing—or "prepping"—for the end of civil society due to a natural disaster or widespread civil unrest), this interested me, and I pressed further to be clear about pistols versus long guns:

LBN: But do you think your life would change if you weren't allowed to conceal carry?
TINA: Not in the here and now. I think it would definitely change if I were ever presented with a situation that I had to use it, yes, but as far as on the day-to-day, probably not. And the statistic is 99% of people who carry firearms never are encountered with a situation they have to use it. So statistically speaking, I probably never will, but having the ability to, if the need arises, is what is important to me.

Being committed to gun ownership meant that Tina was not reluctant to talk about her guns and how they are stored in front of her young nephew, who lives with her part of the time. Indeed, her daughter, not yet three years old, already has a rifle of her own, has been to the gun range, and her first lessons with a BB gun are not far in the future:

TINA: Our daughter is now two-and-a-half-ish, and we've been shooting. . . . [It's] getting close to the age that we will start introducing the smaller BB guns and smaller caliber like .22s and things. We are already starting to try and train her on safety. She realizes, "Okay, that's something I shouldn't touch." If she sees it, and she knows to come and get us if she sees something. We're trying to make sure that both of our kids are raised very much with the safety aspect in mind above anything else. . . . *[S]he is well beyond her years,* as far as demeanor and responsibility is concerned. . . . So I feel like by the time she's probably four or five, we'll start introducing things to her. . . . *We have read several studies on parenting with guns and things and, statistically speaking, again, that's one of those things, the more the child knows, the better off you are.* It's the kids who are hidden from the firearms, who find them, who, out of curiosity, with being a kid, has a lot of issues with having incidents happen. (emphasis mine)

Tina cited her daughter being "well beyond her years" as a reason to introduce her to guns early. She also invokes "statistics" and "studies" that support her decision to have guns in the homes. When pressed, she does not remember where she learned these statistics, but she has a master's degree in statistics, and I have no doubt she reads about gun safety and analyzes the research carefully.

Like Tina, Samantha has been committed to gun ownership since she was very young, her guns have important sentimental value, and she anticipates teaching her children about guns very early. Samantha estimates that she and her husband own about twenty guns. Interviewed via Skype from the "blue" state of Washington (as she reminded me again and again), Samantha understood herself to be an outlier in her general community but her commitment to guns is—like Tina's—relational. When I asked Samantha about her first gun, she said:

SAMANTHA: My first firearm was a gift from my dad from graduating from college. Since then I inherited his collection when he passed away. And my husband also has his own that he owned before we got together, and since then we have a few that have been either purchases or gifts over the years. . . . *I've been shooting with my dad since I was five.*

LBN: Really?

SAMANTHA: Yeah, [but the first firearm I owned] was a graduation gift. I was kind of heading out on my own, moving across the country; starting a new life. He wanted actually to get me a very small Derringer type gun, and I talked him into getting more of a functional, something you could use for target shooting and so forth, that was still small but not huge. But because it was my gift for graduating from college and because it's from my dad and he's no longer alive, and it has critical meaning for me than just something you were to see on a shelf at a store.

LBN: And it sounds like probably all of the guns that he's given you feel
  like that or there more and less ones? Or that . . . Were his . . .
SAMANTHA: Well, it's his collection. He worked really hard on collecting
  and curating with historical value and so forth. I did not take all of his
  collection. It was more than I knew I could safely house, but all the
  ones that I did take upon his death were special to me. Usually things
  we had gone out and shot together when I was growing up that I remember sharing the experience with him.

Samantha talks about "shooting with her dad when she was five," recognizing that his collection was "curated" and had "historical value." These
objects have become symbols or mementos of their shared experiences and
now that he has died, she would not begin to think of selling them. Like
Tina (and other committed gun moms), Samantha is vigilant about how
she stores her guns given that she has a three-year-old son.

SAMANTHA: Ninety-five percent of the time they are stored in the safe.
  They are unloaded, checked by both myself and my husband, stored
  separate from ammunition. The safe is locked, my husband and
  myself have the combination, that's it. . . . The ammunition is stored
  separately, locked up separately in a separate location. When we get
  them out, we hunt, so we do get them out once a year every year and
  go hunting. We have carrying cases that we put them in. When we are
  hunting we always lock them in a vehicle. Generally one of us will stay
  with the vehicle as well. When we're hunting we're typically out in the
  middle of nowhere around no other people so we aren't quite as careful as we would be when we head back into town. We're still careful,
  but we could walk away and come back, there's nobody else literally
  within miles of us. When we get home we again double check, secure,
  clean them, make sure that everything is unloaded, and relock them
  back in the safe.

Gun and ammunition storage practices are very important to Samantha,
and her narrative expresses not just a recognition of how to keep them in
the house, but also careful consideration of what to do when they are out of
the house with the guns, how the context matters, and all the other layers
of security that exist. Given that she is very comfortable and committed to
gun ownership, I wondered if she thought of the guns as being something
that would help keep her safe. When I asked her about the possibility of
using the gun against someone, she said:

SAMANTHA: I don't think it [my gun] would be much good to me in a self-defense way, because the gun and the ammo are separate and frankly *by the time I could open the safe, get out the gun, and load it, I probably would have crawled under the bed and called 911.* I'm sure my husband differs in opinion with me here but to me it's not currently a home self-defense measure because it's not quickly accessible to me. Growing up in my home, we did have two loaded pistols that were accessible. All of us in our family knew where they were and we knew to stay away from them unless it was an actual emergency. But for myself currently, I'm not comfortable doing that with young kids in the house.

Although Tina and Samantha are committed gun owners whose weapons are very sentimental because of the relationships and moments they represent, both endeavor to be (and believe they are) incredibly careful about gun storage and safety. And yet, they differ in one fundamental respect: Tina keeps a loaded unsecured pistol in her home and Samantha would not think of doing that. Although Samantha grew up in a home with a loaded and available weapon for home defense, she does not keep one like that to protect her child's safety. Tina, on the other hand, told me that all the guns were unloaded (though a bullet fell from the chamber of a pistol she was showing me) and secured. She said:

TINA: We have safes for our everyday carry pistols. Both my husband and I have a safe on either side of the bed that we keep those locked up in. We don't have any other firearm. . . . *Well, we have one other firearm in the house, but it is well out of reach and is inaccessible to the children, that is not in the safe.* . . . It's a revolver and we keep it in our kitchen actually. So, if we were to have an intruder or something like that, it's easy access, at that point.

Whereas having children made Samantha a more locked-down gun owner (no unsecured guns in the home ever despite having one in her home growing up and as a young woman), having children made Tina believe that to be a good mom, she needed more weapons and more access to them in the moment:

TINA: Since having kids, I do think I'm a lot more diligent about being aware in certain situations and *I certainly carry a lot more frequently than I did before kids.* . . . But it does make you think more because you have one or more people that you're responsible for, in addition to yourself, at that point.

Tina talked about teaching her daughter to shoot early and proudly displayed her daughter's first rifle. Rummaging through the fifty or so guns in her sixty-four-gun safe, Tina said:

TINA: We actually do have . . . where is it? We have bought our daughter her first rifle. Here it is. . . . She kind of got it as a Christmas present so she may not remember it necessarily . . .
LBN: So, this is not a BB gun?
TINA: No. This is an actual . . . it's a single shot 22 long rifle. So the only way it can be loaded is one at a time here, there is no magazine for it. And just a simple bolt action, so . . .

Figure 6.5. Tina's 2.5-year-old daughter's .22 caliber rifle; photo courtesy Zach Sorensen-Nielsen Photography.

Although they may disagree on which practices maximize safety for their family, committed moms with guns have a history of gun ownership, sentimentality toward the objects as representative of important life stages and relationships, and plans to teach their children about guns relatively early. Tina is a rural Republican with a prepper husband and Samantha is a city-dwelling Democrat in a neighborhood with a moderate level of crime.

Compromising Moms: "You Are Marrying the Guns Too"
Unlike "committed" moms with guns, compromising moms with guns did not grow up around guns or shooting guns, but they married a man

who had, wanted, and/or acquired guns. These moms were skeptical about having guns in the home at all, and that skepticism only became greater when they had children. These moms consider their gun ownership a "compromise" with their husbands. All the compromising moms with guns described their current arrangement as a "compromise." They are not thrilled to have a gun in the home with their young children, but they have conceded to that and use their concession to extract safety measures from their husband. Compromising good moms with guns are involved in ongoing negotiations. New kinds of guns, new technology for safety, and their children's development all go in to the continual process of compromise. Of course, since they have conceded to the weapon being in the home, compromising moms have, to some extent, been "converted" (the next category), but the compromisers have a more robust skepticism and indicate that this is an on-going discussion/fight/tension in the marriage.

The compromising good moms with guns include Denise, a thirty-five-year-old suburban Republican; Harriet, a thirty-year-old suburban social worker who conducts home visits on behalf of the state and identifies as a liberal Democrat; and Linda, a thirty-two-year-old stay-at-home mom who identifies as Libertarian and socially liberal. Linda and Harriet are the more reluctant compromisers, whereas Denise is closer to a "convert."

Denise's home in the suburbs of the southern city in which I conducted the research boasts a manicured lawn complete with blooming flowers in pots and along the walk approaching double oak front doors. Denise's mother opened the door, greeted us, and went to find Denise. We waited in the cathedral-ceilinged entry way and then Denise ushered us into her front sitting room. It was formally appointed, but the family room off the kitchen was visible and strewn with kids' toys. Aside from the toys, the home was immaculate; the baby was napping (Denise was only a few weeks post-partum), and her older children (a toddler and a pre-schooler) played happily with their grandmother. The family is solidly upper-middle class, and Denise sported stylish leggings, gold jewelry, professional highlights, and manicured nails.

Denise told me how she got her first gun:

DENISE: Yeah. I didn't grow up shooting guns . . . it was never part of my life. . . . It wasn't until I went off to college that my dad actually started getting really interested in guns for shooting, and also for protection, and he got my mom involved. And then . . . the next logical step was indoctrinating his daughters. I have a sister as well. So we all started getting really interested in looking at guns, and went to a gun range.

My parents got their concealed carry permit, and with their encouragement, I did the same along with my husband. I think it was more of just peer pressure, or family pressure. But I found that I really enjoyed it. It's just a lot of fun to shoot, and it felt powerful like I wasn't weak anymore.

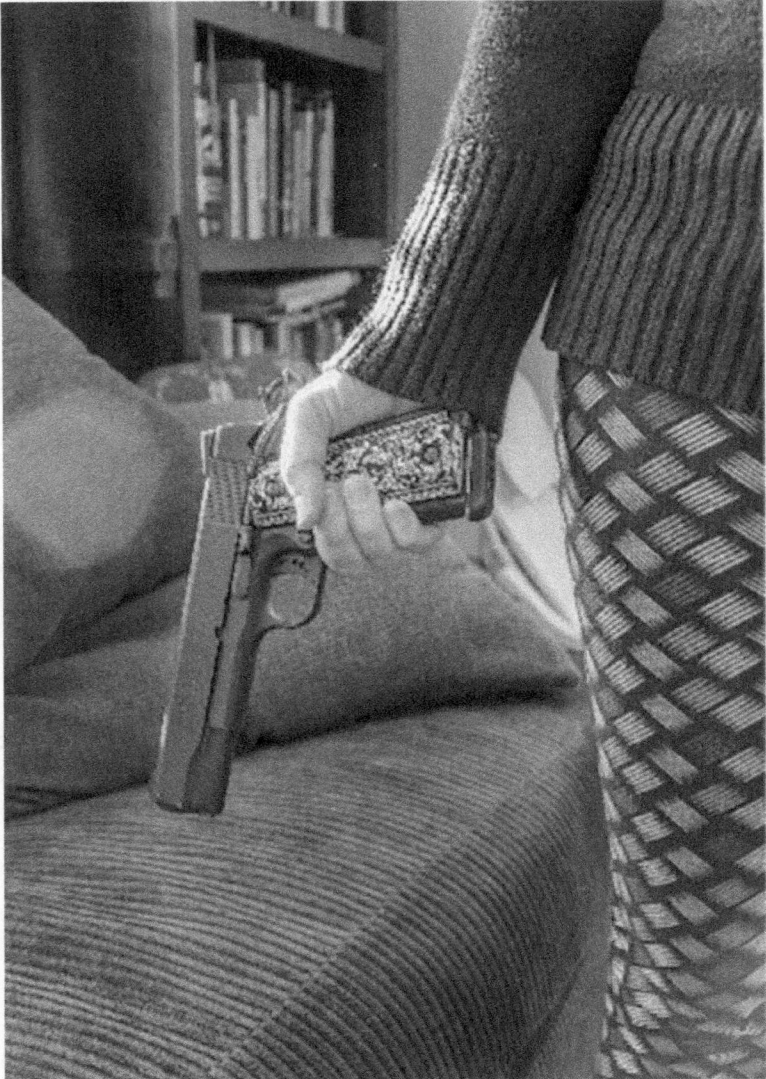

Figure 6.6. Denise's pistol; photo courtesy Zach Sorensen-Nielsen Photography.

Denise enjoys the gun itself and the feeling it gives her. Even though Denise sounds like she is convinced about owning a gun, she has her reservations about safety:

DENISE: We do have the safes . . . [and] a gun lock, for when we're trav-
    eling. Especially with the kids because you know, no boundaries. [The
    lock] threads through the barrel and then out where the chamber is
    so that . . . you can't put anything in, you can't close it, you can't shoot
    it, and it's got a lock on it. Actually, I got one of those from the [Town]
    Police department at a festival. They had a booth that they had all these
    locks for free.
LBN: Oh, cool.
DENISE: That was pretty cool. As far as, so, the gun that I keep at my
    desk I do keep loaded but without a chamber in the round. Or a round
    in the chamber. And I keep the safety on.

Denise wanted to perform "good mothering" to me and did so by explaining all the security and locks and safes her family has (including one safe
in her office so that she can move her gun from the safe by her bed when
she is asleep to the safe by her desk during the day). Some of Denise's
rationales were the same that vendors at gun shows used to address me (a
forty-six-year-old white woman) about ensuring gun safety around children.
Unlike the committed gun owners who plan to teach their children about
guns very young, Denise thinks a safer strategy is to keep the safe itself—as
well as the gun—a secret from the children. She said:

DENISE: I don't even think my kids know that there's a safe there 'cause
    I have it hidden. But if they found it they would still have to get in
    and then if they got in they would still have to figure. . . . They're not
    gonna be strong enough to ever *rack the slide* 'cause it's really, it's hard
    for me to do it and I'm a grown person so I feel like that helps a lot.
    My concealed carry . . . it's really loud. My concealed carry gun doesn't
    have a safety but it's got a really *long trigger pull* so again they would
    have to really be messing with it to get that to fire. 'Cause I have a hard
    time with it.

"Racking the slide" refers to the process in handguns (not pistols) of
propelling the bullet into the chamber before it can fire. It is very difficult
but only needs to be done once in many guns (including the Ruger Seven

9-mm handgun I have been working with) and will then fire everything in the clip (up to twenty bullets). Vendors at gun shows instruct that having a racking gun or a pistol with a long trigger pull is the best idea for safety. Denise has heard the same (although neither she nor I had heard the recommendation from the moms and guns blog that it should also be double-action with a thumb safety). Dealers tell women that their children will not be strong enough to rack the slide, but with a rush of adrenaline (in the event you need to defend yourself), you will have all the strength you need. Similarly, many gun dealers recommend against trigger locks for the same (adrenaline) reason. In "the moment" you won't be able to open the safe or dial a trigger lock.

Denise also is reticent about the safety of carrying a gun day-to-day even though she has a concealed carry permit. Her reluctance is due to "little grabby hands."

DENISE: The thing that really did it for me was reading about, I think it was a two year old was playing in his mom's purse and found her gun and it was loaded, safety off, and he was playing with it and he shot his mom and killed her. And I'm like, "That could have easily been me," because my children have no boundaries.

Denise is worried about having guns in the house with her children and admits that she has them due mainly to "peer pressure" from her husband and father, but when pressed she demonstrates a lot of lay-knowledge about what will make her a safe gun owner.

Harriet, the thirty-year-old social worker from North Carolina, is probably the most reluctant compromiser in the sample. When I asked her to tell me about her first gun, she said:

HARRIET: So it's actually co-owned by my husband and I. . . . It's *our* gun. . . . It's my first gun.
LBN: And was it his first gun as well?
HARRIET: No [emphatically].
LBN: Does he have a long history of guns?
HARRIET: Yeah, yes he does. And I do not. . . . We have kind of an interesting story with guns. My parents are both heart and lung specialists in hospitals. And my mom works mainly in the emergency room . . . [so] she's really only seen guns used for violence. My parents had NO interest in ever owning guns. I was always raised with [the idea], "guns are bad."

Despite her reluctance to own a gun, her and her parents' left-leaning political tendencies, and her parents' experience with the actual harms guns can cause, Harriet and her parents moved to North Carolina, where she fell in love with a gun owner. Harriet loved him very much but as the time to combine households came, she said she told her husband:

HARRIET: "So you know, when we get married, your guns aren't going to be allowed to be in our house." And he was like, "No, no. *You are marrying the guns too and they aren't going to not be in our house."* And I said, "Uhh . . . I don't know how I feel about that." And he said, "You need some new education around that because they can be used for good. And they can be very safe. And they are not going to hurt you." So we did a concealed carry class together and I went out to a friend's farm and I learned to shoot . . . but it is not something I ever thought I would do.

Harriet's story of becoming a compromising gun owner is interesting because she came from a family with real-world experience about the harms of guns and she remains very skeptical about the guns. She never plans to touch it (unlike Denise, who goes target shooting with her husband from time to time). Harriet is extremely reluctant to have guns and she takes a lot of care to secure most of the guns in a biometric safe. Except one:

HARRIET: And then there is a rifle. . . . My husband has said that if some-one were to break into our house he would not use a handgun; he would use a rifle. Hopefully not with the intention to shoot someone but with the intention to scare the hell out of someone. So that's in our closet. It's on these hooks. And like, you can't see it unless you know it's there. So like if the wall is right here, and you are looking into the closet, it's like behind you. So you have to go into the closet and then reach up behind you. So you couldn't see it.

Harriet's compromise might not seem like much of a compromise at all. Rather, her husband got his way and got his way on everything, including an unsecured weapon in the home. Not only are there guns in Harriet's home, there is an unsecured, loaded rifle in her home. Harriet, a social worker with a master's degree, knows how dangerous this is and went to great lengths to convince me (maybe herself) that this was reasonable. Her explanation of where the loaded unsecured rifle is kept is much longer than the above excerpt and included her standing up in the coffee shop where we spoke to pantomime what would be required to access it, but Harriet still is not comfortable with this arrangement. Discussing the loaded rifle in the home, she admitted:

HARRIET: Yeah [chuckles]. There have been a lot of heated conversations about this. Because I am uncomfortable having an unlocked gun. Like, a gun not in a safe. But that was our compromise. It needs to be out of the reach of kids. The kids can't know where it is. It has to be where they can't see it or find it even if they go looking.

Compromising good moms with guns, like committed moms, see their guns as important in their primary relationship with their husbands. And yet, "compromise" may be a misnomer. The way these moms spoke about it, the husbands little more than overruled their partners. And yet, in that concession, the wives retained some power to make certain demands about gun safety in the home.

Compromising moms with guns are engaged in ongoing processes of negotiation with their husbands. They recount discussions of having a weapon in the home, having ammunition, how to store it. But some of the mothers had not yet reached agreement on other difficult matters going forward. For example, I asked Harriet about when they would teach their oldest child about guns in general; she said her husband would like to

start teaching the oldest young. And I don't know how comfortable I am with that. So I don't know. This is all pretty new to me, to be honest with you. But he would start young. He wants them to be proficient and know how to use them.

Sensing her skepticism, I asked why he thinks it is important for a child to learn about guns at an early age. She said:

HARRIET: He [my husband] always tells me this story of this like 8-year-old girl whose father had taught her how to use a shotgun. And, I mean this was in the news. This was a couple years ago. This like 8-year-old girl—I don't remember where she lived—but it was a more rural area and her dad had taught her how to use a shotgun. And these two men broke into her house when her dad was not at home. And he had explained what guns were for and, "If anyone ever comes in this house. You get a gun. And you pull it on them. And you tell them you are going to shoot them. And you shoot them." And so apparently she was standing at the top of the stairs and she said, "Do not come up these stairs or I will shoot you." And they started to come up the stairs. And she shot them both. And he tells me that story and I am like, "Yeah." But at the same time, I don't think I am going to be leaving my eight-year-old at home alone. But there are stories like that and he has so many stories like that because he follows that stuff. I'm like, "Yeah. There is merit to knowing how to use these things safely."

Interviewing Harriet, I had the sense that I was watching her reanalyze all the compromises she had made and will be making in the future as her children get older. Her casual demeanor was occasionally peppered with indecision and frustration followed by resignation. She was almost using me as a sounding board for her beliefs and ideas about gun ownership. She was a feminist, working professional mother who does not seem altogether content with the "compromise" she has made.

Linda, the last compromising mom with a gun, is perhaps the most reticent of the compromisers. When I asked her what kind of gun she owned, she said:

LINDA: We have a revolver in our home. It was one that my husband inherited from his grandfather and after many discussions, it is now in our home. . . . He had brought it up when we were in an apartment and I told him I absolutely was not comfortable. Once we had our home, he asked again, and it took me some convincing because I personally don't feel like there's any need for it. *But you make compromises in marriage, so . . .*

Like Denise and Harriet, Linda did not grow up in a family with guns. After she moved away to college, however, her mother and father became first-time gun owners, which meant that they could go on family outings to the gun range. Interestingly, Linda described a similar relational dynamic between her parents as would later take place between her with her spouse:

LINDA: When I was in college, [my father] bought one, bought a handgun [for his home]. And that was a similar discussion he had with my mom. She totally disagreed and they ended up making a compromise, so it was in the house but not until much later.
LINDA: So you don't think that there's ever gonna be a situation where you would be taking this gun out?

LINDA: I never thought that it would be used for protection and that's part of why I never really wanted it in the first place. . . . And in my mind if an intruder comes into your home by the time you get the gun loaded, do everything you need to, it's too late.

LBN: Right, so that's one of my next questions: how do you store it in the home?

LINDA: It has a trigger lock and then it's in a locked case. The key for the case is in a completely different room of the house. It's up high on a shelf where it's in one of the least used rooms of the house. *I've made it very clear it will never be loaded. And at first I said absolutely no ammunition in the house. We've gotten to the point where I'm okay with having the range ammunition, because I know that the damage that that would do is very different than actual ammunition.* So, I'm okay with the blanks, that kind of thing. But I've made it very clear that there will never . . . it will never be loaded. And part of that was my insisting, and also part of it was the way that my husband views it as well. That he knows it needs to be locked and kept safe. So at that point it made it easier to compromise because I knew that he felt just as strongly about keeping it protected from anyone else or even our son when he gets bigger.

I asked all the women I spoke with whether they think they need a gun or want a gun. Linda was the only one that answered, "Neither." In other words, the compromise is about storage and usage. Owning a gun was a capitulation in the relationship with her husband.

Compromising moms with guns have a unique set of issues to balance. Their husbands are insistent and women want to maintain that relationship, obviously. And yet, they are very aware of the danger and want to keep their children safe. Every news story about a child's accidental shooting can lead these families to reanalyze the compromise about how the gun is stored in the house. Only one of the compromisers (Harriet) allows an unsecured weapon in the house and it clearly makes her very nervous. Both Harriet and Linda have no intention of ever touching the guns that they own with their husbands.

Compromising moms with guns again see the gun itself as relational. If they insisted that it not be in the home, it would do an unacceptable level of harm to their primary partner. The gun itself represents one of the most significant "compromises" they have made to stay in the relationship. And yet, their protests give them capital in the relationship to make other demands. At least that is what they think.

Converted: Bears and Creepy Dudes

The "converted" good moms with guns are women who did not imagine themselves having guns and children together in the home, but they came around to the idea and now are enthusiastic about it. Gina is a thirty-two-year-old stay-at-home mother of two young boys in a southern state who describes herself as a socially liberal, fiscally conservative Libertarian. She grew up with guns in her home but she never used them. They were stored and locked to be used only in an emergency. As an adult, Gina did not want a gun in her house. Nonetheless, she was converted and became enthusiastic about having a gun in the home. Gina's home is in a mixed suburban neighborhood outside the southern city in which I conducted the research. Her home is small and tidy. When I arrived, Gina's husband was working on their car in the driveway and greeted us with greasy hands. He invited us to open the door ourselves (so that he would not smudge it) and we were met by two enthusiastic large dogs. They were both well trained to stand down once Gina gave the OK, and the older pit bull spent the rest of the time at my feet as we sat at the kitchen table and talked about guns. One of her sons napped nearby while the other played video games. When I asked her to tell me about having guns, she said:

GINA: So I was raised with guns. My grandfather had guns. I shot at a very young age, mostly long guns, so rifles, that type thing. I was taught respect for them, so I've never had a problem having one in the household . . . until we had kids and we have two boys, and the four-year-old in particular has major impulse control and that worries me in general.

Her childhood memories of shooting with her grandfather were special, but she did not own a weapon when she got married or when they had children. About six years later in November 2016, Gina lost a bet:

GINA: [My husband had] been wanting a handgun for a while, and I essentially said, "Okay, if Trump wins, you can have one," not thinking that this would really happen. So in the middle of the night I wake up and he's watching the news and he's like, "I'm getting a gun." I was like, "No, you're not." And he was like, "No, Trump won." And I was like, "Okay."

Gina's familiarity with guns may explain why she was not too upset
when she lost the bet with her husband. In addition, Gina's husband travels
often and they both worried for her safety even before the children came
along. That worry is more intense now but they chose not to activate the
alarm system that was already installed in their relatively new home when
they bought it:

GINA: We have a pit bull . . . when we moved in this home, they were
like, "Oh, do you want to sign up for [security system] stuff?" And I
was like "No, I have a pit bull. I'm fine!" She [the dog] tore into someone's leg one day because they trespassed on our property. She's got
us. She is the best dog in the world, but at the same time, especially,
if *he [husband] might travel more and now, that it's not just me. Now, it's
everybody. Now, I'm in charge of all the little humans and the dogs to make
sure everybody's safe.*

Despite her fears, the increased responsibility of being "in charge of
all the little humans," and two large dogs, she was not concerned enough
to activate the home alarm system. Her comfort with the gun is in part
because she grew up shooting with her grandfather (like the committed
moms), but she did not stick with it and she married someone without guns.
Nonetheless, safety is enough of a concern that she has two very well trained
pit bulls. The idea of being victimized is present in her understanding of
why the gun is a good idea. An imagined (male) criminal could be waiting
when her husband is out of town and now she has to protect everyone.

Rachel is also a convert to guns. A divorced mother of two children (ages
eleven and fourteen) and an elementary school teacher, she did not grow
up with guns. Now that she has one, it makes her feel safer and she can't
imagine not having one. When I asked her about her first gun, she said:

RACHEL: I have two guns. The first gun I got was a Ruger Redhawk
Alaskan 44 caliber. And I got it because I was planning on going on
a hiking trip by myself and I have seen the movie *Wild*. So I got it for
two reasons. *The first reason was for bears, and the second reason was
for creepy dudes.* And I was planning on going back country by myself
at that point. So that's why I got that gun. Then after I had that for
probably six months, I decided I wanted a smaller gun to have for
personal protection, after I read more about concealed carry . . . just to
have on my person, especially *since I'm divorced and alone.* So I got a
9-millimeter Smith and Wesson Shield.

Figure 6.7. Rachel's pistol; photo courtesy Zach Sorensen-Nielsen Photography.

Rachel described her conversion like this:

RACHEL: I do feel like we have a right to protect ourselves. Before, I was very . . . I would fall into the left. I was very against guns. I always thought, "Well, why would you need that? There is no reason for that." And I've kind of changed. . . . First it started with the protecting myself against bears and being on my own. Then I thought, well . . . To be really honest, if there was a government revolt right now, of which I would probably be a part of, I would want to be able to protect myself in some way. And I think of how our . . . the Revolutionary War and things like . . . And I know it sounds weird and crazy, but if some such situation came up, I think as a people, we have that right, just in case. And not just in case, but it's kind of a part of what is our history. And I've been in countries where the only people that have weapons are the government, and that doesn't usually bode well for the common folk.

An ardent Bernie Sanders supporter, as she told me later in the interview, Rachel is as "left" as they come but she sees her safety as continually at risk and even is willing to break the law to carry her gun. A teacher in a classroom, Rachel carries her gun to work in her purse where she locks it in her desk. When I asked why, she said:

RACHEL: I'm not comfortable leaving it in my car because if someone
   breaks into my car and steals . . . I'm not comfortable doing that. I
   have it in my purse. My purse has a lock and . . . then I put it in a
   cabinet that also locks. I would be in big trouble and be fired if that
   were found out. Which I understand, but at the same time, I have a
   life when I leave school. . . . If someone steals it out of my car, then [I
   have] the legal responsibility that comes with that. I feel at least if it's
   close to me, I have control over it. I'm almost never out of my classroom, so it is within 30 feet of me all the time. And students don't
   go anywhere near it because they're not allowed behind my desk and
   I'm always there. . . . But I work in an area where people have been
   assaulted walking to their cars. . . . But I'll be running errands at night
   after that, where I don't go home first. And I go back and forth with,
   "It's my right to have that with me and to protect myself."

   Rachel understands the danger to her and the children if she has a
weapon in school. At another point in the interview, she talks about "code
red drills" that are practiced regularly so children know what to do in an
active shooter situation and she asks me, "If we want to be prepared for
that, shouldn't I be prepared?"
   Converted moms enjoy the feeling of security but do not talk about the
"fun" of target shooting very much. These women have serious (whether
well-founded or not is irrelevant) concerns about their personal safety and
the safety of their children that are addressed by gun ownership. Their
guns are for protection from real or imagined future "creepy dudes" that
could come at any time: on the way to work, running errands, or in the
home in the night.

Agreement

All the moms who took part in this research came to their guns in different
ways, but they all are trying to balance their needs with the needs and preferences of their husbands, children, and fathers. Their "right" to a gun is
not primarily the reason they own a gun, and they conceive of the guns as
inherently relational. Of course, since guns are designed to be used by one
person against another person, animal, or target, they are necessarily relational. And yet, there is a remarkable level of agreement among these very
different moms about the role of the state in gun regulation. Republican or
Democrat, committed, convinced, or compromising, married or divorced, all

the moms understand themselves to have a "right" to a gun, but they share a sense of responsibility to their communities and favor the regulation of guns in some ways to protect the safety of everyone. In this sense, then, the "right" to have a gun—in addition to the gun itself—is relational. All these women understand their right to a gun for safety or for fun as something that must be balanced in the interest of public safety.

All the moms with guns understood themselves to have an individual right to have a gun in the sense that *Heller* and *McDonald* articulate. Whether this language came from their own understanding of the law or was taught to them by a family member, a friend, or television, the concept of an individual right permeated the interviews. And yet, like the Supreme Court, these moms understood the right not to be impermeable. Indeed, all the moms I interviewed favored gun control regulations, although they differed on which ones.

Linda, one of the most reluctant gun owners I met with, said it like this:

LINDA: Yeah. So you have a right to own it, but can that right be taken away? Yes. *Just like your right to vote can be taken away.* Those are all things that it's part of our country and the way that we operate. I think of it as an overarching, "Yes, you have the right but that doesn't mean you have the privilege." And so they're trying to pass laws that take away all of the restrictions on people with mental illness and things like that and those are things that terrify me. That I think we have, as citizens, *the right to be protected from people as well who might use the guns for bad.*

A number of the mothers we interviewed made the comparison to other things that the United States allows but regulates, such as driving. But Linda was the only participant who compared gun ownership to something else that would be considered a constitutional right—the right to vote. Although she was ambivalent about her own gun ownership and even felony disenfranchisement, she is a proponent (like all the mothers I interviewed) of restricting gun ownership from some groups of people. Other mothers compared it to driving: something everyone has access to but that requires test-based certification of basic competency. Samantha, a committed gun owner, started by articulating very clearly that gun ownership is an individual right derived directly from the Second Amendment. She even used some of the precise language from it:

SAMANTHA: Well, the Second Amendment, in my opinion, was originated for having a militia at the state level. . . . And so, for me, that means individuals having the right to have the firearms. Whether you're part of the state militia or not, it's still part of one of your rights to participate in it shall the need arise.

When talking about gun control, she told me:

SAMANTHA: It would be very hard for them to completely get rid of the Second Amendment, but at the same time . . . they could put stricter constraints on [gun ownership]. As far as being really gung ho and, "Oh, it's one of my inalienable rights and they can't infringe upon this in any manner?" No; I don't believe that. I do think that everything that's in the Constitution and Bill of Rights and all of those founding documents can be changed.

She doesn't favor a lot of gun control, but:

SAMANTHA: I think guns with giant huge magazines or hooks that hold enormous amounts of ammunition should either be inaccessible to the general public or more . . . like they are with automatic weapons right now where you can go to a certain range and shoot them there but you can't actually own it at your home. I don't think anyone needs a full-on automatic weapon. I don't think anyone needs tanks, artillery, rocket-piercing this and that, either.

Similarly, Linda, one of the most reluctant compromising moms, strongly favors strong gun regulations. She said:

LINDA: Anything semiautomatic has no purpose. I understand guns for hunting. . . . But anything semiautomatic or that could be modified to be, it's just made to kill people and that's it, plain and simple. So there's no need to have that for protection. There's no need to have that for hunting. That's just . . . that's military, that's not for private citizens.

Similarly, all the moms thought gun ownership by felons merits strict scrutiny by the state, although they differ in how well they think the state can actually monitor such things. When I asked about felons with guns,

Linda, perhaps the most reluctant compromiser and least enthusiastic gun owner, said:

LINDA: That's one that I can never make up my mind on. . . . I do believe people deserve a second chance. However, I would say maybe looking at the origin of their felony, if it was a weapon-related felony, you maybe wanna look at that a little bit closer. . . . [For sure restrictions for the] mentally ill. I think age restriction, certainly is [OK]. . . . If you wanna go into safety even more, people who don't see well. If you can't see well enough to drive, you probably shouldn't be trusted to aim a gun at whatever you're supposed to be shooting at.

While she is extremely safety-conscious and does not really even want to own a gun, she is conflicted about the way that gun restrictions, even for felons, will reproduce inequality and prevent people who deserve one from being offered a "second chance" in society. Ironically, Tina, the most committed of the committed, said the opposite about felons:

TINA: I do favor that criminals can't have access to firearms. I do favor the regulations when it comes to purchasing firearms for the forms and the background checks and things like that. I do think that that is something that we need to keep in place. I don't think that it should be a free reign that anyone should be allowed to own a firearm. Because there is a certain amount of responsibility involved in owning a firearm.

And Gina, a strong proponent of her right to own guns, said:

GINA: I don't think that Joe Shmoe should be out and be able to get these automatic rifles that can shoot twenty rounds a second. There's no reason, even if you're hunting big game, you don't need that. You don't need that. So yeah, I'm very in favor of that. You don't need that. But limiting other handguns and the fact that you can buy a long gun without any sort of permit is worrisome. You can still shoot someone with a rifle, or a shotgun, and a handgun, but why is it harder to get a handgun than it is a rifle or shotgun? That bothers me.

All the women believe that mental illness should be a limiting criteria for owning a weapon, and yet two of the respondents have been diagnosed

with post-partum depression at least once. Both have interesting explanations for why post-partum depression should not count as mental illness:

TINA: I've had depression twice now; both of the times [it] has been
     postpartum depression. I'm not considered a risk because that's a de-
     pressive state that is not an ongoing ailment. . . . They do look at that
     and they [ask], "Is this person clinically depressed to the point of sui-
     cide?" . . . If so, then that can throw up a red flag, and you either have
     to go through an additional check of proving that, "No, I'm a responsi-
     ble firearm owner," or they can reject allowing you to have a license.

Although she excludes her type of mental illness from the kind that
should prohibit gun ownership, Tina recognizes the importance of some
gun restrictions.

TINA: I feel like there needs to be something in place that's better about
     deciding who is mentally ill enough. Because my best friend, she has
     depression, can she not have a gun now? Are we considering that
     mentally ill? My mother is bipolar, I would probably not give her a
     gun! But . . . the labels! You're labeled once and then all the sudden,
     you lose all these rights that you might not necessarily need to lose.
     An ADHD person, should they lose their rights? I wholeheartedly
     think he (gesturing toward her child) will be labeled as an ADHD kid
     and that's okay. I was too; so was my husband.

Mental illness is an interesting sticking point for good moms with guns.
They certainly think that "some people" with mental illness should not have
guns, but their gun ownership (and their friends' gun ownership) should
not be affected by a diagnosis of postpartum depression or even general
anxiety or depression.

Whether it is safety measure, bullet caliber, mental illness, or criminal
records, these moms with guns favor legal regulations of gun ownership
because they understand the responsibility of gun owners within society.
Compromises should be made as long as it does not interfere with their
gun ownership, and they believe it will make a difference in protecting
against gun accidents.

Conclusion

Similar to Carlson's subjects, whose gun ownership is tied to their identities as "citizen" and "protector," these good moms with guns teach us that while guns are objects (that must be thoughtfully, consistently, and carefully stored to protect their children), they also are symbolic of relationships with men. These relationships shape their decisions about whether and what kind of gun to have. Women frame their identity around gun ownership in traditionally feminine ways (sentimentality) and also see themselves as "protectors" (a mama bear), but another way to read their decisions about guns in the home is that they are centered on the men in women's lives. Whether it is the approval of their father, the shared familial glow of fun times with another male relative, the preference (or insistence, or coercion) of their husbands, or because of the threat of male violence, all the gun owners interviewed for this project related their gun ownership to men, seeing guns as symbolic of relationships with the men in their lives.

All the women consider themselves to be good mothers and responsible gun owners, but they have very different views on what constitutes "safety" for their weapons and their children. All them have safes, which are expensive, but some say carrying in a purse is unsafe while others say carrying on the body is unsafe. Some mothers cannot abide having all their weapons secured in the event of an intruder, whereas others are so concerned that they will not even allow working ammunition in their home.

All the women interviewed articulate a "right" to gun ownership, and yet it is not the kind of individualized "right" articulated by the Supreme Court. All believe the state should and must regulate gun owners and types of guns. All of them support "common sense" gun regulation. This may be because they do not view themselves as likely to be the objects of state intervention, but three of them (from different states) mentioned with approval the idea of being prepared for some sort of societal collapse.

The politics of gun rights in the United States are entrenched and charged. These good moms with guns complicate our conception of ordinary citizens' understanding of their Second Amendment rights. These women see themselves and their guns as embedded in familial relationships that they cherish and that shape their orientation to guns and rights. And yet this individualized orientation to rights such as the Supreme Court elaborates in *Heller* and *McDonald* is not how they understand this serious social issue. Good moms with guns complicate our conception of ordinary citizens' understandings of Second Amendment rights. These women's orientation to guns and gun rights is embedded in familial relationships—relationships they cherish. In contrast to the individualistic version of the citizen gun owner celebrated in cases like *Heller* and *McDonald,* these women own and use guns as an extension of their role in the family. While their husbands may also see gun ownership as part of their role of protecting their families, it appears that the men in these women's lives carry a more individualistic ideology about gun rights.

This research, like other work I have done on offensive public speech and employment civil rights, suggests the importance of seeing the connection between social relationships and rights consciousness. Individuals identify and use rights in ways shaped by social relationships—whether on the street, in the workplace, in the university, or in the family. For a more complete socio-legal theory of rights, it is necessary to explore the relationships that are the essential underpinning of rights consciousness and rights utilization.

Notes

1. Sarah Larimer, "Mother Fatally Shot by Toddler Who Found Gun in Car," *Washington Post,* April 27, 2016.

2. Stephen Jones, "Horror after Two-Year-Old Police Officer's Son Shoots Himself DEAD with Dad's Gun," *The Mirror,* December 23, 2016.

3. Terence McCoy, "After a Toddler Accidentally Shot and Killed His Older Sister, A Family's Wound Runs Deep," *Washington Post,* December 1, 2016.

4. Editors, "Armed Toddlers Kill Twice as Many Americans Each Year as Terrorists," *Euronews,* January 31, 2017.

5. Christopher Ingraham, "People are Getting Shot by Toddlers on a Weekly Basis This Year," *Washington Post: Wonkblog,* October 14, 2015.

6. Terence McCoy, "The Inside Story of How an Idaho Toddler Shot his Mom at Wal-Mart," *Washington Post: Morning Mix,* December 31, 2014.

7. In *Freakonomics: A Rogue Economist Explores the Hidden Side of Everything* (New York: HarperCollins, 2005), Steven Levitt and Stephen J. Dubner analyze assessment of risk by parents and conclude that a swimming pool is some 100 times more likely to kill a child than a gun in the home (pp. 149–50).

8. http://momsandgunsblog.com/the-simple-solution-to-what-gun-is-right-for-mom/ (spoiler alert: double action pistol with a thumb safety).

9. Taryn W. Morrissey, "Parents' Depressive Symptoms and Gun, Fire, and Motor Vehicle Safety Practices," *Journal of Maternal and Child Health* 20 (2016): 799–807.

10. Ali Rowhani-Rahbar, Joseph A. Simonetti, and Frederic P. Rivera, "Effectiveness of Interventions to Promote Safe Firearm Storage," *Epidemiologic Reviews* 38 (2016): 111–24.

11. Brendan Parent, "Physicians Asking Patients about Guns: Promoting Patient Safety, Respecting Patient Rights," *Journal of General Internal Medicine* 31, no. 10 (2016): 1242–45.

12. Terence E. McDonnell, "Cultural Objects as Objects: Materiality, Urban Space, and the Interpretation of AIDS Campaigns in Accra, Ghana," *American Journal of Sociology* 115, no. 6 (May 2010): 1800–1852.

13. *District of Columbia v. Heller,* 554 U.S. 570 (2008).

14. For more on the transformation of the Second Amendment, see Amanda Hollis-Brusky, *Ideas with Consequences: The Federalist Society and the Conservative Counterrevolution* (New York: Oxford University Press, 2015).

15. *McDonald v. Chicago*, 561 U.S. 742 (2010).

16. Ibid.

17. Jennifer Carlson, *Citizen-Protectors: The Everyday Politics of Guns in an Era of Decline* (New York: Oxford University Press, 2015).

18. Jennifer Carlson, "The Equalizer? Crime, Vulnerability, and Gender in Pro-Gun Discourse," *Feminist Criminology* 9, no. 1 (2014): 59–83.

19. Ibid.

20. Ibid. See also Dan M. Kahan, Donald Braman, John Gastil, Paul Slovic, and C. K. Mertz, "Culture and Identity-Protective Cognition: Explaining the White-Male Effect in Risk Perception," *Journal of Empirical Legal Studies* 4, no. 3 (2007): 465–505.

21. Judith McDonnell, "Women and Guns," in *Guns in American Society: An Encyclopedia of History, Politics, Culture, and the Law*; Laura Browder, *Her Best Shot, Women and Guns in America* (Chapel Hill: University of North Carolina Press, 2006).

22. Wendy Griswold, "A Methodological Framework for the Sociology of Culture," *Sociological Methodology* 17 (1987): 1–35. See also Wendy Griswold, *Frame Analysis* (Cambridge, MA: Harvard University Press, 1974); Wendy Griswold, *Renaissance Revivals: City Comedy and Revenge Tragedy in London Theatre from 1576 to 1980* (Chicago: University of Chicago Press, 1986); Wendy Griswold, "The Fabrication of Meaning: Literary Interpretation in the United States, Great Britain, and the West Indies," *American Journal of Sociology* 92 (1987): 1077–1117.

23. Websites and blogs included http://thewellarmedwoman.com/, https://bearing arms.com/, and http://www.nrawomen.tv/.

Contributors

CARL T. BOGUS is Distinguished Research Professor of Law at Roger Williams University.

JENNIFER CARLSON is Assistant Professor of Sociology at University of Arizona.

SAUL CORNELL is Paul and Diane Guenther Chair in American History at Fordham University.

LAWRENCE DOUGLAS is James J. Grosfeld Professor of Law, Jurisprudence, and Social Thought at Amherst College.

DARRELL A. H. MILLER is Professor of Law at Duke University.

LAURA BETH NIELSEN is a Research Professor at the American Bar Foundation as well as a Professor of Sociology and Director of the Center for Legal Studies at Northwestern University.

AUSTIN SARAT is Associate Dean of the Faculty, the William Nelson Cromwell Professor of Jurisprudence & Political Science, and Professor of Law, Jurisprudence, and Social Thought at Amherst College.

KATHERINE SHAW is an Associate Professor of Law and the Co-Director of the Floersheimer Center for Constitutional Democracy at Cardozo Law School at Yeshiva University.

MARTHA MERRILL UMPHREY is Director of the Center for Humanistic Inquiry and Bertrand H. Snell 1894 Professor in American Government in the Department of Law, Jurisprudence, and Social Thought at Amherst College.

Index

Abolitionist Theory of right to bear arms, 8, 17n33
accidental shootings, 101–3, 164–65
acquaintances, murder and homicide statistics, 100
active-shooter training, 95–96
Act Obliging the White Male Inhabitants of this State to Give Assurances of Allegiance (1777), 17n30
Adams, Samuel, 32–33
Adler, Matt, 56
affray, 27
African Americans: gun ownership and, 50; gun prohibition and, 4, 31, 51; homicide and, 136–37; incarceration of, 135; prejudice against, 15n9; Stand Your Ground laws and, 18n62; War on Crime and, 135, 143
age restrictions, 104, 195
aggravated assault, 110
Alabama, 111
American Revolution: armed travel and, 22; militias and, 3. *See also* founding generation
America's First Freedom (NRA magazine), 136
amicus briefs, 11, 71–74
ammunition storage, 178, 188
Anker, Elizabeth, 2
arguments, 100
Aristotle, 1
Arizona, 54
Arkansas, 17n34, 111

Armed and Prohibited Persons System, 145
armed citizenry, 1
assault weapons, 14, 195; term, 73, 145. *See also* bans: assault weapons
assembly, right of, 25
ATF. *See* Bureau of Alcohol, Tobacco, Firearms and Explosives
Atlanta, Georgia, 103
attention-deficit/hyperactivity disorder (ADHD), 196
Aurora movie theater shooting, 11–12, 74
Australia, 8, 110
autonomy. *See* sovereignty, individual
Aymette v. State, 17n34
Ayres, Ian, 93

background checks, 11–12, 14, 70, 74, 92, 99, 104, 106–8, 120, 130n86, 131n95, 133n141, 134n169; destruction of records relating to, 104
Balance of Power (Patterson), 124–25
balancing model for gun rights, 21–22
bans: assault weapons, 6, 14, 70, 75, 119–20, 135–36, 145, 155; concealed carry, 4–6; firing ranges, 6; firing within city limits, 4; guns, 155; handguns, 71, 125; high-capacity magazines, 11–12, 72–74, 118–19; loaded guns in the home, 4; short-barreled shotguns, 10. *See also* prohibited persons
bears, 190–91